Shaq
Talks
Back

Also by Shaquille O'Neal

Shaq and the Beanstalk and Other Very Tall Tales

Shaq Talks Back

Shaquille O'Neal

ST. MARTIN'S PRESS ✼ NEW YORK

www.stmartins.com

Design by Susan Walsh

ISBN 0-312-27845-4

First Edition: April 2001

10 9 8 7 6 5 4 3 2 1

To My Loved Ones, especially my parents, Philip and Lucille Harrison, and my children, Taahirah and Shareef O'Neal. All of you and my closest friends are really the wind beneath my wings.

CONTENTS

ACKNOWLEDGMENTS

I could not have brought this book home without the help of my agent, Leonard Armato, and the staff at Management Plus Enterprises. Thanks also to David Vigliano for putting the deal together, George Witte and the St. Martin's Press crew for seeing it through, and all my friends and family who made themselves available for interviews. Many thanks to Thomas Gosney, who kept us well fed while we were working on the project, and to Charles Bock, for helping put the book together. The entire Los Angeles Lakers organization deserves credit, too, especially the public-relations staff.

I'd also like to thank my teammates and coaches over the years, past and present, who taught me a lot about the game and even more about life.

And a special acknowledgment goes out to Mike Wise of *The New York Times*, who pulled a lot of these stories out of me over two weeks last summer and made me talk about some things that I've been wanting to talk about for a long time.

Shaq Talks Back

1

Why I Cried

And Why You Should Read My Book

The confetti was coming down. People were chanting, yelling, "MVP! MVP!" Then I saw David Stern, the commissioner, out of the corner of my eye. They were bringing out the shiny trophy, the big golden ball. It was all happening so fast. Everything I ever wanted in basketball was right there in front of me on June 19, 2000, the night I had been waiting for since I first picked up a ball as a five-year-old in Newark, New Jersey.

After we beat the Indiana Pacers in the sixth game of the NBA Finals and the Los Angeles Lakers had won their first title in twelve years—and I had won my first ever—I remember Kobe Bryant leaping into my arms for a few seconds. Then I remember finding my family and friends. I remember my mother sharing the moment with me, right in the middle of the Staples Center floor. So many of the people I grew up with, going crazy, trying to tackle me. My three-year-old daughter kissing her daddy.

It all got to me.

When you're 7'1" and weigh 330-something, you're supposed to be big and strong. You are supposed to take whatever people dish out and keep your emotions to yourself. But I needed to let it out. I needed to show people how I was feeling.

Back in 1992, when I first came into the league, it seemed like everyone embraced me and showered me with praise. How great I was going to be. How much I was going to mean to the game. Besides dominating people on a lot of nights, I was the big man who actually had fun and liked being around people.

But somewhere between my rookie year and the beginning of the 1999–2000 season, I became this player who in a lot of people's eyes had not lived up to his potential. I became this guy who everybody thought cared only about making movies and rap albums.

Never mind that I was putting up big numbers, playing more hurt than anyone knew, and trying to find the right chemistry with my coaches and teammates. Never mind that I was trying to learn how to be an NBA champion. No one wanted to hear about that. After we lost four straight games to the eventual 1999 champion San Antonio Spurs, everybody wanted to talk about what I couldn't do, how Kobe and Shaq still hadn't grown up yet.

Whenever we lost, it was my fault, no matter what I did. I could have a great, monster play-offs, score 29 a game. But if we didn't win, it was, "Y'all got swept and Shaq wasn't playing hard." Nothing was said about the guys who weren't playing defense and I had to play my man, play Robinson, play Tim Duncan and play all these other guys. Just, "Sorry-ass Shaq. Doesn't work hard. Can't hit free throws. Can't guard the pick-and-roll. Can't do this. If he would have stopped doing damn movies and stopped showing off his personal chef on the chef channel, maybe he could win."

OK, when you're the best player on the team, you have to learn to take that kind of criticism. Everything falls on your shoulders. That's the way it is. When you have the good life like I do and make the kind of money I do, I guess you should be immune to criticism. But I'm not lying: I had a hard time with it. The criticism hurt. It made me realize: In this world, whatever you do, it's never enough. And that's how I felt.

And so that's why I cried when I won my first championship.

I didn't cry because I was happy, I cried because I was mad. It wasn't a release. It was the wildness of my father trying to get out, but the calmness of my mother taking over.

Inside, I was like, "Damn everybody that said I couldn't do it, that said I didn't know how to win." A lot of people think I was probably happy. No, I wasn't happy. I was getting my revenge on the critics. All you people that said all this stuff, "Shaq couldn't do this, Shaq couldn't do that." Well, I did it. I proved you wrong. Now what you gonna say?

That's why I cried.

No one knows the struggles I went through to be standing on the court after we beat the Pacers. Where I really came from. How I tried to learn how to mesh my game with young superstar teammates like Kobe and Penny Hardaway. How no one in America hardly knew my name after my junior year of high school. After all the Hack-a-Shaq defenses, where the object was to basically foul the hell out of me and physically rough me up so I had to shoot free throws. After the abdominal injury I suffered two years ago that almost ended my career. Everything was coming back to me, and I let it all out.

Don't worry. I'm not angry anymore. I let go of it that night. I want to have fun and enjoy the rest of my career, whether I play two more seasons or five or more.

But the fact is, there's a lot I want to get across in this book, things I haven't talked about before. And when you read it, you'll get to know a little bit more about me. There's a saying that goes, "Don't always believe what you see on TV." All the marketing surrounding me shows me playing mean, dunking, acting crazy. I'm not really like that—off the court. I've been mostly corporate because that's the politically correct thing to do. My agent, Leonard Armato, has been projecting and protecting my image ever since I've been in the league. He has done a great job. And I would never second-guess him. But there's a part of me that doesn't feel like I've said the things I've really wanted to say—about myself, different players, teammates, coaches and the NBA in general. I've held my tongue a lot over the eight years 'cause it's the diplomatic thing to do. But like that other commercial says, image is reality. And while I hope people see that I'm a nice, genuine person who loves children, who loves being nice to people, at the same time, I'm going to be voicing my opinion on certain issues, and it might not make me the most popular guy on the block.

All I can say is, I'm not trying to embarrass nobody.

I signed a contract extension worth $88.5 million before this season, which means I've got $152 million coming to me over the next seven years. I didn't do this book for money. I did it because I have something to say about my life and my career.

Living the NBA lifestyle is something most people can't possibly imagine. In these pages, I'm gonna try to bring that life home to you. All the stuff I'm talking about is legitimate. Nothing here is made up. This is what I see and how I see it.

Will this book be upsetting to some players in the league? Maybe. But just because I give my opinion on someone based on the time I played with or against him doesn't mean I don't like that person. My opinion can change just like people change over their careers.

Will this book be upsetting to some fans? I'm sure that adults can handle it, but I don't think the whole thing is suitable for children. I'll be honest, there's some cursing in here. Hey, I'm a grown man. I curse every now and then. If we, as parents, teach our children to be leaders and not followers, then they should grow up and be able to handle a few curse words. I want kids to be able to see people make a mistake and say, "You know what, I can't do that."

I know people look up to me as a role model, and I have no problem with that. But I would rather be known as a "real model," someone with flaws and weaknesses, like everyone else.

One more thing. The first championship was just to get people off my back.

This next one? It's gonna be for me.

2

Where I Came From and How I Got So Damn Big

I had to stop trick-or-treating when I was eleven years old. I was about 6'4" and when I would go to the door, people would just stand there, looking at me with their eyes wide open.

"You too big to be trick-or-treating, ain't you?" they would say.

By then, I had gotten used to people either making fun of my height or not believing me when I told them my age.

Already, I was scoring 40 and 50 points in youth-league games, and the other parents were just going crazy. "Damn it, he's not ten," they would say. "I want to see his birth certificate right now."

My mother could tell even more embarrassing stories, but I think the Halloween one hurt the most. It meant I could no longer dress up as Shaquanda—either this sexy girl or a grandma, depending on my mood. Most times it was a grandma, but for a few years, I would put on a wig and ugly lipstick, pretend I had these gigantic breasts. I already had this big ole ghetto booty. Even as a kid, I was a comedian. It was a good way to hide my insecurities about being so big.

I was born in Newark, New Jersey, on March 6, 1972, to Lucille Harrison, the most loyal and loving and sacrificing mother anyone could ever know. I'm biased, sure, but you have to know where the story begins.

My mother's family was from Dublin, Georgia. My great-grandmother, Cillar O'Neal, got married in 1930 at the age of 15 to my great-grandfather, Hilton O'Neal, who was a farmer.

How do I get to be 7'1"? I never met Hilton O'Neal but I was told he was 6'8" or 6'9" tall.

My grandpa Johnny, on the other side of the family, was a farmer, too. He was also about 6'9". My mother's father, Sirlester, is about 6'4" or 6'5".

Cillar, or "Muma" as we call my great-grandmother, grew up in a much different world than I ever knew. Her father killed himself at the age of forty-five, supposedly over another woman. Muma grew up on a farm in Dublin. She picked cotton and pulled corn as a young woman. In those times, she'll tell you straight-up: white folks didn't associate with black people. Hilton, her husband, passed away in 1965. She never remarried. Muma is eighty-three and going strong today in Newark. She can still cook up a storm of Southern food, from black-eyed peas, to collard greens, corn bread, and any kind of pie you can imagine.

Anyway, she gave birth to three children: Reba Mae, Ruby Lee, and my grandfather, Sirlester O'Neal, father of my mother, Lucille. Sirlester married my late grandmother, Odessa Chambliss, who passed away on April 2, 1996, after a long bout with cancer.

Grandma Odessa was, and is, one of the biggest inspirations in my life. Muma always said my grandmother respected her and was one of the kindest women in the world.

One of the most-told stories about me growing up is about Muma and my dad. When I was about three years old and my father was trying to make me hard and not be a baby, Muma used to sneak me a milk bottle at bedtime. She had a little stash of them for me hid in her bedroom. So one time my father snatched me and snatched the bottle and started yelling at me.

"Leave that boy alone!" Muma said. And then she took her shoe and hit him in his head. Just popped him, right in the head.

Yeah, Muma was tough. Still is.

I had a pretty interesting childhood. You could label me from the 'hood, or you could label me an army brat. Either way, you'd be right. I don't remember much from ages zero to two. However, when I got to the age of five and my brothers and sisters were Harrisons and my last name was O'Neal, I asked my mother how come my last name was different. My mother explained to me that she used to date a guy named Joe Toney, who had been a basketball player. He was my biological father.

Joe Toney had been a student at Seton Hall University, who got caught up with the wrong crowd. Since my mom and Joe were never married, she gave me her last name, O'Neal. For our sakes, she left him alone. And so for those first two years, it was just me and my mother.

My mother used to drop me off at a day-care center. She worked at City Hall.

One day she met this guy while she was walking down a street—a nice, clean-cut gentleman who had two kids of his own named Philip Harrison. He was a college student and an all-around good guy. He addressed her, began to make conversation. They were . . . blasé, blasé for a number of months. OK, they fell in love, got married and he joined the army.

When I was five, we moved to Bayonne, New Jersey. That's where my father really began disciplining me. He spanked me. He made me hard. He made me a man from day one. I'll admit, I was a little soft as a child—and very spoiled.

It was hard coming up, but he taught me and my brothers and sisters not to worry about materialistic items. At times he couldn't pay the rent. At night he would have to go to a U-Haul trucking job. Some nights, I've seen him not even sleep.

We were often short on money. Mom was working; he was working. But I don't think they cleared $30,000 a year back then. He also had two daughters from another relationship that he had to take care of. At night, he would drive U-Haul trucks to New York, New Jersey to deliver things, and then come back. I could see he was a hard worker and he was responsible for his family.

He also taught me how to play every sport. Baseball. Basketball.

How to go out there and just have fun and play. Muma always said I was born to play ball, that I was always running around with a football or basketball. My first love was football, but I couldn't catch; I was scared of the ball.

"Don't catch the ball when I throw it," Dad told me one time. Then he threw it, and the ball hit me in the face.

He said, "You see that? That's the worst thing it can do to you. It's gonna hurt for a second, but it ain't gonna hurt bad. Don't be scared of the ball."

To this day, I believe that's why I have good hands.

As I grew older, I started to wonder about my biological father. My mother took me to meet Joe Toney in Newark when I was about nine or ten years old. I think she just wanted me to see him, how he was.

I remember he lived in a little apartment. Didn't have much. We didn't really go into how long he went to jail. He just told me he went to Seton Hall and got caught up in things. After that visit, I never asked to see him again. Phil was the one who took care of me. He was the only father I knew.

The next time I saw Joe Toney's face was about six years ago. I was playing on a team representing the United States in the World Championships in 1994. One day, walking down the street in Chicago, this guy said to me, "You need to talk to your dad. I saw him on the Ricki Lake show."

Phil does a lot of crazy stuff, so I called Mom. "What did Daddy do now?"

She said, "It ain't him, it's Joe Toney. He got on TV."

He was on the show with his little son. "I just want to meet my brother, I love my brother. I just want to get to meet him," the kid said.

Then Joe came on and said, "Yeah, Shaquille is my son. I just want to let him know that I miss him."

We later found out that he was living in Jersey City, New Jersey. My half-brother told me that's why he tried to contact me.

It seemed like there were always reminders of him. I met this guy in Las Vegas one time who came up to me and said, "Yo, I'm your brother."

I thought he meant he was my fraternity brother. "No," he said. "Joe Toney's my father."

He showed me his picture. He pulled me off to the side and said, "I know what he was trying to do because he never tried to contact me ever. He never said nothing to me. So I know why he tried to contact you."

He said, "I'm your brother, I don't want nothing. I just want to let you know we got the same father."

I met this other kid in Newark one time. Same thing. "Joe Toney's my father."

Somebody asked me if I hate him. No, I don't hate him. I'm just going straight. My path was selected. I was tutored by Phil. I'm going that way. I have no desire to see him again.

Lucille Harrison
Orlando, Florida
August 9, 2000

I dated Shaquille's biological father for four years, all through high school. But I don't call him a father. I consider him a sperm donor. That's about all he did that came close to being a father. I was eighteen years old when I gave birth to Shaquille. I was a baby myself, just out of high school. But I grew up and became a woman quick. I knew I had a big, big responsibility then. I wanted to take care of him. I wanted to work. I stayed on welfare for a few months, but then I got a job. I had to support him.

So I started doing clerical work at a youth agency in Newark. I went from there to City Hall, working for the City of Newark. That's where I met Phil, my husband. I never gave it any thought that Shaquille's father wasn't around. I knew I had something to do. The only drawback was, I didn't have a place of my own; I was living with my grandmother when he was first born.

I was not depressed because I didn't have a man, because his biological father wasn't around. It was just the reality of the situation. It was real that I was alone. I had no reason to be depressed. I had my health. I had my life. I had people around me who loved me—my mother, my grandmother, my sisters and brothers.

I'm not going to go into why Shaquille's father and I stopped seeing each other. But much of it was my decision. Basically, I really wanted us to have a life together. But we felt different about parenting. I accepted the responsibility and he did all he could to reject it. I figured, if I'm gonna be doing bad, I can do bad by myself. I don't need you to do bad with me. I said, "See ya." I just went on and took care of business. I'm no saint, but I did the best I could do.

I named him Shaquille Rashaun O'Neal after seeing the first two names in an Islamic book of names. Shaquille means "little one," and Rashaun means "warrior." Little Warrior might not make sense for a boy who grew to be 7' tall and over 300 pounds. But I don't care how big he gets; he's still my little one.

Shaquille was born 7 pounds, 11 ounces on March 6, 1972. His birth weight might sound lucky, but it didn't give me any indication of what he was gonna be like.

He was bad when he was little. I mean, bad. Typical boy: mischievous, curious, all those things.

The most frustrating thing about having a big child like that, though, was how people didn't believe me when I told them his age. I remember when my husband was in the army stationed in Eatontown, New Jersey. We didn't have a car, so I had to travel from Eatontown to Newark by train for work. At that particular time, the half-price train ticket was for children under five. So I used to have to get in an argument with the conductor because he tried to tell me that Shaquille was not under five.

I had to start taking the train with his birth certificate in the palm of my hand just so we could pay the half price.

Whether he was at school, playing sports or walking around the supermarket, everybody would always accuse us of lying about his age. It used to make me so mad. He was always bigger and taller than the kids his age. When Shaquille was twelve or thirteen, we took him to one of the military doctors, and they told my husband that he could grow to be 7'. That's when we really knew we had a large child on our hands.

At first, Shaquille was hard to manage because he was spoiled rotten. We gave him everything he wanted. At the same time, my husband tried to teach him that in life, you don't always get everything that you want. The world treats you different than your parents. Things are not always gonna go your way.

He didn't take to my husband right away. Before it was all of us, it was me and Shaquille. And when Phil came around, Phil kind of invaded our space. Shaquille was just two years old. We had that bond, that special bond with mother and son. His attitude was, "This is my mother, what are you doing here?" I told my husband, "If you want me, you gonna have to take my son." And my son came before him.

It took a little while, but Shaquille and Phil finally warmed up to each other.

Isn't my moms cool?

She is a beautiful, classy woman. When I was growing up, it seemed like she never worried about anything. Even if it was the middle of the month and we don't have any food, she was always, "Don't worry about it, payday isn't so far away." You know, she would always be humble. Never worried. Even to this day, she still doesn't worry about money. Never raises her voice. Always cool as a cucumber, always stays positive. That's where I get that side of me. Oh, and she always babies me. To this day, she still babies me. I was her first son, so as you might expect, she and all my relatives just babied me, gave me whatever I wanted. And I was always mischievous.

One time at age six in my first house at 100 Oak Street in Jersey City, I had a teddy bear. I also found a lighter. You know what happened next. I lit the teddy bear on fire. I was just going to burn him a little bit and put him out. But he went up in smoke. I hid him under the bed. The house was smoky. I was scared. Needless to say, I got a butt-whoopin' for that.

My grandmother, Odessa, was a nurse in Jersey City. My mother lived with her in the early years even though she worked in Newark.

We used to go back and forth between Newark and Jersey City.

And I lived all over Newark. Littleton Avenue. Springfield Avenue. You name it. We basically used to go from relative to relative.

We had to bus every day, and sometimes we'd bus back. If we didn't feel like busing back, we'd stay at Uncle Roy's house, Aunt Vivy's house, Aunt Velma's house, Aunt Anne's house, Aunt Ruby's house or Muma's house. We had a lot of places to stay. They were always low-income, two-bedroom apartments. The projects, really. All the cousins used to sleep on bunk beds, sometimes seven or eight of us in the same room. Some of us would sleep on floors. No air conditioning, nothing.

On those hot, humid nights in the summer when you could hardly breathe, we had a rotating fan in the corner. That was it. Everybody wanted to share the wind, but I would sneak up at night, wait till the fan got to my side, and pull that button up so the fan would stop rotating and stay on me.

We didn't have much in the refrigerator. Army-rationed foods. A lot of sandwich meat. A lot of bread and a lot of chicken, that's all we ate. That's why I love chicken and macaroni so much. A lot of soup. A lot of oatmeal.

My grandmother, Odessa, gave us castor oil when we were little to keep our immune system strong. We had to drink that every morning. A big old country spoonful. We never got sick, actually. We had coats and enough clothes. My parents and relatives provided the essentials for us. We didn't have a lot of things, but we had coats. We had boots. We might have had to wear them for three years straight, but we had them.

Now I have nice, big homes in Beverly Hills and Orlando. But Newark is really still home, where my relatives live, and I can always go back and see the people I grew up with.

When I was five, we moved to Bayonne, New Jersey, and a couple of years later to Eatontown, New Jersey. Halfway through fifth grade, we moved to Fort Stewart, Georgia. A year later, we made the big move—to Germany.

Because Phil was in the army, I was always moving around, trying to fit in with new kids and new cultures. In Newark, I was around black people my whole life. Bayonne, where I lived until I was about nine, was the first time I experienced being in classes with white kids, Indian kids, Puerto Rican kids. It gave me a whole new perspective on the world.

I never disliked white people when I was young. And to this day, I was raised to believe there are two kinds of people in this world: good people and bad people.

But I saw *Roots* a couple times when I was a kid, and that movie based on Alex Haley's book about the slavery in his family's past really left an impression on me. My mother saw how it affected me and finally took me aside one day.

"Times have changed," she said. "You just have to take people for what they're worth. All white people ain't like that no more."

That opened the door for my friendship with Mitch Riles.

He was my best friend growing up in Germany, a white guy who looked just like Larry Bird. He played like Bird. So, of course, I had to be Magic. I had the purple-and-gold Converse Weapons like Magic, and he had the green and white ones like Bird.

We used to go at it every day. We'd fight, kick and punch each other on the court. We had a seven-game series every day. That's when I really started playing basketball. His game was nice. I remember one time I had him defended well. He couldn't do nothing. He was behind the backboard. He shot that ball over the backboard and it went in, just like Bird. Everybody was like, "Oooh."

Lucille Harrison
Orlando, Florida
August 9, 2000

The world can take your child and snatch him up. And if you ever lose him, it'll be so hard to get him back. We tried to raise Shaquille the best way we knew how, but there were times when we worried he was not going to turn out the way we hoped. With Shaquille, and with our other children—Ayesha, Lateefah and Jamal—what was important is that we communicated with each other. We talked to Shaquille, instead of just whooping him all the time. Now he got some whoopings, good whoopings. But there comes a point in time when you have to stop whooping them and you got to start talking and doing plenty of praying. And that's about the best you can do as a parent. And we did a lot of praying, OK?

Shaquille stole things as a youngster. He hung around with the wrong crowd for a while. I never had to go to the jailhouse to get him out of jail. I've never had to go to the police station or anything like that, thank God. But after some rough years, I think he reached a turning point when he was about fifteen years old.

He loved sports so much, especially basketball. It just killed him not to play because of his grades. But "No pass, no play" was the rule in our house. Shaquille wanted to be somebody. He knew that he could be somebody besides a little thug kid, hanging out in the streets. Once he got involved in basketball, he started to dream and use his head to imagine which way he could go, how high he could go. You could see it happen.

A lot of people have said Shaquille has Phil's no-nonsense toughness and my kindness and calmness. All I know is, I wanted my sons to be men. Shaquille didn't have to be an NBA basketball player, but I did want him to be a man. My husband and I groomed him so that he would be a strong man, a responsible man, a loving man. That's what we want.

I'm a Baptist and my husband is Muslim, but that never created problems for us or our children. I pray to God. My husband calls God "Allah." We still connect with that Supreme Being. We have two different religions but we still get to that same point; we just go in different directions.

Not everyone agrees with me on this point, but I think a father in the household is extra, a luxury. It's good if you've got a man; but if you don't have one, then you go on and you work with what you got. You do the best with what you have. That's how it is.

I'm a member of the NBA Mothers organization, a group of women who formed a support group for our sons in the league. A lot of the women I work with raised their sons by themselves and did great jobs.

I learned a few things from women like Magic Johnson's mother, from Charles Barkley's mother and from Michael Jordan's mother. One thing they told me was that I have to learn how to not trust everybody, that not *everybody is who they claim to be. Another thing I know is that I get instant respect because I'm Shaquille's mom. If I wasn't his mom, I'd be a regular black woman walking down the street. I would receive much less attention.*

In many ways, Shaquille is still learning about life. But I would say the main difference I've seen since he came into the league is his maturity. He has grown up. He was still a very young man when he came into the NBA. Over the years, he has stopped trying to please everybody, and has started to please Shaquille. He has realized that you can't be all things to all people.

But one thing he has always been is my protector.

In 1979, I was pregnant with one of my daughters and driving from Newark to Jersey City. My husband used to spend a lot of time in what we call the PO in the army. He wasn't with me.

We were down in the Ironbound section of Newark. I got a flat tire by a railroad track. It was almost pitch-dark down there.

I didn't know how to change a flat tire. I didn't know how I was going to get to Jersey City. I got a carful of kids. I'm a young mother in a bad part of town. The only thing I could do is just get out of the car, sit on the curb and cry.

All of a sudden, Shaquille got out and came up to me. He must have been only seven or eight years old at the time. He didn't cry, even though I was boo-hooing up something awful. I didn't know what I was gonna do.

"Ma, it's gonna be all right," he said.

He comforted me and told me it was gonna be all right. So I knew that I could depend on him from that day.

We sat there for a minute and a man came along and helped me. Shaquille helped the man fix the tire. From that day, Shaquille was always there for me.

He still is there for me. He's my protector.

As for Phil Harrison, my father, I'm glad he came into my life when he did. If it hadn't happened, I probably wouldn't be in basketball. I'd probably be in Jersey, working somewhere that I didn't want to.

If it hadn't been for Phil, I'm not sure what would have happened to me. Because I was so big and awkward, kids called me names.

Sasquatch. Tall Bunyan instead of Paul Bunyan. Shaqueer. Shaquilla the Gorilla. So I became a bully. I learned how to fight.

Whenever we moved from army base to army base, I went to a new school and had to always make my mark, let them know who I am. I always found the baddest cat in school and made my mark. "What'd you call me?" Smack.

I was always resentful of the officers' kids. They had new bikes, good toys. I'd be cutting grass and see a person throw an old bike away. I'd take it to the house, go buy a rim and a tube, paint it and make like a little raggedy bike. The officers' kids, they had Mongooses with the chrome frame and BMX and all that stuff. They had go-carts. I had the raggedy-old bike.

Kids would make fun of me. They'd be like, "Oh, you're big. Didn't you wear those pants yesterday?" Because I had some Monday, Wednesday, Friday jeans. I had to wear them Monday, Wednesday and Friday because the washer was broke or whatever; Mom didn't have time.

"Didn't you wear them jeans yesterday? I was sitting there when you spilled ketchup."

They'd embarrass me in front of everybody. So I'd just take their head right into the desk.

Oops. Two days' suspension. I'd get home, get beat by my father.

"Why you do that?" Phil would say.

"Because he was talking about my clothes."

"Goddamn it, don't worry about that. Block it out. Get your education."

I was a bully until I was about twelve or thirteen years old. It ended when I was in Georgia. This guy ratted me out for throwing something in class. I told him I would see him after school.

I beat him up. He fell. I kicked him. Then he started having an epileptic seizure. I didn't know what I had done. Luckily, someone was there and took care of him. It made me realize how I could really hurt somebody. It scared me.

I used to always get in trouble for having bad grades in school. I didn't have bad grades because I couldn't do the work, I was just a clown. I thought I was cool, wearing my pants off my ass. I had the suede Pumas with the thick shoe laces. I was ten years old and had all Fs on my report card. All Fs. I think part of it was that I used to be ashamed of being tall. I used to try to slouch down and be the size of everybody else. My father always told me, "Be proud. Be proud of being that size." He always used to say, "One day you'll see." But at the time, I didn't care. I was a clown.

Now, I had skipped the first grade, so I wasn't your typical dumb jock. It was more that by the fourth grade, I'd started to goof around and not take school as serious. The teachers at my elementary school had told my mother I had Attention Deficit Disorder. Although I was never diagnosed with ADD, they said I had it because I never paid attention.

To this day, I don't think I had it. I think the schoolwork we had was easy and boring, and after I was finished, I would start messing with the other kids.

It's not that I couldn't pay attention, I didn't want to.

The schoolbooks were old. The films were all grainy and black and white. Nothing made me interested. If they would have had this Internet stuff when I was coming up, I would have been in Harvard by now. Well, maybe not Harvard. But I would have had no problem paying attention.

So I was ten years old, all Fs on my report card. Now I'm afraid to go home. I dropped my books and my report card, ran as far as I could, all the way downtown.

I was in the local arcade. I wasn't playing video games, I was just sitting there because I was scared to go home. Then the Sarge walked in.

"What are you doing?" Phil said.

"I ran away because I didn't want you to beat me no more."

He said, "You know why I beat you? Because you don't listen."

Then he had a talk with me. I started to change.

We left Fort Stewart and moved to Wiesbaden, Germany. We stayed in Wiesbaden for about three months. My father got transferred to a place called Wildflecken, which is about 30 miles from Wurzburg.

It snowed a lot and it was cold. There wasn't much to do. This is when I really made a dramatic change in my life, because there was nothing to do but play basketball.

I tried to work in McDonald's at the base. Two days, that's all I lasted. I was on Fry Detail. At the end of the shift, you'd have to mop up all that gook in the middle of the fries. Nuh-uh. I didn't want that.

So I became a baby-sitter from 8:00 to 5:00 during the summer, watching Ayesha, Lateefah and Jamal. I'd change their diapers, act stupid to entertain them. Feed them. Whatever they needed. That's why I'm good with kids, because I know how to relate to them. I'd clean up their room, clean up my room, wash the dishes, make them take a nap, make them take a bath, take them to the park, protect them. Hey, I'm the original Shaq Daddy. ☺

But while I had this great family life, I had another life that was tugging at me daily.

I was always a follower, liked doing what everybody else did. I used to steal Pumas, steal the hottest sunglasses, steal gold chains, steal Public Enemy Flava Flav clocks, steal tapes. I thought I was cool. I'd go to dances, start trouble, go to the PX, steal something, talk back to the teacher.

Guys I was hanging out with as a young teenager would be like, "Hey, come here, watch my back. I'm gonna get some candy bars." This was during the break-dance era. We'd get into breaking wars, where it was my crew against the other crew. I was actually very good, to the point where a teacher once asked my parents if I had seizures during school.

I was with the Furious Five, and we were battling this crew called Little Manhattan. They lived off the base. I never got beat up, but once they jumped me at a dance. Seven guys pounding on me at once.

In Germany, everybody wanted to be this guy named Cleveland. He was big and strong, used to beat people up. So he'd tell us to do things and we would do them. If we didn't, he would come after us. He had his gang in school. They had little cutoff jean jackets. The only reason I was allowed into the Furious Five was because I could dance and I could fight. They used to call me Shocka D.

The turning point came when these guys I was hanging out with stole a car in Germany on the army base. There were some nice sunglasses on the dashboard. So they busted the window, broke in the door and decided to steal the car.

I just kind of stood back and said, "You know what, I'm not messing with you all today."

One of them said, "You're a punk."

"Yeah, I'm a punk." And I walked away. They got caught. I said to myself later, if I had been with those cats, I would have been done.

That was the end of the Furious Five. I never heard of Cleveland again.

I learned to think for myself that day because of Sarge's discipline.

You can argue all you want about whether his method was right or wrong, but part of the reason I have the self-control I do on the court when I get fouled hard intentionally is because my father prepared me for anything.

When I woke up in the morning, I would have to make my bed up quarter-tight. He'd bounce a quarter right off the bedspread. If the quarter didn't bounce and flip, I'd have to do it again.

Did he walk a fine line now and then? Maybe. But I believe there is a difference between abuse and discipline. If he was hitting me for no reason, out of anger, then maybe you call it abuse. But I was a juvenile delinquent and I did everything from vandalizing to stealing.

That's my way of saying that my father, Philip Harrison, disciplined me physically. He beat me. And when I was a teenager and thought I knew everything about the world, I got to the age where the belt didn't matter anymore. Since I was becoming a man, my father started disciplining me like a man. He was an army supply sergeant, a drill sergeant. So he did what he had to do. Closed fists. Straight smacks to the face. A punch to the chest now and then. He would grab me by the back of the neck. There was no blood or bruises, but I was in pain—more pain than I have ever felt in the NBA. I'm not telling parents to always discipline their children physically. And I don't think I understood it at the time. But looking back, now I know why he did it. He did it because he got me to the point that he wanted me to start thinking, to start listening.

As for drugs, I was never tempted. Part of the reason was because my father told me if he ever caught me doing drugs, he was going to mess me up. But that's not how he said it. It was a little harsher.

Maybe you see that as too harsh in these times when parents are accused of being abusive when they lay their hands on their children. But he wanted me to think before I did stuff because I was always a follower.

Phil was trying to teach me about life's lessons, trying to straighten me out.

Fact is, in my father's home, if you didn't want nothing bad to happen, you behaved.

Philip Harrison
Orlando, Florida
August 14, 2000

People have said my wife, Lucille, once told me, "If you want me, you have to take my child, too." But the truth is, I never looked at it like that. I was going to be with her. That was my duty as a man—to become the father of her son. I asked her to marry me, and Shaquille came along with the package. I felt blessed. In my eyes, Shaquille was always my flesh and blood. Cry with him. Sleep with him. Feed him. Holler at him. Ever since we've been together, he's been my son.

As he got older, he got into more trouble and I tried my best to deal with it the best way I knew how. I'm not going to sugarcoat it. Sometimes I had to beat his ass to keep him in line. That's what I was taught, and that's what I taught him.

The last time I hit him, he was about thirteen years old. He had gotten into some trouble at school, and it was after a parent-teacher conference. I beat his ass in the school bathroom.

People might say, that's wrong. But my attitude was, I would rather have me do it than someone on the street. Out there, they would try to kill him.

He began going to class after that, doing what he had to do, playing ball. He was fine. His juvenile-delinquent days were over. Well, if they weren't, I didn't catch him again. I broke him down and built him back up. If I had to do it again, I would bring him up the same way, the right way. Respect your elders. Respect yourself. Respect people. It's the name of the ball game.

My father, who is from Jamaica, disciplined me worse than I disciplined Shaquille. I was the oldest out of seven brothers and sisters. I had to take care of them. When they did wrong, I got punished. We were supposed to be home at 5:00 one day. I got home at 5:10, and my sister wasn't with me. I got beaten.

I wouldn't treat my children like that. My dad meant well. He's a good person, but he was from the islands, and he believed in the old ways. And even though he could be harsh, I learned responsibility from him.

Why was I hard on Shaquille? I didn't go to class. I took the hard road. I made things harder for myself when I was young. I was in the student lounge in college, playing cards, running around, acting crazy, chasing girls. I wanted to make sure my children benefited from my shortcomings, to know what the bad side of life was. Honestly, I was a gangster. I'm not proud of all the things I did in life. But I set myself straight, turned things around. I got tired of my crazy Newark life and joined the military.

General George Patton's philosophy was that his men didn't have to love him as long as they respected him and did what he told them to do. And eventually they would love him because they realized he saved their asses.

I'm not going to hurt you physically or abuse you, but I want you to be prepared for whatever comes up in life. That's what my dad did to me.

I loved basketball when I was growing up and played as best I could. I even got my teeth knocked out by Dave Cowens in a pickup game when we were fighting for a loose ball.

Shaquille used to come to the gym with me. I tried to teach him to play all sports. I put him at fullback in football. I tried to teach him to pass out of the high post when he was young. When it became obvious that he had the size to be a basketball player, I tried to pattern his game after all the great players. Wes Unseld's passing from the outside. Bill Russell's blocked shots. Jerry West's jump shot. He could do all that kind of stuff when he was young. When he ended up at LSU, they made him a box man. But he's still got a lot of that old-school in his game.

I don't have a problem with some of the young players. But when the old brothers played, they played basketball. There wasn't all this bullsh**. The attitude was, if you don't play right, I'm gonna beat your ass because you hurt my team. You see? Now it's all this finesse, off-the-wall crap.

You might have guessed I'm a little old-school at fifty-two years old. I'm also protective of my son. Maybe overprotective.

If you thought Shaquille was upset about all the criticism over the years, you ain't seen nothing. He worked hard and played hard and that wasn't enough for everyone. He plays only one way: all out, team ball. And people were still taking him down. Sometimes it makes me crazy, the way players hold and grab him. It upsets me when Shaquille gets hit all the time. They say he's big and he can take it. But he's flesh and blood like everybody else. He loves contact—that's what he was taught—but there is no reason to hurt a man physically because he's better and bigger than you.

Anyone can tell you, I can be hard to deal with sometimes. Shaquille's agent, Leonard Armato, found that out the first time I spoke to him. Shaquille was still in college, about to go pro. I told Leonard straight up, "You mess with my son, I'll kill you." Just like that. He looked at me like I was crazy. Then he looked at my wife and she said, "He's not lying."

That was extreme, but too many people could get to him at that age. I was putting my son's faith in this man's hands. I felt like, hey, don't mess us over. Because if you do, I'm going to mess you over.

After Shaquille's rookie year in the NBA, I retired as a staff sergeant. But don't be fooled. My family is a military family. We were used to living payday to payday, and we were tight. I was in the army for twenty-one years. I could have retired with a higher rank, but I never kissed anybody's behind, got in fights all the time. Thank God, I never had to go to war. The closest I came was during Desert Storm. I was on a list to go before the Gulf War ended.

As I said, we're blessed. And not just with Shaquille. Two of my daugh-

ters attend Florida A&M in Tallahassee, and Shaquille's brother Jamal attends LSU.

Am I little emotional sometimes? You could say that. Sometimes it gets me in trouble.

I was ready to fight Phil Jackson last year. I was watching a game against San Antonio at the end of the regular season, and I'm wondering why Phil is keeping Shaquille in the game after David Robinson is out and the Spurs send in Felton Spencer to basically try and beat up on Shaquille. The Lakers didn't need that game to clinch home-court advantage for the play-offs or anything, but Phil left him in.

I'm thinking, Get my son out of the game—they're trying to hurt him. And Phil just left him in there. I was so damn angry, I ran onto the court after the game.

"What was that all about?" I started screaming.

Phil turned around a little shocked and wanted to know what the hell I'm doing on the court.

Jerome Crawford, Shaquille's bodyguard and surrogate uncle since the Newark days, pulled me away.

That's the closest I came to meeting Phil. I found out later that his philosophy was to see how players adjust to certain situations. That's why he left Shaquille in. That was good. I understood. It was a protection thing with me, though.

During the 2000 finals, after Game 2, Phil came up to me and said, "We still have some unfinished business to talk about."

We started laughing and I walked away. Water under the bridge.

I don't know if I'm a Little League parent. But I'm a parent. I'm involved with my children. Even now. When Shaquille won the championship and he cried, I'm crying right along with him. When he is on that court playing, I'm right inside his body playing along with him.

I often wondered what life would have been like if my son didn't listen to me and his mother. I wouldn't be living in this nice home in this nice neighborhood in Orlando, enjoying my children, grandchildren, and retirement with my lovely wife. I would probably be in Newark or someplace else.

You might think all I am is hard and strict. But I tried to teach Shaquille about compassion, too. If people need money for food on the street, I give it to them. If someone is down-and-out, I try to help them. Because it could easily be us in that same situation. I know that.

I can remember the day I met Shaquille's mother, the day my life changed.

She was working for the Payroll Department in City Hall. She's twenty. I'm twenty-six. I was playing ball, wasn't doing nothing. I was trying to get a job at the watershed in Newark. Had my Chevy Nova hatchback, driving to City Hall to talk to one of the counselors.

She was walking down the street. You know that saying, Love at first sight? The whole block just lit up when I saw her.

"Can I talk to you for a minute?" I said.

"Who, me?"

I asked if I could come by after work that night. That's how it all started.

I knew Shaquille's biological father growing up. Me and Joe Toney played ball against one another in high school. I knew Joe very well.

One summer I came home from Fort Lee, Virginia, where I was attending supply-sergeant school. Some of my partners were going to New York, and they dropped me off in Newark on their way.

I got home and saw Joe down at the park. We got to talking about Shaquille, who was then about fourteen years old.

"Listen, Phil," he told me. "We know each other. Our word of mouth is a bond. Shaquille is your son. You take care of him. I've got my own son to take care of now."

I said, "OK." I shook his hand and moved on.

When Shaquille was at LSU, I started to get calls from the school that Joe Toney was trying to get in touch with him. Then he's on the Ricki Lake show. After all these years, Joe was trying to get back in his life.

I wasn't sure what to do or how to react to something like that. But Shaquille took care of it. One day one of my daughters came home and said, "Daddy, listen to this song. This song is about you."

Shaquille had made a rap album, and one of the songs was called, "My Biological Didn't Bother." It talked about how I had raised him from a boy to a man, how I had raised him and changed his life for the better.

When I heard that song, I felt like the tallest man in the world. At that point, I had no idea he felt that way about me.

"Phil's my father, my biological didn't bother."

The father issue was over after that. Joe Toney missed out on having a great son. I still cry whenever I hear the words to that song.

I wasn't good enough to make the high-school team in my sophomore year. I was going to the gym, working hard. But I wasn't getting any better. I was 6'8", 6'9", but I couldn't even dunk. I was still growing into my body. It was then that my father told me about an American college coach who was giving a clinic down at the base where we were living in Wildfleken, Germany. The gym was located on a steep hill on the base. I walked in and sat up front. The visiting coach was Dale Brown of Louisiana State University.

At one point, he said, "You're a strong guy. I want to see if you can throw this ball from this court to that court."

I took the ball, threw it almost the length of the court and it almost went in.

After everybody left and Dale stopped to sign his autographs, I went up to him. "Coach, can you send me some weight-lifting gear? Can you tell me what to do to strengthen my legs? I'm 6'8", 6'9". I got cut from the sophomore team this year, and I can't play. Can't dunk. I'm not that good."

Coach Brown said, "Well, how long you been in the army, soldier?"

I said, "I'm not in the army. I'm only fourteen."

"What?!! Where's your father? I want to meet your father right now."

He was talking scholarships. My father said that could wait. "He might be a good player, might not. I want a college education for him." Dale said he liked and respected my father for his opinion. "I'm going to be watching your son closely," he said.

We moved back to the States in the middle of my sophomore year of high school. I had grown to 6'11". I told everybody who would listen how good I was in Germany, but since I hadn't gone to any of the basketball camps in the United States, nobody knew anything about me. "Yeah, OK, whatever, we never heard of you." But I knew about me. I knew I wanted to play pro basketball.

My father had taken me to Madison Square Garden in 1985 to watch the Knicks and 76ers play. Finally, I would get to see my idol, Dr. J. We sat way up, in the last row of the nosebleed section. Before the game, I went down to that store beside the Garden to try to get some size-14, -15, sneakers because my feet were growing so fast. They didn't have any, but I bought a Dr. J jersey.

My dad didn't have a lot of money but he did the best he could. We tried to get down to the floor, but we never made it. But I got to see my man, the Doctor, in person.

My dad used to run a gym. One day he stole a little raggedy-ball from the gym. "This is your ball," he told me. "You play with it, you dribble with it, you dream with it. Don't take it to school because I don't want to hear from your teachers. Don't let nobody steal it from you. And don't dribble it in the house. I'll kick your ass if I catch you messing up my furniture."

He told me, "Dream with it," and I did. My sister Ayesha still likes to tell the story of how I used that ball as a pillow. It's true. Little, old raggedy ball.

This is how it started, everything coming together. But man it took a long time.

What I mean is, like my mom already said, when I was real young, I grew so fast that it was almost embarrassing. I was dominating kids my age on the playground. I was a little kid, and everyone was saying I'm already the best. Then, as a teenager, I still was big, but I wasn't getting the finer things in life. I still didn't have the girls. I still didn't have the lunch money. But I was big. And I saw that hey, this can get you somewhere.

Now, no youngster enjoys banging and physical contact, no matter how big he is. You have to get adjusted to it.

Other big guys in the NBA, you can tell that they don't like getting hit because they're probably not used to it. Probably being tall all the time, they did tall-people things. But I did little people things, too. Skateboarding. Riding bikes, jumping ramps. I used to bust my ass a lot. But since I couldn't cry when I was out hanging with my boys, this also helped me develop a high pain tolerance. This is why I can take the Hack-a-Shaq and getting beat up now, because I'm used to it. Meanwhile, you could look at most of the big guys' personalities in the NBA, you can tell that they didn't go through that. Look at David Robinson. Just from how he talks and acts, you can tell he has no street in him at all. That's not a knock against David, because he's a great guy, a great person. He just has no street in him. None.

When I saw little kids break dancing, I was out there. I was dancing, doing flips, jumping off roofs, busting my knees up. You can see it in my game now. When I'm playing, it's all about rhythm. I could dance. That's partly why my moves are smooth, like the Hakeem shake. If I was stiff and couldn't dance, I couldn't do none of that.

I remember one time I was break dancing. I got carried away and crashed into a window, came down on both my knees, and was hurting real bad.

That's when I had developed osteitis. When you grow up too fast, it stretches the bones. The area between them gets inflammation, gets liquid in it. So first time I got liquid on my knee, I was like, "Damn."

My mom was like, "See, I told you about break dancing."

But my father, he told me, "Be proud. Just 'cause they're little, *you* ain't got to walk little. You can do that stuff. You want to dance, go ahead."

So, even though I was getting banged up, it was all starting to come together. I'm getting tough now. I'm coordinated. At Cole High School in San Antonio, I finally learned how to dunk. I discovered TBS, too. Every Tuesday they used to show the NBA games. I used to watch the games, then study. Every night. I would watch how the announcers would praise them, exploit them, how some guys would make it and others wouldn't.

"OK, he's making a lot of money, but he's doing drugs. He's broke now. That's not going to be me." I would actually say those things to myself.

Who am I talking about? Guys like Micheal Ray Richardson,

who was banned from the NBA because of drug use. Chris Washburn. Lloyd Daniels. Guys who took the bad roads like that, who the media would just kill. I told myself that wasn't going to be me.

I knew that to get to the pros, I had to get a scholarship, but I made only a 680 on the SAT. I tried to take courses, prepare for the tests. But I didn't know a lot of that stuff.

I was good at math. I was pretty good at history. But when it came to the vocabulary words, I'm from the brick city, Newark, New Jersey. I don't know what "perturbed" means. I don't know what a philanthropologist is.

People always stressed getting an education, but it all falls back to money. If you don't have any money, you ain't going to school. They give only two types of scholarships that I know of: athletic and academic. They may give a music scholarship, but I can't play the trumpet. They might give certain grants, but there's a million other people trying to get grants and aids and loans and all that. There are doctors still paying their college loans to this day. My parents didn't have any credit. Who's gonna cosign the loan? If I didn't get a basketball scholarship, I don't know where I'd be.

This is kind of sad and hard to admit, but I ended up taking the SAT test rhyme-style. I was like, A to the B, B to the C, give me an E, back to the B. Multiple guess.

But you can't get into no college with a 680. Luckily, I made a 15 on the ACT, which back then was good enough for you to play.

Even before I got a college scholarship, I would daydream about being famous. I mean, I have the same autograph right now that I had in Cole High School. I'd sit in class, practicing it. I would do it to keep myself going. "I'm gonna be a star," just saying it jokingly, "I'm gonna be in the NBA, I'm gonna have my own shoe." Meanwhile, deep down in the back of my head, I was always wondering, "What if I don't?"

I was a scared dreamer. I was 6'9" and couldn't dunk. I'd go to the gym, they don't even pick me. I got this little stutter.

Now, today, I've made it. I am somebody. And every now and then in practice, Kobe Bryant will tell me, "If I was 6'10", I would dunk on you." I've heard this my whole life, guys saying if they were taller, if I was shorter. I always answer, "No, you wouldn't. You wouldn't do nothing." I worked hard to become the MVP of the league.

I have all kinds of skills I haven't shown. I used to bring it up and shoot my jumper. See, my father was an excellent shooter. He could shoot his butt off. To this day, he can shoot. I was taught the fundamentals. Right now, I can cross it up, come down under control, pull up, shoot the jumper. There are tapes from me in high school running the three-on-two fast break correctly, giving up the ball at the free-throw line. I had all that game, and I still have it. Once you learn it, it's always there.

But I was forced to become dominant. They told me: "You're 6'11", we don't want you shooting that jumper. The farther you are away from the basket, the lower your percentage." Shooting that far from the basket, every now and then, you have an off game. But down low, there *is* no off game. Especially when you're taking high-percentage shots like dunking back misses.

So now I'm coming up, 6'10", 6'11", yeah, a jumper's nice but can you dunk on somebody? So now I dunk it. They like to see you dunk. "Dunk, don't lay it up, damn it." Dunk. Dunk, dunk, dunk, dunk, dunk. Jump hook, jump hook, jump hook. Guys were like: "Get the rebound. That's not your outlet. Don't dribble. Be mean. He elbows you? You 'bow him back. Get them 'bows up when you stand.

"Dunk, dunk, dunk, dunk."

When I started doing that, I could see in other guys' eyes: If he can play like that, we're in trouble. All of a sudden, I'm finding out what it's like to become a big man.

But right at the beginning of my senior year, I went to the BCI tournament, one of the showcases of high-school talent. Shawn Bradley was there, Kenny Anderson, Conrad McRae, Jimmy Jackson, Allan Houston, all the guys that are in the NBA. Nobody heard of this kid from Texas. I played on the San Antonio team. Nobody knew any of us.

I had to work. I'm going into my senior year, only letters I'm getting are from Southwest Texas State and UTSA (University of Texas at San Antonio). Screw that. I need the big colleges. I want Georgetown. All the coaches are there. Everybody's there. Now it's time for me to do work. I tore up the competition.

Soon as I got home, letters were piling up. For the first time, someone wrote an article about me. The reporter was talking about all the players, Kenny Anderson, the people in Texas. He said I was the best.

My dad ran home. He said, "Did you see this? I told you you can do it. Stay out of trouble and listen. You can do it."

These days, I never keep or read articles. But that probably was the best article ever written about me. I have it framed in my home in Orlando. It changed my life, 'cause once I saw that, and once the letters started pouring in, I'm like, "OK, now they offer me a scholarship, I'm gonna get a scholarship. Phew."

Someone even sent a video crew to check me out, from one of them High-School All-America shows. The camera panned up to me, I put on a mean face, looking into the lens. The first thing I ever said into a camera?

"Dummies don't go nowhere."

After that, I was in the San Antonio paper every day. I actually got cocky, believing my own press. I was getting fan mail, and the girls were beginning to come around. But once I got to high school, my friends were like, "All right, you gonna act like you're big-time, eat by yourself, practice by yourself."

My high-school coach, Dave Madura, didn't like hotdogging. So in one practice, I was standing on the side, talking to girls.

Madura says, "You need some mustard with that hotdog? I'll tell you what. Why don't you get on a line and run about fifty suicides."

I had to keep running and I was pissed off and wanted to curse him out.

But remember. Mentally I'm saying to myself, "Yo, if I don't get this scholarship, brother . . . that's it."

Coach made me run until I almost threw up.

Now, I'm glad Madura didn't treat me like a prima donna. There's a lot of guys in the NBA that got treated like prima donnas in high school and before then, they can't handle it now. Some of these million-dollar cats you can't even yell at. But people like Dave Madura made sure I didn't wind up like that. My junior year, we went 35–1. Lost to a bunch of white dudes shooting nothing but jumpers. They played harder and smarter. But we learned our lesson.

My senior year of high school, I led Cole to an undefeated 36–0 season. Three years after meeting Dale Brown, I committed to attend Louisiana State. America found out who I was. And if they didn't know, Dick Vitale, the college basketball announcer on ESPN, told them one afternoon on national television.

I was still relatively unknown when I showed up for the McDonald's High School All-American game. All these big-time players were in that game, from Kenny Anderson to Jim Jackson. Sonny Vaccaro, who was working with Nike at the time, was passing out nice gear to all of them. Brand-new shoes and sweats. I'm just this dude from Texas who he hadn't heard of. I don't get anything. Mitchell Butler, Tracy Murray, these guys are getting all the hype, getting Nike jackets, the red-and-black Jordans. Sonny finally gives in. He gives me a pair of raggedy green Nikes.

I said, "OK." That's when I went up to Dick Vitale. I said, "Mr. Vitale, remember this name: Shaquille O'Neal."

So at the game the next day, I just took off. In the opening minutes, I blocked a shot by Conrad McRae on one end and started dribbling downcourt. I kept dribbling and dribbling and took off just inside the free-throw line, dunking hard over about three dudes. Vitale went crazy. "Did you see that?!!! Are you serious!!! Dale Brown, you got a Diaper Dandy, baby! Welcome to LSU, Shaquille O'Neal!"

Bobby Hurley and Shaquille "Air Ugly Green Nikes" O'Neal shared the MVP. Suddenly, I wasn't a juvenile delinquent going nowhere anymore. I was going to college, on a basketball scholarship.

Even before then, I knew what I wanted. My friends and I started paying $5 to go see the San Antonio Spurs games. We would sit way up there in the Alamodome, nosebleeds, so far up you could barely see the floor. We'd sneak down to the court and try and get inside the locker rooms.

Sometimes we would follow the players home, to see where they lived.

One time, me and my friends followed Frank Brickowski, this journeyman forward playing for the Spurs. He lived in a nice neighborhood. Big house. Nice front lawn. I'm like, "Frank Brickowski got a house like this?"

I want this life.

Forget about Southwest Texas State and University of Texas–San Antonio. All the major schools had started to notice by now. Big Ten schools. The ACC.

I visited N.C. State and Illinois. I even visited North Carolina. Chapel Hill is supposed to be one of those basketball heavens, but my visit wasn't that great. Dean Smith kind of turned me off. "You can be like Michael and Sam Perkins, blah, blah, blah." And Rick Fox may be one of my Laker running buddies right now, but back then, he ain't show me no love. He and J. R. Reid—who played for Carolina at the time—basically said, "Hey, what's up?" and did their own thing. I had to hang out with King Rice. King Rice! We didn't do anything. We just stayed at the hotel.

Not that it mattered. LSU already had me hooked. The other schools all tried to recruit me with the same pitch: "You're gonna be blah, blah, blah." But Dale Brown told me straight up. "Look, you might play at LSU. We got Chris Jackson and we got Stanley Roberts right now. You *might* play."

Besides Dale, I saw all them beautiful light-skinned Creole women. Just as important, Baton Rouge was exactly six hours from the crib in San Antonio, so I would be able to drive home or fly Southwest Airlines. At that time, Southwest cost only $100 to fly both ways. And since Southwest didn't have a first class or business, just first-come first-serve, all I had to do was get there early and get my seat.

I don't know why colleges try all kinds of crazy recruiting tactics to get the best players. Sometimes, all we need are the simple things. Good coach. Good program. Close to home. Where do I sign?

Like I said, one of the main reasons I went to LSU was because Dale challenged me. In high school, I was the star. I was it. So when I got to college, I had to learn how to adjust. A lot of NBA players can't adjust. Even to this day, a lot of cats who have been stars in high school and college, they can't adjust. It messes them up.

Now, when I got to LSU, I didn't get no girls. I didn't have a car. I couldn't get into the clubs because I was only seventeen. They just treated me like I was normal. In fact, the whole town knew I was seventeen. All the college bars were worried about getting raided, so they wouldn't let me in. I had to wait outside for the guys.

Some of my teammates used to get twisted: Vernell Singleton, Stanley Roberts, Maurice Williamson; they used to blast their heads off. I would have to drive them all home. I would drop them off with the car keys and then walk back to my house. Vernell wouldn't let me keep his burgundy Beretta. Chris had a Grand Am. Stanley had some little Cadillac. They didn't want me keeping their cars overnight, so after I got done playing designated-responsible-driver cat, they made me drop off the car and walk back home.

Anyway, that first year Coach Brown sat me down and said, "Look, we have Chris and we have Stan. They're our go-to guys. I need you to play defense. I need you to rebound." I listened and learned. Also, I had some other inspiration.

When I left home, my father told me, "You mess this up, you're on your own."

Dale Brown was a disciplinarian. He meant what he said. He was hard. If we missed class, we would have to get up at 5:30 in the morning and run. Seven laps in twelve minutes.

Coach Brown also trusted his players and wanted us to get better on our own. He gave us a key to the gym. I started spending a lot of time on my own, working on my moves. I used to watch Rony Seikaly, Patrick Ewing and David Robinson. Whatever they did, I just went to the gym and emulated them. Especially that first year when I was only seventeen. While the guys are at the clubs, I'm at the gym working on my Hakeem move, working on my Ewing move, practicing the jump hook just like I saw them do it, working on my dunking, getting my knees up like Rony Seikaly used to do at Syracuse.

I'm not a big David Robinson fan on every page of this book, but I do have to give him credit for helping me develop my game. I watched an NCAA tournament game when Navy played against Kentucky. The Admiral would do a spin move against the man guarding him. He would wait till the guy put his weight on him; then he would spin away from him, catch the lob and dunk. He did it about eight times in the game, I think.

Once me and my man started doing that, it was all over. Guys want to lean and push; I spin right off and catch the lob. Since my Orlando days, Brian Shaw and I have been using this move. It was nicknamed the ShawShaq Redemption, but I feel like Dave should get some credit.

This is where I started to believe I could become an NBA player.

With Chris Jackson, Stanley Roberts, and me, we had the makings of a powerhouse. We lasted only one season together, but I remember it well.

Chris was always very silent, very to himself. He was one of them lightning-bug little guards who could shoot the hell out of the ball. He had that one herky-jerky move that always got him open. He would put the ball between his legs and step back and shoot. Just shoot and shoot and shoot. I'd be posting up. He'd never throw the ball because he was always open. Most times the ball went in, so you couldn't go to the coach and say, "Yo, Chris isn't passing it to me."

Chris returned to the NBA this season after being out of the league a few years. After embracing Islam, he changed his name to Mahmoud Abdul-Rauf several years ago. Even though he hasn't had a Hall of Fame career, he's had to deal with Tourette's Syndrome his whole life, so I consider him successful. When we were in college, I never really saw him have any bad twitches, but you knew it was always there.

Just to show you how cruel people can be, in my freshman year, a bunch of the LSU players tricked me into sitting next to Chris on the team plane. "Go ahead," they said. "You can sit by Chris." I was cool with it because Chris was the man. But then, when I tried to sleep, he started tapping me.

I'd go, "Huh?"

He'd go, "Nothing."

This happened about twenty times.

"What?"

"Nothing."

It was a three-hour flight to Ole Miss. Afterward, all the players were laughing at me.

I thought Stanley Roberts was going to be a dominating player. Stanley could shoot the jumper, he could put it on the floor, go to the hole, back you down and dunk on you. We used to have a lot of battles in the gym. When I got that son-of-a-gun mad, he was hard to stop. The only thing, if you didn't get him mad, he was just content with being OK. I don't think Stanley really, really cared about much. If he would have had that ferociousness and could have learned how to turn that ferociousness on and off, I think he would have been a dominant player.

Anyway, Stanley flunked out of LSU, and after my freshman year, Chris left for the NBA.

Instantly, I became the man, averaging 27.6 points and 14.7 rebounds, dunking on anyone I wanted. I was an eighteen-year-old sophomore, and it was starting to look like I was going to be drafted very high.

By my junior year, I was getting hacked and whacked by every little dude in the Southeastern Conference. Because of all the defenses designed to stop me, Dale Brown began to encourage me to turn pro. He was worried about me getting hurt and not having a pro career.

With every game, my profile was getting bigger. All the experts kept saying I was going to be the No. 1 pick. It was hard to handle. In a lot of ways, I still felt like a college kid who needed to learn a lot more about life before I went out into the working world for good.

In fact, I was acting like a stupid college kid.

In my last year at LSU, a guy named Clarence Caesar, one of my teammates, was allegedly messing with a football player's girlfriend. I was in the lunchroom one day when I overheard some of the football players say, "We gonna beat his ass."

Being a responsible teammate (and a naïve dummy), I went over there and said, "Y'all ain't gonna do nothing."

"Shaq," they said, "we'll beat your ass, too."

I started to worry. I went upstairs to talk to the football captains, trying to be diplomatic and work it out.

Anthony Marshall, this big linebacker dude, was having none of it. He started acting all crazy. "Yo," he told me, "I know you ain't come up here to talk. What you want to do? You want to fight?"

Now, Anthony Marshall was a big, mean cat. But I felt like he was backing me into a corner in front of everyone. So . . .

I punched him in his face. Gave him a two-piece. And then I ran back downstairs.

Not the smartest thing in the world.

Five minutes later, the whole football team was after me, chanting, "We want Shaq! We want Shaq!"

Did I mention that the basketball players lived at the bottom of a dorm where the rest of the floors were all football players? Anthony Marshall and a couple of his boys broke down our door. Me and him started fighting again.

Then the cops showed. When the football players started beating up the cops, I snuck out the back and hightailed it to my girlfriend's house.

The football coach showed up at the athletic dorm. Dale Brown showed up. Then *they* were about ready to fight.

It was mayhem. Everyone mad. All our football players got arrested—which made people even more angry. A lot of people were saying, "Shaquille O'Neal was fighting, too. He didn't get arrested. The basketball players have special privileges."

Because of the fight, we got kicked out of the dorm and had to live off campus my junior year. That taught me responsibility, because now I had to pay my own bills.

At least I had money coming in. My construction job paid $15 an hour, although $8 of it came while we were working, and we received the other $7 per hour during the basketball season (so we had some spending money then). I also had money from a Pell grant. Even though I was on athletic scholarship, I got the Pell grant because it was based on my parents' income. I wasn't dirt-poor, but I was kind of struggling. Like gravel-poor, maybe.

Why was I so strapped? Because I refused to take money from agents.

The NCAA was watching. They even paid me a visit one day. How about this story: It takes place before everybody started having cell phones—they were still expensive back then. I wanted to impress girls, so I had this big, clunky thing that looked just like a cell phone. It was called Cell-U-Clone. Whenever I'd walk through the quad, I'd press it and it would start ringing. I'd act like I was talking, "Yeah, what's up?"

Well, Dale Brown called me in his office one day. Sure enough, there was an NCAA investigator waiting.

"Shaq, you got a phone?" Coach Brown asked.

"Yeah, I got a phone," I said.

The NCAA dude asked how much it cost.

"Ten dollars," I said.

"Who did you get it from? Who's paying your bill?"

"I ain't got no bill."

"How do you have a cell phone and no bill?"

I pulled it out and showed him my phony-ass cell phone. He was embarrassed for coming all the way down to the school. True story.

Even though I didn't take money, I was still acting like I was getting paid. My work checks and my Pell grant check would be about $500. I would get three $100 bills and then two hundred $1 bills and make my money wad look fat. I'd stand in the middle of campus, just counting my chipparoos, and people would walk by. "Damn, Shaq's getting paid."

It was all an act. When you're All-American, you're supposed to have the dopest cars, all the girls. Well, I didn't have either but I wanted to make people think I did.

I did have a used Bronco II in my junior year. I took out a loan to buy it for $6,000. Since I knew I was getting drafted, I figured I'd just pay it off when I got my money.

My days of pretending were just about over.

3

Almost Magic, Almost a Title

I left college for the NBA in 1992, and signed the largest rookie contract in the history of sports: $41 million for seven years. Michael Jordan had come knocking on my door in Orlando, to see if I was home before he played a round of golf on the course next to my new lakefront home. ESPN wanted a few minutes of my time. The *New York Times* wanted a week of interviews. I had met Muhammad Ali, rapped on late-night TV, dunked on Patrick Ewing so viciously. It was all a blur.

One minute, I was playing for Dale Brown at LSU, learning the game, trying to fight through triple-teams and keep from getting hurt by all these cats who just kept fouling me because they couldn't stop me. The next, I'm the No. 1 pick in the draft, playing pickup ball with Magic Johnson in L.A., making a shoe commercial for Reebok and costarring in a movie with Nick Nolte.

In less than five years, I went from Shaquille, troublemaking son of Sergeant Phil Harrison and his wife, Lucille, to Shaq—Rookie of the Year candidate by night and entertainment empire by day.

Did I mention I was only nineteen years old? My head was spinning.

With the right people around me, I managed to keep my focus.

I tried to find a balance between enjoying life as a youngster in the NBA with my job as center of the Orlando Magic. I tried to be a kid off the court and an adult on it. Less than three years after turning pro, I thought I had the perfect recipe for success.

It was 1995, my third year in the league, and the Magic had a chance to win a championship. Everybody knew each other, and our team had been together for a while. Anfernee "Penny" Hardaway was just two years out of college, but already people were making Jordan comparisons. It wasn't right or fair, but Penny did so many things well as a young point guard. He was 6'7", with these long arms and big-time hops. Could stop and shoot from anywhere, could break you down with his dribble, spot you out of the corner of his eye for an alley-oop dunk. Penny was the truth back then, and together we had a nice one-two combination.

We were young, energetic, with an inside game and an outside game. Throw in Horace Grant, Nick Anderson and Dennis Scott—the Magic had all the weapons.

Only one problem: We set our goals high, but not high enough.

Everybody was talking about making it to the NBA finals, but nobody talked about wanting to win a championship. Then the unbelievable happened: We went on this great playoff run, beat the Chicago Bulls in six games the year Jordan came out of retirement. We were the last team to knock Jordan out of the playoffs. Then, with the best player out of the picture, we beat Indiana in seven games to go to the finals.

We felt it was over. We're gonna win a championship. The teams out West were still playing. So we had a lot of time between winning the East and playing in the finals. Too much time. Six years after the city of Orlando got its first real pro team, the Magic were in the finals. We had a parade; everybody was enjoying the moment. From the media to the fans, it made you feel on top of the world. I got caught up in it. There were times when I thought I was bigger than Disney.

But as the saying goes; the bigger they are, the harder they fall.

Leading up to the finals, guys were partying, talking to the media every day, joking around. We had lackadaisical practices. Some guys were flying girls in, eating whatever they wanted, hanging out. I could sort of see the championship slipping away. It was hard to keep that hunger when you have that kind of time off.

Let me tell you: Whenever a young team has that many days off, trouble is around the corner. We were mentally so relaxed we didn't think the Houston Rockets had anyone to match up with us. They were the sixth-seeded team in the Western Conference, hadn't even won 50 games during the regular season, and had to get out of some serious scrapes just to make it to the finals. They had some old, great players. They got Hakeem Olajuwon, and that's about it. Their other players? I'm thinking, Robert Horry. I played against that chump in college. He ain't gonna do nothing. Kenny Smith is a bum. Mario Elie? I don't even know who he is. Sam Cassell got a lot of herky-jerky moves, but I wasn't worried. Otis Thorpe? I'm gonna bust his ass, too. We got this thing, right?

It just shows how being young and too confident can lead to your downfall. It's late in Game 1 of the finals, and we're in front of our home crowd, leading and feeling good about ourselves. But Hakeem is busting out with moves I didn't know he had. I'm neutralizing him, playing him as tough as I can. At the end of the game, we had a 3-point lead. All Nick Anderson has to do is hit one out of four free throws to clinch a win for us. He misses all four. Then Kenny Smith, well, he didn't turn out to be such a bum. He fooled Penny with a pump fake and dropped in a 3-pointer, sending the game into overtime.

In many ways, that was the series. Mentally, after those free throws and Kenny's 3-pointer, we were shell-shocked. In Game 1, the shot just drained us so bad that Houston pulled it out in overtime. In Game 2, Horry didn't turn out to be a chump, and pulled some threes out of his ear, dropped in these serious prayers from all over the court. Now we're going back to Houston down 0–2. These old dudes are showing us heart we didn't know they had, taking it to us youngsters. They're calling Houston "Clutch City." Game 3, Clyde Drexler took over and out come the damn brooms. A couple guys on my team start arguing. Nick didn't want to shoot free throws anymore; he just wanted to shoot threes. Nobody's going to the hole; the ball isn't coming inside. It's over.

Game 4, Houston's whole team is having fun; they're loose now. They just destroyed us and won their second title in a row. Rudy Tomjanovich, Houston's coach, took the microphone at the end of the game and said, "Never underestimate the heart of a champion."

Brooms are smacking our charter bus on the way out of the arena and I'm sitting there, pissed off. Our coach, Brian Hill, is telling us to remember this feeling when we return to the finals. Some of the assistant coaches are talking about how we're a young team, it's OK, we gave our best. Everybody thought Penny and Shaq and the Magic would have a lot more chances to win a title, that Orlando could be a dynasty in the making. But it wasn't OK. It turned out, that was our one shot. And we let it get away.

I took Brian's words to heart and always remembered that depressing feeling. As I'm riding the bus through that mob in Houston, I vowed to myself that if I ever got back to the finals, I would win the championship. No use coming that close and leaving with nothing.

Now, if Nick made one free throw, maybe we win Game 2 and it's a better series. I don't know if we would have won because we really got caught up in just being there, and didn't concentrate enough on winning. That was partly my fault. One of the reasons we lost is because I respected Hakeem too much. Wasn't 'bowing him, wasn't fouling him, wasn't talking my usual smack. I was just being nice, respecting my elder. Whenever I hit him, I'd ask him, "You OK, Hakeem?"

Hakeem never said anything. He just took the pounding and came back at you. He'd go into a herky-jerky move. You'd be over here, he'd be over there, shooting a fade-away jumper. When he had that Dream Shake going, it was lights out, buddy.

To this day, I regret that in my first finals, I didn't treat my opponent as an equal. It was the first lesson I learned in Orlando. The others—money, ego and bad management—I learned later on.

Those lessons would be even harder to accept, and eventually led to me signing with the Lakers in the summer of 1996.

How did everything that seemed so good turn so bad? Over the years, I've taken my turns blaming Penny and management. But lately, I've thought about what I could have done differently.

In this world that we live in, the No. 1 player gets all of the blame. It's not something I've ever tried to shy away from; it's just life. Two people get the blame: the top player and the coach, and the player gets it first. When the next season came around and we lost to a hungrier Jordan and the Bulls, I used to hate going to the airport, reading the articles, listening to guys on TV: "Shaq's not a leader."

That's what I heard. Like a broken record.

Maybe then I didn't understand everything it took to be a leader. At that time, all I knew was to lead by example. Besides, whenever I yelled at guys, it was like they went into their shell. You can't yell at Penny and you couldn't yell at Nick. They're too sensitive to take that kind of criticism. Their games would just fall apart. Since there wasn't any point to screaming, I figured if I worked hard and put up numbers, that was enough. Maybe it wasn't. I know that now.

So yeah, maybe I should have spoken up more. But I didn't get much help from the Magic. There weren't any generals around to make sure that the troops obeyed the drill sergeant's law, set the GIs straight.

Before I left, it got ugly.

In March 1996, my world was turned upside down. I had called home to speak to my grandmother, Odessa Chambliss, for a few months. But every time I called, the family would tell me she wasn't there. "She's at the hospital," they would say, and I didn't think anything of it because Grandma worked as a nurse.

But I missed hearing her voice.

Grandma Odessa, my mother's mother, helped raise me. She was always that comfort zone in my life. Whenever I would get in trouble and get a whooping, she always used to sneak in the room with some cake and ice cream. "Don't worry about it," she would say.

She never had a care or worry herself. She went to church every Sunday, always prayed, never swore and never complained. I moved her from Jersey City to Newark when I got my first contract. I bought these two houses in Newark, and I put them together. I had it fixed up. The house was like a mansion, and it made me happy to do something for her after all she had done for me growing up.

Deep down, when I couldn't get hold of her, I knew she was sick. But the family didn't want to tell me she was dying of cancer. They knew I would worry. They didn't tell me until March.

When the doctors told her she was dying, she probably knew she wasn't gonna last long. But she never showed it. A week before she died, I came up to New Jersey to visit. She was real thin and weak, but she had enough energy to speak.

The last thing she said to me was, "You want to fight me?" And then she smiled. I had to go.

I came back up about a week later, on April 2. We were supposed to play the Knicks the next day. I got to the house about 3:00. She was already in a coma. The nurse came and said she was going to die soon.

I went downstairs and cried by myself for three hours. I couldn't believe it. I had never lost anyone close to me. I cried and cried, from about 3:00 P.M. to 6:00 P.M. But then I realized I had to be strong because my mother was there.

I knew that she was gonna lose it. So I had to be there for her and all my aunts. They were already crying in the other room, trying to console each other. I was so sad.

After she passed away, I had wanted to give her the best mausoleum. I wanted to give her a big memorial, with gold on everything. She didn't want that. She wanted something simple. A little headstone right next to Grandpa.

It was the first funeral I ever attended. I still have mementos of her everywhere. I have her old perfume and her old spectacles underneath a glass case in my Orlando home. I have a plaque in her memory in my bedroom in Los Angeles.

Since she passed away, I have privately dedicated every game played on April 2 to her. I go to work for her that day. I once scored 50 points against the Nets on April 2, but I never told anyone what motivated me. Odessa Chambliss *still* motivates me. She was a great woman, and sometimes I still can't believe she's gone.

After my grandmother died, I was a twenty-four-year-old kid trying to put all my feelings together. I was even considering taking a month off just to get my world straight. I left for the funeral on a Thursday, and we were playing the Bulls on a Sunday. I didn't call the Magic. They knew where I was. They knew what I was doing. But for some reason, they turned this into how unprofessional I was.

"Shaq didn't call us, so if he comes to the game Sunday, he's not going to play." That was their attitude. My mother called and asked me what I was doing. "You got a game today. Come on, let's go." Meanwhile, Brian Hill is trying to be a tough guy. "He's not going to play. He hasn't contacted me."

It bothered me. Look. My grandmother had just died, I'm upset, and now I have to deal with the team's questioning my loyalty—the same team I led to the finals the year before, the same damn management I'd told to make sure we got Penny Hardaway instead of Chris Webber, figuring he was the guard we needed. I mean, when Horace Grant was pissed off at Bulls management, I helped recruit the dude, telling him how much we needed him. To this day, I feel like I had a lot to do with not only our wins, but also with putting that team together.

And they're making a big deal out of me not calling after my grandmother, the woman who helped raise me, had died? Nuh-uh. I called up and said, "Yo, they don't let me play today, I ain't playing no more." I showed up in the second quarter and played, but was still upset. I had no desire to play for the Magic. None whatsoever.

That's when I did something to turn the town against me. My contract was about up at the time. Now, every good businessman knows that in negotiations, you start high. When you negotiate and you start high, even if the number may sound astronomical, the worst they can do is say no. It's a starting point. So, out of frustration and, I admit, maybe some calculation, too, I threw out that I would not re-sign with Orlando for anything less than $150 million. I did this knowing full well that no one in the game was getting that kind of money, and knowing damn well I wasn't getting it from anyone.

Soon there were billboards in the city, polls in the newspaper, e-mails. "Does Shaq deserve 150?" They put a billboard up near my mom's house. Eighty-five percent of Orlando, or whoever voted, said I didn't deserve that money. Fifteen percent said I did. And the spectacle didn't stop there. When I announced I was going to be the father of my baby girl, Taahirah, an Orlando radio station started up with, "If you know who Shaq's baby's mama is, call."

Never mind that I was having the baby with my girlfriend of several years, a woman who I'm friends with to this day. Girls would call up, "I saw his Suburban over here on Kirkman Road the other day. I think he messing with the girl in Apartment 2E."

Another girl would call up and say, "He sent some girl that works in my office some money. She had a raggedy car, now she got a nice Lexus."

The gossip and rumors were just killing me, blowing me up inside. One night, I was at a club and saw the deejay who started all of it. I stood over this little tiny chump and, with all my self-control, said, "Man, you lucky you little. . . ."

The team and town were just laying the groundwork for me to leave. The incidents involving Penny—and the Magic's attitude— put the roof on it. For almost three years, we'd worked together well, but by 1996, he was starting to believe everything his identical twin of an agent was telling him, he was starting to think he really was the man. I saw for real what kind of guy Penny was when it came time for new contracts.

It went down like this. In 1996, Penny's contract was up. During his new negotiations, John Gabriel, our general manager, told me, "Look, Penny and his agent want to get more than you." Knowing economics, I knew I was gonna get mine soon enough. So I said, "That's fine. He deserves it; he's been having a great year." Penny decides to sit out a couple of weeks, makes a fuss. When he comes back, the whole city is booing him. The one guy who stuck up for him? Me. I even got on TV and said, "It's Penny's team," just to kill all that. So now it's my turn, I'm trying to get my new contract, and Penny is nowhere to be found. This is the guy who I filmed the movie *Blue Chips* with the summer before his rookie year, the guy I came to know and trust as a teammate. Dude was on the same Olympic team I was on, and he never said anything to the media about the Magic taking care of Shaq. Nothing.

People always thought I had a problem with Penny, but I never had a serious problem with him. I've never been the type to be mad at a guy because he's getting more press than me. If you watch the old tapes, we played great together. Every pass he threw me, every lob he threw, I was there to catch it and we made each other look good. When Magic and Kareem were playing, you never heard people talking about whose team it was. That was how I looked at things, that every great team has to have a great one-two punch.

I think Penny saw things differently.

Penny's a great player and I respect his game, but I think he needs someone other than himself to be the focal point, the leader of the team. Penny just doesn't have the qualities to be that kind of person or player. That's not sour grapes because it didn't work for us; that's just how it is. To this day, I like and respect Penny.

We had a nice team in Orlando. I think we could have been strong for a while. We really could have. But then I left and Penny left. Now they're starting over with Grant Hill and Tracy McGrady. I wish those brothers luck. I hope they can work it out and coexist.

We almost did. Why did I end up on the Lakers? Actually, in the summer of 1996, John Gabriel sealed me going to L.A. Like I said, I was the highest-paid player on the team until Penny signed his deal. I was happy for Penny. Figured my payday was around the corner. Then Gabriel said, "We can't give you more than Penny. We don't want to upset Penny."

When he said that, I was out. Nobody knew that at the time, but I'll tell you what: When John said that, I told him calmly, "OK, you're right. I'll sign with you tomorrow. I'll have Leonard call you tomorrow. He'll handle it."

Inside, I was fuming. I said to myself, I'm not messing with these guys. They're worried about *Penny's* feelings being hurt? Leonard, get Jerry West on the phone.

The whole time we're negotiating, Orlando kept messing around. I kept telling them, "Let's get the deal done." They must have had their spies out. I'm sure they knew I was building a twenty-car garage and a new gym at my lakefront mansion in Isleworth, where Tiger Woods, Ken Griffey, Jr., and a lot of celebrities live. So I guess they're thinking: he's not gonna leave, he's comfortable. But deep down, I'm a businessman. The Lakers were turning their team upside down and went after me hard.

Orlando offered me $69 million over seven years. Jerry West, the Lakers president, was talking $98 million. He was cutting guys left and right to make room for my salary. After I heard Alonzo Mourning was getting $110 million, my leverage was increasing by the day. When the Magic found out what the Lakers could do, then they tried to come back.

"Okay, the Lakers will give you 98, we'll give you 99." All those little games.

I said, "Look, man, I'm done with this."

Believe it or not, it was a one-day thing. I made my decision to become a Laker in one day.

Jerry got rid of George Lynch, sent him to Vancouver, and they were able to get the money up to $121 million.

All of a sudden, 'Zo wasn't making more than Shaq. So I said, "All right, I'll take 121. Let's do this." And I signed.

Jerry flew down to Atlanta during the Olympics. I guess he was more surprised than anything because he was shaking when we met him. He let us know he couldn't believe that I was coming to L.A.

And the truth is, I really had no intention of going there until the games with Orlando started. Like I said, it was a one-day decision. Jerry had this great reputation as the best general manager in the league. He could put teams together like no one else. Sometimes I wonder what would have happened if I said I wasn't coming. Would he have been ruined? Probably not, but the Lakers would have been a much different team. Everything happens for a reason. I'm glad I went there. It helped me to be myself and grow as a person.

At the end, in Orlando, I couldn't even ride around in this city without people passing on information about my life. Meanwhile, in L.A., I could just blend in. I could be in a cigar bar with Leonardo DiCaprio. I don't smoke cigars or smoke anything, but I could be sitting there acting like I'm smoking a cigar, pretend like I'm this big, cool cat, just chilling with a stogie. Now, in Orlando, it would have been, "Oooh, he was in a bar smoking—that's why he was tired in the fourth quarter. His lungs are probably black." But in L.A., you won't even hear nothing about it.

After I signed, there were guys in Orlando with boats putting FOR SALE signs on the house, calling my mom's office. "Shaq took the money and ran," all that stuff. They were so hurt I left they couldn't appreciate those early years when Orlando Arena was rocking with noise.

Now, maybe you're reading all these wild numbers and thinking, "Damn, Shaq, just be happy with $98 million. Shut up and play." But what if somebody who worked in the same business as you— who wasn't as good at what they do as you are—announced to the world that they were being paid more than you are? You would probably say, "That's messed up." Right? Well, I did.

I called up Leonard and said, "Listen, man. I need more than 'Zo. Simple as that." If a BMW getting $110 million, what's a Benz gonna get? Right? When people like 'Zo and Juwan Howard started getting over $100 million, they set the market.

The truth is, as much as a lot of players won't admit it, money equals respect and loyalty in the NBA. And if a player who's not as good as you is making more, then everybody talks about what a stupid deal your agent got you, and how you're not even making as much as So-and-so.

Also, I was tired of Orlando. And I think everything in life happens for a reason. I know it was a good move for me because it helped me start all over. If I would have stayed, I think I would have gone crazy. There's nothing to do in Orlando.

People in Orlando said, "Shaq left for the money; he didn't show no loyalty." The whole town turned on me in a lot of ways, and forgot about all the good times we had those first few years. One of my boys is convinced some crazy fan poisoned my pit bull, Die Hard, who turned up dead right around that time.

I don't know if that's true, but I did find out how many small-minded people live in that town. It was like I committed a felony or something, instead of leaving for a flat-out better situation.

Bye-bye, Small Market. Hello, Hollywood.

When I think about all the things took that team apart, I also have to mention Black Jesus*—Michael Jordan. We were getting stronger and stronger. We took the Bulls out of the playoffs the year he came back from baseball. Then he got mad. Came back the next year and swept us. That helped break the team apart. Once we lost to Jordan, things started to go downhill.

Brian Hill was a good guy, a good coach. He'd been an assistant coach ever since Orlando got a franchise, and was promoted through the ranks. But for me, he wasn't hard enough. He'd be soft on some guys, hard on others. We just didn't respect him. Sometimes he went from nice to hard-core and people were looking around, like, "This ain't the guy we know."

You know what was crazy about Orlando? I told them to get Chuck Daly years before they ever signed him. It was my idea.

*The original Black Jesus was "Earl the Pearl" Monroe.

Chuck was a championship coach with the Detroit Pistons and he was retired, thinking about getting back into the game. When I went to management, they were like, "No, B. Hill led you to the finals. We want to keep him." So after I leave, they sign up Chuck, and he and Penny have problems. If I was there, I would have squashed that. There wouldn't have been no problems. A championship coach that knows how to get us to the next level? I would have had to punch Penny, tell the cat, "Listen, now we got the coach you want, let's do this."

I have been gone from Orlando four, almost five years. It was a great learning experience. It helped me grow as a person. It helped me grow businesswise. It helped me learn a lot about people. I learned that when everything is going good, everybody's on your side. Miss a jumper when you're down by one, they'll kill you. Penny was talking all that noise, "Shaq's a traitor. Blah, blah, blah." Then they started doing the same thing to him. Eventually he left.

In the end, the town was small and had a small-town mentality. Being realistic, I'm a young guy, I got to go out, do some things. The nightlife there wasn't that great, maybe only one club to go to.

Don't get me wrong. My parents live there, and I have a summer home there, where after every season I can just kick back and enjoy life.

Fact is, when I was on the Magic, we had our good times, crazy times and some emotional moments.

I knew the NBA was going to be wild my first year, when our coach Matty Guokas and Jerry "Ice" Reynolds got into it during a game. Matty had all these plays drawn up so that Jerry could stop Dale Ellis, telling him, "Listen, this is the first couple plays they're gonna run. I want you to stick him; don't let him catch the ball."

So Dale Ellis comes off the screen, hits a couple 3-pointers in a row. Matty is pissed. He called a time-out, looks at Jerry Reynolds and says, "What are you doing?!"

Jerry Reynolds grabbed the clipboard, threw it down. "That motherf***er can't guard me, either. Draw some plays up for me! I know he has some game, but draw up some motherf***in' plays for me."

You can kind of see how Matty didn't feel much like coaching after that season.

My second year, I had a wild brawl in practice. I mean, wild. A couple of guys on my team, they would be acting like they're playing hard, be yelling and screaming, acting like they were leaders in front of the coach. Just a bunch of talk. Scotty Skiles, then the team's starting point guard and now the coach at Phoenix, was a leader. But Larry Krystkowiak, Tom Tolbert, Greg Kite, guys like that, talking out loud in front of the coach? It just looked fake.

So we lost to the Clippers. The next day, we're practicing at the Forum in L.A. and our coach, Brian Hill, comes in. "You aren't playing any defense," he said. "You have to play defense." So it's a rough practice, and Kite and some other dudes like Krystkowiak weren't moving their feet, they were just hitting, hacking me to death.

I finally said to Greg, "Listen, you hit me like that again, I'm gonna punch you in the face."

So now Larry hacks me and I just lose it. I punch Larry in the face. Then Scott Skiles—this dude was little, but he had a big heart—charges me, jumps in and tries to break it up. I gave him a two-piece. Bing-bing. Everybody is going crazy, the whole team falling over each other in the front row of the Forum, an all-out brawl. I don't remember much more than that, except Greg Kite's big head. I hit him square in his head, and I was like, "Ahhhh, that hurts." With that big blockhead of his, he didn't even move and I damn near broke my hand.

We played the Lakers the next day and destroyed them.

Now, I don't recommend physically going after your teammates, but getting out that aggression helped break the ice for us.

We had a lot of cliques on that team. Dennis Scott and I were hanging out. Anthony Bowie and Donald Royal were a clique. All the white guys stuck together, and Nick and Penny were either by themselves or hung out together. It was a funny team. A lot of arguments. A lot of acting crazy. When I look back, we were just kids. We had cruel nicknames and everything, busting on each other like kids in grade school do. Like, Nick had this skin irritation where he would get bumps on the back of his neck. So we started calling Nick, "Morse Code Neck."

And that wasn't even the meanest or most embarrassing nickname. We called Anthony Bowie "B.H.D." I can't tell you what that meant (my agent would take it out anyway), but it shows you how young and immature we were. We would make fun of physical appearances, anything. It didn't matter.

When you're in your early twenties and growing up in the NBA, sometimes the only family you got is your team. Black or white, whether you're from the country or the 'hood, it doesn't matter. Teammates become your brothers. And Dennis Scott was my closest brother. I never got closer to a teammate than I got to my man, D.

When I first got to Orlando, I used to live forty-five minutes away from downtown, out by Disney. D was the only one who came out and picked me up, showed me around the town, showed me where I should live, introduced me to people. We had the same interests: trucks, rims, music. He would show me where I could get rims for my car, things like that. On the court, we were close, too. When I got doubled, I was looking for him to drop in that 3-pointer. He was one of the best long-distance shooters in the league, a guy who could break down a defense by hitting that jumper.

I have a lot of memories of our time together, but one of the most unforgettable came during a road trip in the middle of the season. He was sitting in the back of the bus on the phone and I heard him say, "What?" He just dropped the phone and he hit the window.

I picked up the phone, I was like, "Hello?"

The person on the other end delivered the bad news: "D's father just died."

There were a lot of unanswered questions, but basically the authorities said it was a drug overdose. I felt so bad for him. I went up to the front of the bus and told B. Hill.

When we got to the hotel, D was so shaken up, I wasn't sure what he would do. I didn't want him to do something crazy alone in his hotel room. So we're in this five-star place, and I just ripped the mattress off my bed, dragged it down to his room, and put it on the floor. I was staying with him all night, no matter what. He sat up all night. I was getting tired, but I didn't want to leave. Every time he moved, I would go, "Where you going, boy!"

He's like, "No, I'm going to walk around."

I'm like, "I'm going with you."

I probably don't have to tell this to people who have lost someone close to them. But when you're young and a family member passes on, it shakes your world like nothing you can imagine. So much pain, so much anger comes out. I didn't know how he felt until my grandmother died on April 2, 1996. Then I knew. You're angry at the world because other people still have their daddies and grandmas around, and you don't. You think it's not fair, it's not right.

After that experience, D and I became even closer. In this league, you got all these crazy coaches who talk about not hanging out with the enemy and separating your friendship from competition. Pat Riley does that. And when you get on the court, you are competitors. (Call D. Scott right now, ask him what I did to him in Dallas when he tried to lay it up—I tried to pin his weak shot against the glass, that's what.) But don't tell me not to hang out with a friend when we've been through the kind of life experiences that D and I have. There's real life, and there's NBA life. And D and I found out together they don't compare.

We won an Eastern Conference championship in Orlando and we put excitement in that town. I won't ever forget that. One of my last memories from Orlando came one day when I walked into the locker room and met this young high-school kid who everybody was saying was gonna be a great player.

His favorite player at that time was Penny. When they introduced the kid to Penny, he asked if he could have a picture with him. Penny said, "Yeah, come on, hurry up."

Penny took the picture, signed something real quick and walked off. Didn't say hi to him, didn't ask him where he was going to college, see what he was really about.

I was standing right there and couldn't believe it, Penny dogging him out, treating him like some autograph hound. Afterward, I walked up to the kid. "What's up, man, how you doing? You all right? Everything all right?"

I was there for maybe five minutes, getting to know him a little because he seemed like a real bright young kid who was happy to meet me. His dad even played in the NBA at one point.

"Nice to meet you," I told this young kid before he left. "Good luck, dog. See you in the NBA."

I don't know why, but I knew I was going to see that young cat again. I just knew.

4

Growing Pains

Why the Old Lakers Couldn't Win the Big One

L.A. was a new lease on life for me. I knew everybody on the West Coast was gonna be excited after the Lakers signed me in the summer of 1996. The last time any of their sports teams had won a title was back in 1988, when the Lakers beat the Pistons in the finals and the Dodgers won the World Series. Both the NFL teams were gone by the time I got there. They didn't even have pro football. In truth, L.A. wasn't close to the same town where Magic Johnson had won five titles during the 1980s. A lot had gone down, and not just in sports. You had the hangover from the O. J. Simpson trial, the Rodney King beatings. Riots. An earthquake. It's not like I thought about that stuff when I got there, but let's just say it wasn't La-La Land.

So this big 7'1" kid shows up, smiling, ready to dominate, just what the people wanted—something to take their mind off things, make them think about the days when Magic, Kareem and James Worthy were running the Forum and making everybody stand up and start singing that goofy song, "I Love L.A. . . . We love it!"

I felt comfortable right away. I'd been going to L.A. the last four summers, so I already had a house on the beach. Right after our seasons ended, I used to fly out to Hollywood and make movies.

Even before I came to Orlando, I was out in L.A. because Leonard, my agent, lives and is based there. So I knew all the stars, all the girls, knew all the clubs. I knew all the fellas. I knew all the dogs. Which barbershop. Where to eat. In some ways, it was just like I was coming home. Plus, I was already burned out from doing everything. The movies. The records. It wasn't new to me anymore. I do think if I would have played my first four years out here in Hollywood, I probably would have been in trouble, maybe got too caught up in the fast lane.

I look at it like this: My first four years in Orlando was just like another college, LSU all over again. But going to the Lakers, I felt I was going into the real world. It wasn't that my life was gonna change that much. But my career was going to change. I knew it would. I felt like I was starting over, getting out of a small town, playing with a new crew. I knew what mistakes were made, and now I knew what to do, what not to do.

I wanted so bad for everything to work right away. And nothing did. I mean, nothing. In my first three years in Los Angeles, we won games, and I put up big numbers, had some great times. But as far as being a championship team, it wasn't going to happen. We had no chemistry, a bunch of me-me-me guys and a couple of coaches who had trouble gaining respect.

A team of knuckleheads, is what we had.

We always won fifty, sixty games; we just couldn't get over certain people in the playoffs. It's not like the Utah Jazz and the San Antonio Spurs were more hungry. It's not like they beat us at our best. It's that their teams were more together. They believed in each other.

The Lakers? Sometimes we hated each other.

Everybody wanted to be the man. You know that I wanted to be the hero. Nick Van Exel, our little stop-and-pop point guard those first few years, he wanted to shoot. Eddie Jones, our slash-and-burn shooting guard, he was mad because he wasn't getting shots. Eddie was mad because a youngster named Kobe Bryant was turning into a bigger option than him. Eddie was mad because he heard trade rumors. Eddie was mad because he was gonna try to ask for more money than Kobe, and everybody knew Kobe was the future and the Lakers weren't gonna do it. Basically, Eddie was always mad.

Nick knew he was getting traded. Elden Campbell? He was just lazy. Cedric Ceballos, I guess management didn't like him. He was a good little garbage player and a basket hanger, that's about it.

It seems like we were feuding every day.

One time, we're playing against the Clippers, and Maurice Taylor is killing Elden. Just destroying him. Now, Del Harris, our coach, is this white-haired, mid-60s-looking cat, looks like Leslie Nielsen in the *Naked Gun* movies. He was always so cool and calm, it was like hearing your grandfather talk sometimes. But not that night. At half-time, Del said, "Hey, Elden, you can't guard him?"

Elden says, "Why don't you fuckin' send help? We always got to double-team the guards."

Del just threw a chair in the locker room, threw a chair at the chalkboard. "Shut the fuck up and guard him, Elden! You're 6'11", he's six-fucking-seven. You can't fucking guard him? Play some fucking defense."

"Fuck that," Elden answered in a kind of whiny voice. "Send help. We always got to double down on the guard. How come the guards can't double down on us?"

So I'm like, "Enough already, I'll guard him." I'll stop Maurice Taylor. How tough can he be?

We go back out, Maurice hits two threes in my face. Del calls a time-out. "Can anybody fucking guard this guy? We're playing the fucking Clippers."

It wasn't just Del and Elden. Del and Nick used to go at it all the time. One time in practice, Del just started messing with Nick, pointing out everything he did wrong. Nick finally said, "Listen, man, I know what the fuck I'm doing. Leave me alone."

Del came up to him, pushed him. "What the fuck did you say?"

Nick said, "Don't you ever fucking put your hands on me again, bitch."

Del wouldn't quit. "I'll beat your fuckin' punk-ass. Get your punk-ass out of my practice."

So boom, Nick jets the practice.

Hearing Del talk like that blew everyone away. I guess he'd been watching a lot of TV and wanted to try to get in with the brothers. I don't think any of us expected some white-haired old man to say something like, "What you gonna do, punk bitch?" But I have to admit: it was good entertainment.

I found out later that that wasn't the real Del. He later recommitted his life to Christ and became very religious. Del is a good family man and a great person.

After that blowup, Derek Fisher was given the starting point-guard job. Fisher was playing well and Nick was coming off the bench, and didn't even try to get his starting position back. He just sat there. You could tell Nick wasn't a fighter then. And Elden didn't show me much, either. I am not saying he ever fouled-shaved, but at times it looked that way to me. A lot of guys foul-shave when they've been out all night. Anyway, I'm not saying that's what Elden was doing, but sometimes he was a funny cat.

Another time, we're playing the Pacers—this was when they had both the Davises, Dale and Antonio, two of the roughest forwards in the game. So I had to guard Dale Davis. Elden had to guard Antonio Davis. We were running down the court and Elden tells me, "Yo, get Antonio. That motherf***er is playing too aggressive."

Antonio was elbowing him, throwing him around, catching his shots off the board, playing hard, because they were trying to beat us. (Memo to Elden: That's what hardworking NBA players do.)

So I had to get Antonio. Elden just didn't want any part of him.

For anyone scoring at home, now you've got Nick and Del fighting, Eddie and Del fighting, Elden cursing Del out, Ceballos and Del fighting. . . .

Once, when things weren't going well, I got everybody dancing on the team charter plane. Remember that song, "The Macarena"? In this world, the stupidest songs get played the most. "Macarena" and "Whoop, There It Is" are two of those songs.

Anyway, so we're at 35,000 feet in the air, cruising along, and all of a sudden I started freaking it. Because, see, white people do "The Macarena" a certain way. But I did a ghetto hip-hop remix of "The Macarena."

I was freaking it, mumbling, "Hey, Macarena." Except I changed the words. I had the whole team doing it and singing.

I don't want to say what I changed the words to in this book, but let's just say it was pretty funny.

And also, with all of us in a conga line dancing down the aisle, the charter plane started to sway back and forth. Maybe it was just turbulence, but it was a wild time in Laker land.

After all these expectations when I came to L.A., I'm thinking to myself, "What the hell is going on with this team? Orlando wasn't this crazy." I knew we weren't gonna win.

Maybe you're saying to yourself, "Damn Shaq, you are making all that money, step up and be a leader." It isn't as simple as that. You can't lead if you don't have people to follow. Nick and Eddie thought they knew it all. Like I said, Elden was lazy, although he looks like he's turned his career around in Charlotte. Cedric was mad because he wasn't getting enough shots. Plus, I'm not too proud of myself here, but I admit it: I didn't give Kurt Rambis or Del Harris my all.

Why? I just didn't respect those guys, especially during tough situations.

Whenever we'd play Utah, Del had us run two- and three-hour practices playing against the pick-and-roll. That's all we did. We focused so much on Karl Malone's stock that the other guys ate us up. Malone's always gonna get his points. Malone's like me. No matter what you do, I'm gonna get above 27 a game. We went over twenty different coverages, and by the end of a practice, we'd be like, "What the hell did he just say?" No one knows whether they should rotate back to John Stockton or to Jeff Hornacek or to Bryon Russell.

In our second season together, we were starting to look sweet against Seattle, taking the Sonics apart in the second round. Then Utah beat us like a drum, four straight, busting our ass again, sweeping us in the Western Conference finals.

"I'm very frustrated," I told reporters after the final game, showing my anger for one of the first times. "I'm very angry. I've got to go home and live with it. Guys just have to step up. They don't want to play, they need to ask for a trade. They don't want to play, they can get the f*** off my team."

Were the players to blame? Definitely. We had a lot of personal agendas that got in our way. But when things were going bad, we didn't get much help from the bench.

There are things I didn't like about Del Harris as a coach. For one, in a practice, he would spend thirty minutes on one player's mistake. Then he would start telling stories from his old days as a coach with the Bucks. "In Milwaukee . . ." It was like that old colonel in the cartoon. He'd be telling some crazy story about his adventures overseas, and the dude next to him would be nodding off. While Del was trying to teach, we were getting stiff. After a while, guys just didn't feel like practicing any more for Del. Players couldn't take him. And if you don't respect a man, you're not going to give your all for him.

So Del gets fired in the middle of the 1999 season. Kurt Rambis, who was sort of like Brian Hill, takes over. Kurt was one of those all-out, hustle role players on Magic's teams. After he retired, he became an assistant coach. I thought Kurt was cool. You could talk to Kurt. After Del was fired, I was the one who called upstairs, said, "OK, do Kurt. Make Kurt the man."

Kurt is a good guy. But he was in a no-win situation.

We win ten straight games as soon as he takes over. Things are looking good, the Lakers are turning the corner during the lockout season.

But we start falling apart again, and the pressure starts to get to Kurt. He's always been a nice guy, but now he starts coming to practice like a hard-ass. "I want you to sprint and run, and hard," he said. "And, Shaq, you're gonna practice."

One day in practice, I hurt myself dunking. All of a sudden, there was this pain down my side. Hurt to the point where I could barely run. I know you're not supposed to talk back to the coach, but I was in real pain. I told him he wasn't getting both a hard practice and a hard game out of me. I physically couldn't do it. I shouldn't have been playing at that point.

"Dammit Shaq, you never want to practice."

"It's not that I never want to practice," I said. "I can't run."

He's starting to act crazy, starting to be someone that everyone knows he isn't. He kept pushing the wrong buttons. Everybody knows Kurt has never been that type of guy. So now the guys are really angry, and they lose respect for him.

Truth is, the thing that hurt him the most turned out to be his relationship with Kobe Bryant.

Kobe is the son of Joe "Jellybean" Bryant, the former NBA player. He'd skipped college altogether and arrived for his rookie year with the Lakers as a seventeen-year-old kid out of Lower Merion High School, outside of Philadelphia. Even then, Kobe could do things above the rim that other players in the NBA only dreamed about.

But before he won his first slam-dunk contest or became the youngest All-Star in history, Kobe was still trying to figure out the game. Even though I was still growing up in a lot of ways myself, there was a lot of pressure for both us to deliver right away.

Now, most times in the NBA, the head coaches who end up making friends with the best players on the team end up surviving. An All-Star has your back. He goes to management and says, "Look, I'm not playing for anybody else," and all of a sudden you got a five-year deal. Life is looking good. That's happened with a lot of coaches in the league who probably didn't deserve to be around as long as they were.

But when Kurt started letting Kobe do whatever he wanted to do, and we lost a bunch of games, it backfired on him. The guys on the team were not happy.

Kobe comes down, doing that Michael Jordan unorthodox stuff, and guys couldn't stand it. Nobody knew what Kobe was gonna do. And while Kurt would yell at everybody else, he'd treat Kobe differently.

After we'd lose a game and we'd been on a roll, we'd be getting off the team plane and Kurt would be kneeling in front of Kobe's car, talking to him, "Blah, blah, blah."

Then one day, right before we were getting ready to play Sacramento in February 1999, I said, "Man, we need to have a meeting." And everybody just starting going off on Kobe, really criticizing him for his selfishness on the court. People might say we were harsh, but it wasn't personal. We wanted to win games and set the kid straight. That's all.

Anyway, Kurt gets up and says, "When you guys were young, I'm sure you made mistakes."

Now I'm pissed. Whenever this kid makes a mistake, he's blaming it on, "He's young." This is this cat's third year, OK? And I could understand missing someone once under the basket. Because my thing is if you come down and you miss a guy once or twice, it's an accident. But when you miss a guy six or seven times in a row, you're being selfish. I don't care who it is. You're being selfish.

My feeling was, he has to learn, and you got to teach him right now. Don't let him do whatever he wants to do. Don't be doing all that high-school stuff. This isn't high school. We're trying to win. So I go off in this meeting in Sacramento, said, "You know what, I don't want to hear that. This is Kobe's third year. Guys don't like playing with the cat. Some guys on the team think he's selfish. Yeah, he's a great player. But he's gonna need us; he's gonna have to use us."

That's why people think me and Kobe had a problem—because of that incident. They had it all wrong. I liked the way Kobe played. The only problem I had is, you got to use what you got to get what you want. At that point, we'd been knocked out of the playoffs twice by the Jazz, and everybody was wondering if we were ever going to get our act together. I saw another season of potential going down the drain.

And Kurt's babying Kobe wasn't the only sign.

After the lockout ended, a lot of players came to camp out of shape. Including myself. We had no idea when we were going to play or whether the whole season was going to be canceled. Teams like the Knicks were taking wild chances, trading for Latrell Sprewell, trying to get some new life in their roster. The Lakers went out on a limb, too. Just to show how desperate we were, we took a gamble on Dennis Rodman. We picked him up that season, hoping he could give us the rebounding we needed to get over the hump. But D. Rod had a lot going on his life, too much to be a full-time ballplayer. He was taking off, not showing up for practice. He was weird. On the court, he did his job. But off the court, I think he took Madonna marketing too far.

D. Rod didn't respect Kurt, either. The game would start at 7:30, the media would leave at 6:45, and Rodman would come in at 7:15, wearing some crazy-ass outfit, eating a chicken plate.

Kurt would be saying, "This is how we're going to play the pick-and-roll."

Rodman would go, "No, that's not how you play the pick-and-roll. Let them motherf***ers shoot."

At first, the organization sucked up to him too much. They let him get away with anything. He'd just come in whenever he wanted to, and he did what he wanted to. He didn't practice. He told Kurt one day, "I don't shoot, so why the fuck am I practicing?"

D. Rodman would talk back to Kurt all the time. Like one time we lost a game, Kurt came in the locker room and got on us. D. said, "Can I say something?"

"Go ahead, Dennis," Kurt said.

"It's not the players' fault," Rodman said. "It's *your* fucking fault." Then he went off on Kurt. "I ain't used to this sh**. You ain't got no organization. When I fucking played with Phil Jackson, Phil told us how we was gonna play the pick-and-roll, who does what. You don't do sh**. Just fucking come in and put some bullsh** on the board and tell us to guard. That's why we lost. You ain't sh**. You a sorry-ass coach."

Rodman was wild, but a lot of the players in the locker room agreed with him. After that night, they were laughing, saying, "You exactly right."

The next practice, D. Rod was gone. And Kurt tried to be even more hard-core. "Goddamn it, we're gonna do a three-man weave, you better run."

I was so fed up with everything at that point, I turned into a young knucklehead again.

"I'm not doing it," I told Kurt.

"Just like I thought, Shaq."

"Kurt, you're trying to come with this mad-dog attitude 'cause D. Rodman told you off, no? Then you let Kobe do whatever he wants to do. My stomach is messed up, and I'm in pain, and I'm not running. So fine me."

Jerry West had to come down and talk to me and tell me to do it.

I can't say D. Rodman was a great teammate. In fact, he wasn't. He did get about 17 rebounds a game for us and made my life easier under the basket. But you never knew when he was showing up. Plus, the dude was phony. While we were teammates, he talked some mess about me to the media. I guess he wanted to make himself seem tough. I'm not gonna lie to you, I wanted to punch him in his face so many times. But Jerry West just told me to be cool and calm. "Don't worry about it." So I kept my cool.

In a way, I kind of felt sorry for D. Rod. A cat like that will never get his due as one of the great role players of his time because of all the crazy off-the-court stuff. I was watching some NBA classic tapes when the Pistons were playing the Lakers. Rodman had no tattoos back then. He didn't say nothing. He was just a nice, hard-working player. Then after he start messing with crazy Madonna, she taught him how to market himself. Then the media shows up at his wedding. The son-of-a-gun puts on a dress and marries himself.

I'll give him this: he was funny. Like, he never took a shower after the game. After a hard game playing forty minutes, he'd just put his stuff on and walk right out. Next thing I know, I'd see him at some club that night with about thirty girls on him—those crazy, techno, ecstasy highlight parties. I once walked into one of those parties. Leonardo DiCaprio's there. Robert Downey, Jr., he's there. All these cats making weird faces. It's dark as hell. People are drinking. D. Rod popping Cristalle champagne, showing off. A lot of stars. A lot of girls, some of them taking their tops off. I just got out of there. Quick.

Being from the streets and all, I knew that's the kind of crowd you can get hurt in and not even know who hurt you. I was getting nervous walking around there. Two minutes in D. Rod's world, and I wanted out.

Even in rough times, I got good vibes from the people of L.A. They stuck with me. Every time we'd lose, I'd go out and people would say, "We'll get 'em next year, dog." They stuck with me. I'll never forget that.

Sometimes I would go out, people would say, "What is Del Harris doing? Why didn't he pass you the ball? Why did Kobe take it? Why did he take the last three shots in a row and they all didn't go in."

I would say, "Man, don't worry about it."

The fans were real patient. They saw that I was a hard worker. However much money they paid to see me play, they knew I was giving it my all and I was doing it for them. They knew I was busting my ass. They knew I wasn't one of those guys who worry about getting all that money and ain't worth the money, doesn't do anything, a guy like Juwan Howard. The ticket price was gonna be raised to $50. They knew they'd pay $50 to come get a show.

"Let's come to watch Shaq tear the rim off, talk trash, rough people up, win games." OK, maybe that's a little reach. But the truth is, the fans were more patient than me.

I wish I could have done more for them my first few years in L.A., but it wasn't going to happen. And the team wasn't the only thing falling apart; so was my body. The most frustrating part for me was injuries. I wasn't myself for much of the first three seasons as a Laker. I was the S-h-a-c-k and not the S-h-a-q. The difference? Shack is just being out there. Still good enough to put up All-Star numbers, but not the dominating man in the middle. The S-h-a-q is the dominant, everybody-scared-of-me-dunking-on-their-head cat, that type of guy.

First season in L.A., I missed thirty-one games with sprained ligaments in my left knee. I was scared to move. I had this big knee brace. I was out there with the guys and putting up OK numbers, but I didn't want to twist it. I was going about 89 percent, which was still good enough to do certain work. But I couldn't play defense.

That's why Greg Ostertag was scoring and getting easy baskets. I couldn't box out, couldn't step-slide, couldn't show on a pick-and-roll against Utah. Then, in Minnesota, I hyperextended my right knee all the way back. I was out six to eight weeks then.

And knee injuries were nothing compared to the abdominal strain I suffered in my second year. I've never told anyone this, but from December 1997 until the summer of 1998, I was scared I would never be able to play basketball like I once did.

What happened? Well, I was on this sit-up kick. Del would talk for thirty minutes and I would try to get ten sets of fifty sit-ups done to get my six-pack going. Then Del says, "All right, get up and go." No stretching, nothing.

The first day of training camp before the 1997 season, we were on a 3-on-2 break. I'm trying to Vince-Carter-cuff-dunk on Elden's ass. I brought the ball all the way back. But I was way too far from the basket. I overstretched and tore my abdominal muscles. I missed 22 games that season. They call it a sports hernia. The doctors said I ripped the lower quadrant of the abdominal wall on the left side. No one knows this, but it was diagnosed as career-threatening. The doctors told me that if the tissue doesn't heal and isn't rehabbed properly, that's it. You're done. At least three of them said I was risking permanent damage if I continued to play and ripped the muscles further.

I missed the season opener, and the injury was killing me all the way into the playoffs. And to top things off, I was rehabilitating it the wrong way. The Lakers trainer, Gary Vitti, and team physician, Dr. Steve Lombardo, had no clue how to treat the injury. No one knew what was going on.

The strange thing about the injury was that I could walk, but I couldn't reach for anything. I couldn't reach to block shots, I couldn't stretch to rebound. It hurt to go to my jump hook or to dunk hard. I had to wear this belt with a tight strap around my waist. I took three cortisone shots for the pain and other antiinflammatory pills. During the game, with the adrenaline going, it was OK. But when I woke up the next day, I couldn't move. I would have to call my acupuncturist, Shen Hsu, early in the morning just so I could get up.

For a while, I wasn't sure I was going to beat the injury. I got to the point where I was thinking about, "What if I am like Charles Barkley or Malone and Stockton? What if it just isn't meant to be?"

I mean, I wanted to be labeled as a great player, but I didn't want to be labeled as a great player who didn't win and who couldn't win. And a couple times I said to myself, "Maybe I *am* going to be like that."

Fed up with my own team doctors, I went to three of the best abdominal specialists. One of them told me I should have surgery. Leonard tracked down this one physical therapist from Vancouver who worked with Paul Kariya of the National Hockey League's Anaheim Mighty Ducks. So I checked out some of these guys on the Internet. This hockey-physical-therapist dude turns out to be a forty-something, 5'9" Scottish guy with white hair.

Alex McKechnie turned out to be one of the most important people in my career. He had done a lot of work with hockey and soccer players suffering from abdominal, pelvic and groin injuries. He was the physical therapist for Canada's national soccer team. The Lakers didn't know what to make of him. But they had no idea how to fix the injury themselves, so they just took a chance. McKechnie would use these big balls, elastic bands and balance boards, talking about "core strength" and "building my center of gravity." One of the first things he did was move my muscles a certain way so I could feel where it hurt. I would look over to the Lakers trainer and say, "How come these guys don't know this stuff?"

I'll admit it: I lost confidence in the Lakers doctors. I stopped going to them for advice on the injury after they told me it was something else. I was seriously worried, wondering if I would ever fully recover from the injury. I was scared emotionally and mentally. I'd ask Alex over and over, "Will I ever get over this? Is this pain going to go away?"

Alex told me straight up: "Even if you have surgery, you still could reinjure yourself. Let's just strengthen your back up."

So I kept working with him. And on his advice, I continued to play with the injury, missed only one game under his care. He came to L.A., started traveling with us on the road. After a while, I got to a point where I wouldn't do anything unless he was there. I was working out with him all last year during the lockout. In the summer of 1998, I didn't do any movies or anything. We rented a house up in Vancouver off a time share, stayed up there like a month and a half, and I just worked out with him. Got my stomach strong. I was ready to play at full strength again, just like when I was healthy in Orlando.

I hold certain coaches in high regard because they moved me, motivated me. Dave Madura, at Cole High School in San Antonio, moved me because he was hard. Dale Brown at LSU moved me because he was hard. To this day, I owe a lot of my success to those two men.

Madura, our high-school coach, walked around with chewing tobacco in his mouth. He would tell you to grab the net with your teeth. If you didn't do it, you would be running suicides until you threw up. When he said something, he meant it.

But some of the coaches I played for, they said something and they didn't mean it. I don't know if they were in awe of me and they felt like they had to be my friend to keep their jobs, or if they just did things differently than I was used to. Maybe they were used to dealing with professionals, and what they ended up coaching was a bunch of hardheaded kids.

Either way, the teams I was on in Orlando and L.A. wanted and needed discipline. When I saw Matty Guokas get talked back to constantly, I lost respect for him. When Brian Hill went from good-guy assistant to hard-ass head coach, I lost respect for him. We wouldn't have won with Kurt. We wouldn't have won with Del. Everyone knew it.

When the Spurs swept us in 1999, teams I had played on had been swept five out of the last seven years. After we lost to San Antonio, Mark Whicker, this columnist from the *Orange County Register,* wrote, "It's time again to make broom for Shaquille O'Neal."

He was just being funny, but what could I say? It was out there. "Shaq can't even win a playoff game."

I wasn't gonna make any excuses. I'm not gonna say, "I never had the coach that Bill Russell had." I would never do that. At the end of my career, if I stopped playing and didn't have a ring, then what could I do? It just didn't happen.

But after three years in L.A., none of my dreams about getting a ring were closer to coming true. So I wanted to make sure I made every effort to get the best coach available in the summer of 1999.

There were three coaches I called Leonard about. Chuck Daly, who got sick of Penny in Orlando and re-retired, was the number-one option. Chuck was under contract to consult for three more years; but since we lived in the same neighborhood in Orlando, once the season had ended, I drove to his house unannounced.

The number-two option was Bob Hill. But Jerry didn't like Bob Hill. For some reason, nobody likes Bob Hill. I don't know what it's about. Bob was our assistant when we made it to the finals in Orlando. He told it like it was, helped B. Hill keep the players in line. He coached David Robinson in San Antonio, Rik Smits in Indiana. I thought that he would get the Clippers job a while back, but he didn't. Now he's the head coach at Fordham University in New York.

Our last option, of course, was Phil Jackson. Phil left Chicago after the 1997–98 season, thanks to a bunch of problems with Chicago GM Jerry Krause. Krause messed that up. When a man's got you six titles, why wouldn't you give him everything he wants? Anyway, Phil said he wasn't coming back. He took off for a year, and there were no guarantees that he would ever coach again. So I figured he would be a long shot. That's why he was my third choice.

Anyway, I'm glad Krause got so arrogant to the point where he thought *he* was the guy responsible for all those titles in Chicago. He forced Phil to leave. Helped get me my ring.

I didn't want to tell Jerry West about my feelings about a new coach because I don't like to be the bad guy. But behind closed doors, I told Leonard, "Listen, tell him I'm not playing for Kurt. Nobody wants to play for Kurt. If Kurt's coaching next year, I ain't playing."

Jerry promised me he was gonna talk to Phil. He was going to try and get me the coach I thought could get the most out of me and my teammates. Whenever things got crazy, Jerry always found a way to make things better. Always.

The best example of this was after the low point of my Laker career in 1998. The Jazz had just swept us. After the final game, I'm mad as hell, I'm about to go through another off-season of people saying I can't lead a team to the finals. I go back into the Forum weight room, and I start ripping the stalls off the doors. I'm throwing ice bags around, cursing people out. This was the day I told the media that certain players could "get the f∗∗∗ off my team" if they didn't want to play. I usually never sound off like that, but I was angrier than I've ever been in the NBA. I was trying to break every-thing but the mirrors because I didn't want seven years' bad luck. I'm even telling Jerome, my bodyguard, and one of the people who looked after me growing up in Newark, "Leave me alone. Get out of here."

All of a sudden, Jerry walks in and surveys the wreckage.

"Calm down, don't hurt yourself," was the first thing he said.

He asked me, "What the hell are you mad about? The other guys didn't help you, plain and simple. You haven't got it together yet. But trust me, we will."

And then he said something that changed my whole perspective about my career, something that gave me hope. I knew a lot about Jerry West as a GM, but it turns out I didn't know enough about him as a player.

"You know I went to the finals nine times before I won?" he said.

That eased the pain. I remember driving home that day, thinking, "Damn, this would be a good commercial."

Jerry told me, "You're going to be all right. You haven't got the right team. I'm going to get you some pieces, I promise you."

Nine times to the finals and no ring? He hurt a lot worse than me. Compared to Jerry West, I didn't even know what pain was.

From that moment, I felt a lot better about the future. I stopped trying to destroy the weight room and started to think about fixing my career.

5

Summit Meeting

How That Zen Cat Kicked Our Be-Hinds and Made Us See What We Wanted

When I first talked with my new coach, he didn't ask me to be a leader, get more rebounds, lose weight, or get along with Kobe or else. All that would come later. The first challenge Phil Jackson put in front of me?

"You see that tree?" he asked. "Move it."

It was the summer of 1999, and I was just coming off a tough play-off loss. With injuries and chemistry problems, I was worried our crew was never going to figure out what it took to win a title.

So I'm in Kalispell, Montana, where I'm doing a rap show for about 15,000 people. There's this beautiful-ass lake. It's clear. Biggest freshwater lake in the world. And guess who has a log cabin just a boat ride away?

Phil didn't even have to go to the Mountain. I came to him.

He had just gotten the Lakers job when I showed up unannounced. Me and my bodyguard Jerome find the place. His summer house was nice. You could see these big front windows from far away, and all of the golden balls there, duplicates of the six championship trophies Phil won when he coached Michael Jordan, Scottie Pippen and the Bulls dynasty. The sun hit them and they were gleaming.

"I'm sorry to come unannounced," I told his wife. "I'm just waiting for Phil."

She's like, "He's on his bike; he went somewhere. He should be back any minute."

So I meet his daughter, Chelsea. I meet his son. He has a trampoline there. I'm jumping on the trampoline, I'm acting crazy. They're worried because they think I'm gonna bust the trampoline. His son started doing trampoline tricks. Me and his mom, we're joking around. I go in the house, he's got all these Zen books and all the championship balls, all his rings right there.

Then I come back out. I decide I'm gonna take a swim. She gives me some shorts. I jump in the lake. It's freezing. So I start doing flips off the dock. They were laughing at me because I'm not completing my flips, landing on my back like some knucklehead at the community-center pool.

So I'm having a good time, until Phil comes out and sees me in the water and asks me to move some dead tree that floated up on his property.

First he ties a rope around this tree in his yard. And while he's pulling it with the boat, all of us were pushing the tree. He took the damn tree way, way out, and I'm hanging on to the bark, making sure it's going. And then I had to swim back from this damn island. It was far— I don't know how far, but it was far. And you know what I'm thinking? This man is challenging me, just like my Dad when he threw me in Hayes Home Pool in Newark, New Jersey, and taught me how to swim. I'm thinking, Phil Jackson means business.

I get back to his house, take my clothes off and take a shower. He sees that I'm big. I'm pumping weights all summer, taking Creatine and other muscle-building stuff. I was huge, more than 350 pounds of solid bulk.

"How much you weigh?" he asked.

"I don't know," I said.

"I want you to lose about fifteen pounds," he said. "The bigger you are, the harder it's gonna be on your knees, and I want you playing forty minutes a game."

"OK."

That's all I said. That's all he said. We didn't talk about basketball. He said, "Listen, I need to talk to you and Kobe when I get back."

That was it. The beginning of the Lakers' championship season didn't start in a gym during training camp. It started that day in Montana. Just from that short visit, I knew Phil Jackson would guide us to a championship in L.A.

Everybody talks about all that Zen stuff when it comes to Phil. Yoga, Native-American chants, handing out books to people. I was cool with that, but I was more impressed that Phil just laid it out, straight up. No sugarcoating.

He asked me, "How come you can't get it going in the play-offs? You do great during the season, but then come play-off time, you guys just fall and fail."

I was like, "I don't know, I can't explain it."

"What's your problem with Kobe?" he wanted to know.

"I don't have a problem with Kobe," I said. "It's just that 'cause he's young, people like to revert back to that, make excuses for him."

He said, "You've got to be patient with a kid like that," using that word I hate so much: "Patient."

I said, "OK, if that's the way you want it."

See, Phil didn't know that me and Kobe didn't really have that much of a problem, but he saw the play-offs and how we'd played, and he'd been hearing a lot of things. And the first thing he did was to bridge the Kobe-Shaq gap.

He understood how to push buttons and cut out all the nonsense and make us do what he wanted us to do to get to the finals.

We got down to L.A. and right before our physicals, he met with me and Kobe and Ron Harper, who had been on Phil's teams in Chicago. He told us how it's gonna be. He told us every great team has a one-two punch. He says, "This is your team, Shaq. And, Kobe, you're gonna be our floor leader."

He said, "Shaq and Ron, you're gonna be the captains. Kobe, you listen to Ron."

Then Phil said, "You guys don't like that, let me know now and

I'll trade you now. You're gonna do what I say, and if you don't, you're outta here."

So I'm sitting there thinking, "Oh, yes, this is the type of stuff I like. We gonna be all right."

Kurt Rambis, our coach before Phil, never said that. Del Harris, who was replaced by Kurt, never said that. Del had Eddie Jones coming down shooting off one leg, fade-away, Rex Chapman threes.

A lot of guys in the NBA talk about wanting to play for coaches they really like and who get the label of "players' coaches." But down deep, a lot of us players want someone to kick us in the ass—because we already got everything we need in life. We want discipline. We want a challenge. Those who don't usually end up in the lottery. Besides, with my dad, I was used to it. I craved it.

And Phil was just what we needed. At the time he got the job, we had been swept in the play-offs enough times that people were saying, "Shaq can't win a play-off game." I mean, we're winning play-off games, but now they're saying, "Shaq can't win *important* play-off games."

And I don't want to be one of those players—"He's a great player but . . ." I don't want no buts behind my name. I've been telling people that all my career.

We have the crew, but we're not playing. Because? No chemistry. Right or wrong, we had no respect for a coach like Rambis. And no real heart. The pressure's getting to me, but I'm more concerned about shutting people up.

Now we got Phil, and I know deep down inside it's gonna work now. Now that I got the coach that I want, now it's time for me to get the players I want. And I know we're gonna do it. In a couple years' time.

Did I think we were gonna win the whole thing in our first year? Honestly? No.

But now I got the man that I want. Now it's time to really go to work. I don't have any more injuries, no excuses, I'm coming in ready, playing for the greatest coach in the game today.

To me, pressure is where your next meal is coming from. So while I wasn't under real-life pressure to win a title, I knew it was gonna be hard to win it. I knew that everything had to be right, especially with Tim Duncan and the Spurs ready to defend their championship.

A lot of people believed that's what motivated me, because people were saying Duncan was the best player in the game. That wasn't it. Would they ever give me that title? Probably not. Tim has a nice all-around game. My game is more dominant in the middle. But there was an ego aspect to my desire to win a title, and it had nothing to do with Tim.

I'm thinking, Punk-ass David Robinson got one before I did? That made me really mad. Oh, man. David Robinson had a ring before me. I'm crushed and I'm hurt.

Me and Dave have history. I looked up to him when I was at Cole High in San Antonio and he was just starting out with the Spurs. I was a player-of-the-year for my high school. He was player-of-the-year for the Spurs. One time I asked him for an autograph.

He wrote his name real quick and was like, "Yeah, come on, hurry up." He kind of dogged me out. He was my favorite player. That's OK. I said to myself, "When I see you, I'm gonna get you."

Then my second year in the league, I was gonna beat Robinson for the scoring title. On the last day of the regular season, as I see it, Bill Fitch, the coach for the Clippers, let him get 71 points to beat me out. I feel Fitch told his team not to play defense. Or at least it looked that way. Now I ask you, is that good for the game?

I got some revenge at the 1995 All-Star Game at the Alamodome, dunking on Robinson as hard as I've ever dunked and knocking him to the ground. That was a message. I wanted to show him that he'll never be able to stop me, especially when I'm coming like that. I kind of showed the rock to him, then had to bring it back a little bit, and I just threw the thing down, right on him. *Wha-pah!* And when he fell, I just looked at him. "Stay down, don't get up."

It was a knockout.

Then they gave the MVP to Mike. I had a great game in the city where I played high-school ball, but they still gave the MVP award to Jordan, who didn't even play in the fourth quarter.

I know this sounds like sour grapes, but it's my book, and right now I feel like venting some. Like the All-Star Game's MVP trophy, which I shared with Tim Duncan last year at Golden State. To me, it should be my second or third one. I might take a little heat for this, but the truth is, I sat out the fourth quarter purposely just to see if they would give it to me like they gave it to Jordan back in 1995. That was my stubbornness getting to me, and I regret it now. At the same time, that's how much I felt like people didn't want me to win that award.

The year after the San Antonio game, I was named as one of the Fifty Greatest Players of All Time. I was really shocked. I didn't know what to say. Then a couple guys got mad, saying I didn't deserve it, like I voted myself on.

I don't know what it is, whether people wanted me to be like D. Rob and talk perfect English and be Mr. Goody Two-Shoes or what. But for a guy who was trying to have fun and stand out, I felt like this young outlaw that no one wanted to join their elite crew.

I know I hadn't won a title yet, and was getting a lot of endorsement deals, but I thought there was some double-standard stuff going on. This one writer from GQ summed it up like this: He was talking about how Dave likes to play the jazz saxophone, how everyone is like, "Oh, look at David Robinson, he's so well-rounded and knows so much more about the world than just basketball. He's not a thug. He's a gentleman and a scholar."

But I make a rap album and it's like, "There go Shaq again, no dedication or focus. Hanging out with the hoods when he should be taking a thousand free throws a day."

I don't hate Dave off the court. I just had to dominate him on it because I got tired of the Goody Two-Shoes image he was throwing out there. He was this crossover guy everyone liked. And I was the big, bad wolf, dunking on everyone. Everyone was trying to make it out be black and white, and it didn't seem right. So I had to do him like that.

We respected Phil because he was a former player on those Knicks championship teams from the early 1970s, and because he had them rings from Chicago, and especially and most of all, because he told it like it was. I knew that with Phil's résumé, the guys were gonna work a lot harder. I knew Phil would have guys playing over their head. He's gonna have Rick Fox pulling shots out of his ear. Gonna have Derek Fisher hounding people in the backcourt. A.C. Green playing well. I knew he was gonna have John Salley doing stuff. Phil had that kind of respect. He said, "Do yoga," and we were out there before every play-off game, stretching muscles we didn't know we had because he said to do it. That's how it was.

When he got hired, I heard stories about how he was going to put some incense in my locker or do some new-age stuff that was going to trip me out, like I was going back to the sixties and tie-dye. But he never went that far.

He did give me a book by Friedrich Nietzsche, some German philosopher cat who wrote about the idea of Superman. Being a fan of the Man of Steel since I was a comic-book–readin' kid, I was interested.

If Phil reads a book that's similar to your personality, he'll give it to you. And Fred Nietzsche was a guy who was so intelligent that they thought he was weird. He used to do things so different that they put him in a crazy home. Anyway, that's what I think happened.

And here I am. I'm 7' 1" can dance, can move, can do movies, can rap. I'm weird. So me and Nietzsche, we had something in common. Phil saw that.

He would come in and bang on his Indian drum, light some incense, and spread it around the room.

"This will get out all the evil spirits," Phil would say.

It wasn't just his shtick. Phil believed that stuff. He brought down this one guy, George Mumford. George taught us how to breathe and how to get and achieve what you want through the power of envisioning it in your own mind.

It's actually all the stuff I've been doing from day one, but I've been doing it on the homeboy level.

These guys coming in with doctorates and their Harvard degrees have names for it. I call it "dreamful attraction." You dream about what you're going to do.

When Phil wasn't banging drums, burning incense, or trying to conjure up spirits to help with my free throws, he was being straight up with us.

One day early on, he came in and said, "Listen, if Michael Jordan, Scottie Pippen didn't have no egos, didn't talk back to me, none of you guys should ever say sh** to me. Period." He said that.

People might see the swearing and take it, like, "We didn't know the great Phil Jackson could use that language." But this is professional sports, and we're talking about a closed-door situation in a locker room. That stuff gets said by probably every coach in the league. That's not crude or rude in the NBA. That's reality. Sorry to say, but that's how you get people motivated. The truth is, Phil talked to us like we wanted and needed to be talked to. He was unlike other coaches we had.

Well, OK, he didn't talk like that to A.C. because he understood A.C. was a born-again Christian who didn't like to hear curse words. When he used to get ready to say something crazy, Phil would say, "No disrespect, A.C., but you guys played like some pussies tonight. You played like Broadway whores. You let people penetrate your defense. Played like some idiots. Don't talk to me." Then we'd have to have a meeting and make everything better.

Growing up with the Sarge coming down on me, Phil really didn't have to tell me much. Whatever he told me, I responded. I didn't get mad when he cursed me out. I knew he was trying to make me better.

I'm not saying that Kurt Rambis and Del Harris didn't try. Maybe we were too young and stubborn to listen. But they just didn't get the respect Phil did. We didn't have the organization. We'd have lousy practices; we'd have guys on the team talking about each other. Everybody was mad because Kobe was taking all the shots.

With Phil and his staff, we had organization. We'd watch tape, and they'd tell us what we were doing wrong. They'd show us, not tell us. Del would tell us and talk about it. And we got accustomed to hating his voice. Whenever he'd stop practice, whenever we'd go through our one-hour drills, whenever he started talking, nobody felt like practicing.

With Kurt, he just turned into a different person when he got the head-coaching job. Before he was named head coach, we all respected him as a normal, regular guy in the organization, and we knew that he had done a lot of the dirty work on Magic's Showtime teams. But when he took over for Del, he started being all phony, trying to be hard and strict with us. We were like, "That's not the Kurt we knew." Plus, he was always making excuses for Kobe.

Phil? He would just tell us flat-out, "Kobe, you're a great player, but you're going to be greater once you learn how to kick it to Glen." He would tell him. He would show us on the tape.

Before Phil, everybody wasn't working together. And two people were going to get blamed: me and the coach.

Del got blamed; he got fired. They didn't really do much with Kurt because it was his first year, but he got fired because it was time and I wanted somebody else. I'm not going to lie. I let Leonard know I was unhappy, and he let the powers that be know. Jordan once got rid of Doug Collins in Chicago, and along came Phil. Magic got rid of Paul Westhead, and along came Pat Riley. I lobbied hard for the Lakers to go after Phil.

I didn't dislike the other people who coached me during my career. Brian Hill in Orlando. Del. Kurt. They were all good guys. But that respect level wasn't there. I had gotten so big, they were almost overshadowed by me. With Phil, it wasn't like that.

It wasn't just the way Phil cut through the b.s. and was always straight with us. It was also that he knew when our bodies needed a day off. And he knew how to push us enough to motivate us, but not so hard that we got angry and didn't want to play for him.

Which gets to the best thing about Phil. He never panics. And because he never panics, we have confidence when we need it most. Every time we had a crisis last season, he put an end to it—quick.

Here's an example. In the finals, Glen Rice's wife started saying her husband wasn't getting enough shots and that Phil didn't like him. She said something to a paper in Charlotte. Then the *L.A. Times* went crazy with the story. It was like Phil vs. Glen and His Wife instead of us against the Pacers. His wife is Cuban, so some of the reporters were calling it the Cuban Mrs. Crisis.

Now, from watching Glen's career, anyone can tell you that Glen's the type of player who's always had plays called for him. And Phil didn't have no offense like that. I guess it kind of got to Glen. After all, Kobe gets 20 shots a game, I'm getting 20 shots a game, and everybody else just has to play their role. I don't think Glen liked that (which, by the way, is why he was finally traded, this off-season: he just couldn't fit in). So there's some truth to the story. At the same time, it's Glen's wife who is complaining, not Glen. And we're up three games to one when she's choosing to bitch.

Phil handled it quick. "Listen, I'm not going to get into this back-and-forth; all we need is one more game." That's what he said. "I'm not gonna get into this. I've never got into this, so I'm not going to get into it now. One more game."

I respected him so much that I even called him "My White Father." He didn't teach me the lessons Sarge did growing up or anything, but he was one of the main reasons I was so focused and ready to win a championship.

Phil had a presence. Just the way he looked, the way he walked. Bad back. Don't care about how big you think you are. Talked to anybody any kind of way. He cared about what he cared about. If he didn't care about it, he let you know he didn't care about it. He blew us away sometimes.

From that day in Montana to the last game of the season and even now, Phil taught me lessons about becoming a champion. He helped me see what I really wanted in basketball and how to get it. Lose weight. Play more minutes. Block more shots. Become more of a force. He told me what to do and I did it.

The greatest lesson he taught me was poise. Not to take myself out of a game because I was frustrated and wanted to punch somebody. Just go with it. Trust the offense, he always said.

I can't tell you how big that was when we were about to throw the whole damn season away against Portland in Game 7 of the Western Conference finals. We were down 15 points in the fourth quarter after blowing a 3-games-to-1 lead in the series.

Instead of screaming, "What are we gonna do about the pick-and-roll?" or starting to panic, Phil was like, "Listen, Shaq, this is what you got to do." He came up to us at the end of the third quarter and told all my gun-shy teammates, "Forget about Shaq. If he's double- and triple-teamed, don't try and force the ball in there. If your own shot is there, take it."

Know why General George C. Patton was so smooth? He never panicked. My man Patton was a smooth, cigar-smoking, sitting-at-the-back-of-the-tent, never-panicking general. That's why he always did well in the war. When your general doesn't panic, the troops don't panic. Even in Game 7, when we were down to Portland, and Phil was mad, he didn't panic. He just said, "Hey, this is how you fuckin' guys want it to end? This is how you really want it to end? They're just playing above their head, but I know they're gonna go cold."

We had another situation like that in the first round against Sacramento. We were up 2–0 and then we lost two straight to force Game 5 in L.A. We didn't even practice between Game 4 and Game 5. We just watched tape. Phil told us, "Listen: This is all we have to do, and we'll be all right." Phil told us to hold the ball the first three plays of the deciding game and told us to yell at the referees because the Sacramento players were playing illegal defense. And that's what we did. Guess what: We got calls right off the bat. He got them out of their game first. Which made the rest of the game much easier.

It was a crime last year that he didn't get Coach of the Year, a flat-out crime. They gave it to Doc Rivers in Orlando, who did a nice job with a bunch of nobodies but didn't even get to the play-offs. Phil won 67 games.

You can say what you want about him always having the talent, with Michael and Scottie and now me and Kobe, but you know what? Not everyone can coach talent.

You need a cigar-smoking, sitting-at-the-back-of-the-tent, smooth general. You need a man who has no problem telling a 7'1", 350-pound multimillionaire with a mean streak to hurry up and move a dead tree off his property.

Time Out

Free Throws: My Kryptonite

I've received letters from people all over the world, giving me every piece of unreal advice you can imagine. Try crystals. Try a psychologist. Try special herbs. Try to make a stupid free throw.

Next to a layup, it's supposed to be the easiest shot in the game. No obstacles. Just you and the rim, your form and your confidence. The problem is, my form and confidence are severely lacking at the line. I admit it.

I've made only 53 percent of my shots from the foul line in eight years in the league. I'm not proud of it. I have to take whatever criticism the media dishes out on this subject, whatever anyone writes about my misses. There's no arguing. I miss the damn things.

I heard Jerry West once say something about free throws. "You ask a lot of players, and they'll tell you that they'd rather shoot a jumper with three guys on them than stand there with the ball as the only thing people are looking at and trying to hit a free throw," he said. "A free throw can be the toughest shot in the game."

He is not lying.

I can say that my hand has an anatomical defect that has something to do with missing. Every one knows that in order to be a good shooter, your hand has to line up with your elbow. My fingers don't line up perfectly with my elbow. It goes back to when I was young. I was climbing up a tree, fell and messed up my wrist. It never grew back straight. My wrist does not bend all the way back like most people's wrists.

It's not a great excuse, because I would get like 50, 60 in a row in high school. And I don't know what it is. Maybe it's a concentration thing or maybe I'm tired. Maybe my arms are messing things up.

I worked with Stan Morrison, the old USC coach who coached Leonard a long time ago. And during all of last season, I would make 100 every night before I went home. One hundred clean ones, right through the net. Sometimes I would be there for fifteen minutes, sometimes I would be there for an hour and a half.

My boys will tell you I could make free throws in practice all day. But in the game, I really haven't figured out why I can't.

It's not like Chris Dudley, the worst free-throw shooter in NBA history, who just can't shoot. I can shoot. You can tell by my fade-away jumper, I can shoot.

But I think I can understand a little bit about what Dudley goes through at the line. I mean, he's a bruising center and I'm a bruising center. And when your whole time on the floor is spent mostly banging, and then all of a sudden you have to separate physical contact from this skill-level thing, it's a difficult adjustment. You go from aggression to trying to have a feathery touch.

You ask why other centers who bang shoot well? I don't know. I'm reaching here. Some people have said my hands are too big for the ball. That has nothing to do with it.

The stupidest advice I ever got? Rick Barry telling me to shoot underhand. I told one of the league's best free-throw shooters of all time to kiss my ass. I would never copy his style and shoot underhand. I'd shoot zero percent before I switched to underhand.

I'm not afraid to admit I would be self-conscious about bowling my free throws. I'm a hip-hop kid. That's not me. For example, my father taught me the skyhook. It's an unstoppable move proven by Kareem, but that's not me. That's why I'm jump-hooking. Like Hakeem and Patrick Ewing did. I don't want to look funny. I'm too big and dominant to be looking funny. Sorry.

So this is what I'm going to do to improve my free-throw shooting this year: I'm going back to the creator of my game, my pops. I'm gonna go back to some old high-school tape, focus on the rim. That's all I'm doing for the rest of my career.

I did a lot last year. I didn't know I was one of only three players to be MVP of the regular season, All-Star Game and the finals in the same season. I didn't know I was third ranked in play-off scoring ever. A lot of what I did, I didn't know about until after the season. The only thing I didn't do that Phil Jackson wanted me to do was shoot 60, 70 percent from the line. Everything else, I did it and I mastered it.

Funny, too. Because if I wanted to, I could blame Phil for all my problems at the line. Well, sort of.

See, Phil started that Hack-a-Shaq defense when he was in Chicago. He had something called the Three-Headed Monster. The Bulls didn't have an All-Star center, so Phil would get Bill Wennington, Will Perdue, and Luc Longley to use all eighteen of their combined fouls.

I look at the Hack-a-Shaq as paying homage to my game. But it is bad for the league. It slows the game down. And it hurts. One more thing. The Hack-a-Shaq doesn't work. Through December 2000, the Lakers are 30–9 when I shoot more than 16 free throws in a game. I make them when they count. Look it up.

I've been very poised the past few years when guys went at me and put me on the line with hard fouls. Instead of retaliating with force and getting thrown out, I was on a mission.

If I had to go home, it was gonna be because another team beat us. I wasn't gonna fight and turn around and get suspended in a game. My team needs me. If I'm not on the court, the Lakers are in trouble. It's no secret. And I could just see the headlines. "Stupid-ass Shaq, he fought. Lakers lost Game 3 and 4 to Sacramento and they lost. He didn't play Game 5 and they lost, they're out. Shaq's an idiot."

I'd be like Patrick Ewing or Alonzo Mourning getting suspended for fighting or leaving the bench. I don't want to have to wait a season to redeem myself. And over time, I guess I got used to being fouled.

When I was young, I used to get beat up; high school, too. In college, that's why I left college early, guys were basically tackling me. That Lloyds of London insurance policy—that $2 million— that wasn't gonna do nothing. I had to go pro.

But now that I have a championship ring, let me say this: If I feel someone is trying to hurt me, I will take action.

Foul me hard under the basket, and I've got something for you.

Because it's gotten out of control. It's about, "You can't stop this guy basketball-wise, so forget basketball. Let's go to the WWF now. Let's just put him in a choke hold." That's what it's become. And a lot of referees think, "You're big, you're strong, you can take it." People always think it's like a Volkswagen running into a Mack truck. But you know what? I pinch you, it's gonna hurt. You pinch me, it's gonna hurt. So what if I'm big and strong? Pain is pain.

David Stern could stop it if he wants to. But he hasn't done it yet. And the NBA's new vice president of operations, Stu Jackson, isn't gonna do anything. Because he's a cool cat. He's happy to have his job.

Stu replaced Rod Thorn. Rod used to be in charge of disciplining players for violence. Now he's running the New Jersey Nets. He told me once, "I know you get fouled every time, but you're big and strong. You can take it. We can't call a foul every time."

I got hurt one time 'cause of Hack-a-Shaq, when Matt Geiger broke my thumb when he raked his meat-hook arms across mine. But I promise you I won't get hurt again without someone else getting hurt. I guarantee you, a lot more guys are gonna get hurt before I get hurt.

You think I'm talking smack here, but watch, one day, somebody's gonna foul me hard and I'm gonna go crazy. I don't think the league knows that. I don't think they know that I will fight.

Well, now they should know.

6

The Big Little Brother

Or How Kobe and I Learned to Swim Instead of Sink

Remember that skinny, little, polite kid who visited the Orlando Magic locker room in the early 1990s, the kid who I spent five or so minutes talking with?

Yep, Kobe Bryant.

Penny should have been a little nicer to him back then. It's like when David Robinson dogged me out in high school. You remember that stuff when you take the court as a young player. And there hasn't been a young player like Kobe in a while. Maybe ever.

You probably heard about the problems between me and Kobe earlier this year. I don't want to go into everything that happened, but basically I wanted to make sure people knew that we won 67 games last year by playing an inside-outside game. I just didn't feel we were a better team trying to break people down and shooting jumpers on the perimeter all the time.

It wasn't about me being the man or Kobe being the man. It's actually more simple than that. I'm a dominant big man and there are only a few bona fide centers in the league. If my team isn't taking advantage of that, then we're not being as good as we can be. That's it.

I got a little emotional about things at the time. I said, "If the big dog don't get fed, the house won't get guarded—period." It was also reported that I asked for a trade in late December. That was wrong. I mean, I was fed up and frustrated. I felt like Dikembe Mutombo running up and down the court blocking shots, grabbing rebounds, but taking no shots. But I have never wanted to leave the Lakers.

Will Kobe and I continue to have problems? I don't have a problem. Just like all teammates that don't always get along, we'll probably still have our struggles now and then. All I can say is, you try to work things out the best you can. Just like a marriage. And I'm not even married. It's an ongoing process.

You just hope the rewards are worth the sacrifice.

My first real memory of playing with Kobe comes from the 1997 play-offs. It was our first season together, and we were about to be eliminated by the Utah Jazz in the second round. With the game—and our season—on the line, and a bunch of veterans in the game, Del Harris made everyone blink. Our coach called a play for Kobe, who was not only a rookie, but an eighteen-year-old rookie.

Everybody remembers what happened next: Kobe shot three airballs in a row, the crowd's laughing at him, and we go on to lose the series in five.

A lot of my teammates were shaking their heads, wondering what the hell Kobe was doing, why he took those shots. But when the buzzer sounded, I wanted to make sure he knew that I believed in him as a teammate. I went up to him and, just like Brian Hill said to me after we lost the finals in Orlando, said, "Listen, see how these jokers are laughing? Make sure you remember this and come back next year and dog them out. Remember."

I've gotten on Kobe a lot, it's true. We've had our problems these last five years. Because of egos, endorsements, and the fact that both of us were basically growing up in the league at the same time, a lot of people thought Kobe and I couldn't play on the same team for more than a few years. They thought we would eventually blow up, just like all those other combinations that couldn't find a way to stay together. Kevin Garnett and Stephon Marbury in Minnesota. Allen Iverson and Jerry Stackhouse in Philadelphia. Jimmy Jackson, Jason

Kidd and Jamal Mashburn in Dallas a few years ago. Vince Carter and Tracy McGrady in Toronto this year. Me and Penny in Orlando. You can look them up. Whether it was about money, ego, or whatever, something wasn't right. Someone didn't put the team before themselves. But after all these years, I still feel like I did on the court in Utah. I still believe in my teammate.

So how did Kobe and I go from a slap fight in practice in January 1999 to when he jumped into my arms after we won the title last June? I'm not going to lie to you. It was a long, hard journey. In many ways, it's still going on.

Kobe and I are very different people. Me, I'm wild. When I was nineteen, I was talking to every girl, I was buying every car. And when I first got my NBA money, I'm buying the freshest Benz, I'm getting the rims. I got the system, I got the windows down, I got the gold chain. I'm back in the 'hood letting all the boys know I made it. Ron Harper says I have a unique ability to destroy very nice things. He might be right. I was the first to get a Mercedes-Benz and destroy it, turn it into a homeboy special. I was the first to ghetto-out a Rolls-Royce. I took a perfectly clean Rolls-Royce, took out the steering wheel, and put on a chrome Superman-shaped steering wheel.

Kobe? Stays in the house, reads.

He's just intelligent—sort of a nerd, actually. He's the only brother I know who made a 1420 on the SAT. I don't think Chris Dudley did that, and Mr. Smarty Pants went to Yale. Kobe doesn't hang out. He doesn't go out to the clubs. He doesn't ride around. He doesn't put rims on his car. He's just him. He's a sophisticated kid. Damn mature for his age.

Now, the cross-this-cat-up, one-on-one, I-ain't-lookin'-for-nobody-to-kick-out-to attitude? That bothered me. I yelled at him a lot, and I couldn't wait for him to grow up as a player. No matter if he was eighteen or thirty-six, I wanted him to understand the game yesterday. That's how I am. He was learning how to play the game, and I was impatient.

Last year was the first time the heroics worked. Remember Phoenix, Game 2? He did that crossover stuff, double-pump, hit the jumper, win the game. That was the first time he made the game winner. All those games, all those years, all the other times he'd tried to be a hero, the ball would come hard off the glass, he'd shoot an airball or lose it in traffic.

I'm not saying I wasn't partly to blame. I respected Kobe and his game, yeah. He was unreal some nights, throwing down nasty dunks from all angles. It wasn't just Kobe's dunks, either. The cat could take you off the dribble, pull up from anywhere inside 18 feet, and whap! All drawers. Unlike a lot of young players, he got after you on defense, too. He used that 6'8", slinky body to just swarm whoever he was guarding. He wasn't just about showing up on ESPN at 11:00. He competed.

I knew he was a great player, and that he had a lot of great moves to get to the basket. My problem with him was, when he got to the basket, he didn't know what to do. He tried to score every time. Instead of just laying it up or dishing it off, he tried all that freaky, herky-jerky high-school stuff. I wanted him to get other guys involved. Give me the ball every now and then, drop it off. Kobe always tried to be a hero. But you know, as the saying goes, a hero ain't nothing but a sandwich.

Maybe in this league you have to go through that period. I don't know. Every now and then I said certain things in the local media, and Jerry West got mad at me. But, again, it wasn't because Kobe was a bad person. He just had to be taught. He came from high school where he was the man; it was all about him.

In a lot of ways, the media wanted us to be at war. It was a good story. "Oooooh, Kobe and Shaq goin' at it, don't like each other, competing on and off the court for shots and endorsements." And it didn't help that my agent, Leonard Armato, and Kobe's agent, Arn Tellem, were on opposite sides of the way the NBA lockout went down.

Jerry West even said in the paper once that there was "sort of a professional jealousy" involved. That pissed me off. What was there to be jealous over? I already had my soda deal. I was the first one to get a movie deal in the new era, even before Jordan. I was the first to get my own shoe in the new era, the first to do music.

I realized that times have changed. My deals were ending and his were coming in. There was no jealousy because he was making money. For what? I did that already. I think guys should be able to take advantage of opportunities and do what they want to do. But there was this crazy thought out there, like, "Kobe's getting all the attention, now Shaq's mad." Mad at what? We were both rich beyond our wildest dreams. My feeling was, this cat has got to play right. When I'm under the basket after he draws the double-team, he better throw it. I'm not busting my ass for nothing. I got to fight and cut through two big-ass forwards' arms so he can shoot a jumper with three people on him? No. Don't work like that. That's why I got mad. It had nothing to do with professional jealousy.

Look, I want him to be better than Michael Jordan; I really do. Because he's on my team. That play against Portland, when he crossed over and threw it up for the alley-oop? That was me on the other end. I was the beneficiary of Kobe's move. So why would I try to bring him down?

That said, I was growing more frustrated over the Kobe situation. I didn't blame Kobe, I blamed the people around him who were afraid to tell him how to play and instead let him do what he wanted. I'm pretty hard on Del Harris for a lot of things, but he tried when it came to Kobe. Del actually tried to discipline him and teach him and bring him along slowly; he really did. I give him that. But every time Del put him on the bench, somebody would run downstairs. "Buss said, 'Put him back in the game now.'"

Kurt Rambis was even worse. After taking over for Del in February of 1998, he let Kobe do whatever he wanted to do. No questions asked. Kurt would defend everything he did instead of just being man enough to tell Kobe, "Look, this is what you got to do if we're gonna win." But I am sure that Kurt, being a first year coach, had pressure from upstairs, too.

The truth is, before Phil came along, no one wanted to play with Kobe.

Phil and Ron Harper brought him along. Harp was the good cop; Phil was the bad cop.

Phil would embarrass him in practice, rewinding tape ten times to show him what he did wrong.

"Kobe, what are you doing here?"

"Yeah, I thought I could cross him over."

"Yeah, you *did* cross him over and get to the basket. But if you aren't gonna dunk it, why don't you drop it off to Shaq, let him dunk it?"

The thing about Kobe, he's a smart kid, but you really couldn't tell him anything. You would have to show him. You would have to show him in front of everybody. It was good for Kobe because Kobe got to see and Phil would yell at him and tell him that. A couple times they'd go back and forth.

One day Phil even said, "Now I know why the guys don't like playing with you. You got to play together."

That's what Kobe needed. That's what he got.

And look what happened last season? He was an All-Star, second-leading scorer and first-team All-Defense. In my opinion, there is not a better shooting guard in the game right now.

Everyone says I led the Lakers to a championship, but there is no way I got my first ring without Kobe. In Game 4 of the finals, I fouled out in overtime and had to watch from the bench in the final minutes.

What I saw—what the world saw—was Kobe taking over at age twenty-one. He scored 8 of his 28 points in overtime, including this sweet put-back reverse layup when Brian Shaw missed a runner in the lane. He basically won the game.

Still, we had to get past a lot of hurdles before that moment, including a little altercation. In January 1999, a bunch of the Lakers were working out before practice officially started. We were running at Southwest College in L.A., going up and down the floor, trying to get in shape before the fifty-game season started.

There was an article in the *L.A. Times* that day that basically said, "Kobe is the next Jordan." I thought it was kind of funny, like, Why put all the pressure on him now?

Until we got to practice.

Suddenly, you can't touch him in practice. He's acting like Jordan, where some players thought you couldn't touch Mike. Whenever somebody ripped Kobe, he'd call a foul.

After a while, I'm like, "Listen, man, you don't have to start calling that punk sh**."

Kobe puffs his chest up: "You ain't gonna be calling me too many more punks, motherf***er."

"What'd you say?"

I lunged at him, gave him a little karate push in the head. Same thing I did sometimes to people I was upset with but really didn't want to hurt, only a little less because he was my teammate.

See, when a little guy acts tough, I like to see if he really *is* tough. Well, Kobe didn't back down. He came at me. Then they broke it up, and it was over, and we kept playing.

I guess at that point, I felt Kobe was starting to believe the hype. Kurt was not helping the situation at all. And I'm thinking, "We're gonna be in trouble."

This dream I had of us coming together and being this great one-two punch, it's falling by the wayside because he's trying to do it on his own, and it's all about him now. Every arena we're going to, they're chanting his name, and that's all he hears. They want to see crazy dunks and crossover stuff rather than play team ball.

Thank God for Phil. If we still would have had Kurt, we would have lost to Sacramento in the first round.

Phil made a couple moves that made a big difference not only in the relationship between me and Kobe, but also in the relationship between Kobe and the team. It happened when Kobe suffered a broken wrist in preseason and missed the first fifteen games of the regular season. While he sits on the bench and watches us play team ball, we go 12–3. He's about to come back and no one knows what's going to happen, how the chemistry might change and everything.

So Phil calls me up on December 1, the morning before Kobe comes back. Tells me to meet him at Jerry's Deli in Marina del Rey.

We sit down at a table at the back. He orders some mushroom-type omelet and I get my regular sausage-and-cheese omelet.

Phil is like, "You know Glen is gonna be upset because Kobe's gonna take most of the shots. I'll handle that. Don't worry about it."

Then we started talking about Kobe. He asked me, "What don't you like about Kobe?"

I said, "Well, I don't like that he doesn't get everybody involved."

He said, "Yeah, I see that."

Then he said, "I'm not gonna get on Kobe all the time. Because Kobe's not the type of player you should treat like that. You should let him go and play his game. Whenever he gets out of hand, then I'll say something to him. Let him go. Let him learn by himself.

"I'm not gonna yell at Kobe every day," Phil said. "This kid can play. I know what I'm talking about—this kid can play."

That's when he first said to me, "Just be patient." If it came from the general, it's like, "All right, boss, no problem. You say be patient, then I'm patient."

In December, we're starting to roll. We're 20–5 heading into Toronto. Everybody—I mean, everybody—is talking about Vince Carter. The Sunday before Christmas, Vince is hyped. We're hyped.

In the locker room before the game, Kobe told me, "Yo, watch today. I'm taking it to this cat." He scored 26 points and kept Vince in check, and we ended up winning, 94–88. Kobe took it to him like he said he would. Kobe and I may be different in a lot of ways, but we both love a challenge. And Vince Carter was his challenge.

It seemed like we were coming together on the floor like we never had before. Little stuff would happen. Before we played Seattle last January, Seattle's Ruben Patterson was going off about how he could stop Kobe, how he used to stop him in practice when he was with the Lakers.

In the locker room before the game, we're all joking around. Phil's writing on the chalkboard. I turned around and said, "Oh, yeah, they have the Kobe stopper." Then Phil dropped the chalk. "Kobe, bust his ass."

In the huddle before the game, I'm yelling, "All right, Kobe, bust his ass! Bust his ass!"

He gets on the floor, starts throwing it behind his back, dunking, shooting threes, looking at the crowd, going, "Motherf***er can't stop me." He was shaking his head, like, "Uh-uh. Not today." He dropped 31 points on Ruben Patterson and the SuperSonics and we won our fourteenth straight game. Got me so excited, I felt like chanting, "Kobe, Kobe, Kobe."

There were still some tough times and learning experiences. Like we got beat by Cleveland at home in late January. Bobby Sura was lighting Kobe up. Kobe was trying to be too cute instead of just playing, and Sura stole the ball from him, just ripped him. Afterward, Phil goes off in front of everyone in the locker room.

"Listen," he told Kobe, "you can't be playing with people, we can't be having that. You can't be coming out, throwing it between your legs. Glen was open. You should have passed it to him. You guys don't deserve to win that game."

Part of the problem was that Kobe is so competitive. In this league, everybody gets scored on. Somebody hits a shot in your face, and you get that look, "Oh, you score on me? I'm coming right back, bitch." All that street stuff comes out. And that happened with Kobe a lot. He couldn't just come down, try to exploit the mismatches first and play team ball.

When he did, everything clicked. One night I will always remember is March 6, 2000. My twenty-eighth birthday.

We're going up against the Clippers at the Staples Center. I'm already in a competitive mood because the Clippers wouldn't give me extra tickets for my family and friends. Which is stupid. I mean, why do you think the building is sold out? Because people want to see Michael Olowokandi and the Clippers play? Plus, Kareem Abdul-Jabbar is on the Clippers bench as an assistant. He always had something critical to say about my game, and now he's giving the Clippers' big men tips on how to guard me.

Uh-oh. Shaq Daddy's a little mad.

By the end of the third quarter, I've got 42 points. Now people are saying, "Get 50," so I get 50 and then it's like, let's go for more.

Kobe is giving it up and I keep scoring. Now I'm at 59 points and Kobe penetrates and people think he ain't gonna get it to me.

What does he do? He doesn't even think twice. Feeds me for my 61st point, the most I ever scored in an NBA game. On my birthday, too.

My plan was if I get 61, I was gonna come down and shoot the three. So I get it, and the crowd is going crazy. I'm dribbling across half-court and I stop. I look at the basket, but I see Kobe breaking toward the rim. So I throw him a lob. He catches it, cocks it back, throws down a reverse alley-oop dunk. That was my way of showing Kobe, "Thanks for helping me get 61. This one's for you."

Once we did that together, we were tight. We bonded that night.

We'll probably never be close as friends because we're so different, but on the court there is no problem.

The biggest thing I would say to players worried about the other star on their team is, you can't let outside forces tear you apart. You can't let your boys tear you apart. You can't let your agent tear you apart. Luckily, my crew and my agent understood the game and never got involved in that. But that's what happens to a lot of franchises. They let outside forces tear them apart.

I look at it like a shipwreck in the middle of the ocean. You either sink or swim together. I'm untradeable, and he's untradeable. So it was either gonna get better or it was gonna get worse. Only way one of us would go is if we'd make a fuss. I ain't making no fuss. I'd just left Orlando a few years back. I like L.A. I don't want to start all over again. So we were gonna have to work.

Kobe still has a lot of learning to do, especially when it comes to drawing and kicking out to your teammates. But he did a lot of that last year, and it's only going to get better.

Kobe may have had outside forces telling him, "Shaq's just mad; don't worry about it. It's gonna be your team."

And one day, Phil's gonna have enough confidence in him where it's gonna be his team, and I'll accept that because it should be a guard's team. And one day Phil's probably gonna say, "Kobe, you know what. It's your team." And I'm gonna accept that. I have no problems with that.

A lot of people don't know that we have two-way pagers. Whenever Kobe has a good game, I'll say, "Good game." And even if I don't like some of the things he does on the court, I won't stand for other people taking him apart. See, the better Kobe gets, the more people are trying to take him out of his game. Muscle him. I'll run to him after somebody fouls him hard. "You want me to mess him up for you?" He'll either tell me, "Yeah" or "No." For real. I'm his enforcer.

After our game with the Knicks last season, I told him, "If I was there for the Chris Childs incident, it wouldn't have went down like that." But I had the ball and I was making a move.

See, Kobe and Childs squared off last year during a game in L.A., and Childs got the best of him. Kobe put his elbow on him, and he didn't have his guard up. Mistake. You got to know who you're going up against. Everybody that knows anything about the streets, you know Chris Childs is street.

You can't walk up on a street cat like that. You could do that to a Shawn Bradley, to Greg Ostertag. They're not street. They're not gonna fight. They're worried about getting fined.

By the time Childs threw the first two punches, everybody was in there trying to break it up. Kobe tried to swing back, but he couldn't get it.

But look closer at the tape. You'll see me trying to take the attention away from him getting hit. Right after the altercation, I pushed Patrick Ewing. I wanted Ewing to come back. I was gonna mess Ewing up. I promise you I was.

I had a lot of resentment built up about Patrick over the years. If he stepped up, I was gonna give Ewing a two-piece. I was gonna knock Patrick out, hit him with a bip-bip-bip. For real. Just to take the attention off Kobe's getting hit. But Ewing didn't budge at all. He was looking at them the whole time. He didn't want a piece of me.

People always ask me if I think Kobe can be one of the greatest players that ever played. Do you think he has "Michael" potential?

I don't know what greatness is. Is greatness what you do, the numbers you put up? Or what a person who has a great reputation says about you?

Even though Karl Malone and John Stockton don't have championships, I think they're two of the greatest players ever, and one of the greatest one-two punches ever. I often get asked, "Do you have to have a championship to be considered great?" In my eyes, no. You have to be on a great team to be a champion. You can't do it by yourself.

But do I think Kobe is a great player? Yes. He's a great one-on-one player; he has a lot of moves.

I'm sure Kobe watches Mike and tries to pattern his game after Mike. But I don't think Kobe wants to be like Mike. I think Kobe should just worry about becoming Kobe. So far, that's worked pretty well.

I think back to when he shot those air balls against Utah. On one hand, I think that was Del's fault 'cause Del called the play for a youngster who really wasn't ready to go through that yet.

But I also remember the huddle back then, too, what everybody was doing. Nick Van Exel was looking around. He wanted to be a hero, but he didn't know how to be one. Jeff Hornacek was killing Eddie Jones. I could look at Eddie's face and tell he didn't want the ball. And Del didn't want me to have the thing because I shoot 40 percent from the free-throw line, and ain't gonna make the free throw.

So it's basically up to this eighteen-year-old. A lot of players in the NBA spend their whole careers trying to avoid taking a shot like that. At eighteen years old, Kobe had the courage to take those shots. The Big Little Brother stepped up and did his best.

No matter what happens, I was proud to be his teammate then, and I'm proud to be his teammate now.

7

Dead Presidents and Free Agents

Usually, when someone asks me about the latest team and their trade for an All-Star player, I don't listen. My time is too valuable to waste it worrying about teams trying to match up with us. But I have to admit: The summer after we won the championship, I was starting to wonder what was going on.

Portland was reloading. They had traded for Shawn Kemp, so they had another big body to help move me away from the rim. Miami got Brian Grant and Anthony Mason to help Alonzo Mourning on the front line. Tim Duncan would be healthy again in a few months after coming off knee surgery; so with David Robinson returning, the twin towers were back. And all of a sudden, Patrick Ewing is in the West, playing for Seattle.

A.C. Green didn't have much left and could not carry the load for us again.

So here we are, the defending champions, with no real power forward to help me down low against these big monsters from the Western Conference. I'm thinking, me, Kobe and the fellas might be in a little trouble if the Lakers don't do something.

So I did the reverse Superman thing; hopped into a phone booth with my Lakers uniform on, and came out in a suit and tie. Just call me Shaq Kent—player by night, GM by day.

Maybe I'm giving myself too much credit, but sometimes as a franchise player you have to take matters into your own hands during the off-season. You not only have to work out and keep your body right, but, sometimes, you have to play general manager, too.

Magic Johnson did it with the Lakers, reworking his own contract so the team could sign better players. Michael Jordan. Larry Bird. Isiah Thomas. They all had input into who coached them and who they played with.

I don't want to take all the credit for bringing Horace Grant to L.A., but from this recorded conversation I had with Mitch Kup-chak, the Lakers general manager, in mid-August, well, you can see I had a little to do with it. I wasn't actually in a three-piece, but sitting in my summer home in Orlando, about to go jet-skiing with my friends. Mitch was back in L.A., working the phones, trying to help make us better.

The day after Jerry West resigned, Mitch called me up. He wanted me to talk to Kendall Gill, who told us he was coming to L.A. Now Mitch was telling us he was signing for more money and staying with the Nets. Time to recruit.

We also had to deal with Glen Rice. He wanted a new contract and was sick of playing in Phil's triangle offense.

Here's our conversation from last August:

Me: Congratulations, Mitch.

Mitch: Yeah, thanks. Kind of a weird week, you know? I know you were close to Jerry, but I was really close to him, too.

Me: No, I understand.

Mitch: After forty years, working with this guy for twenty, I have a certain, you know, void that I feel right now. But I saw him on Sunday night, he looked great. Happy. He looked rested. So I think he's at peace with himself.

Me: All right. I'm sure that you will do a good job. I know you're gonna take care of me. I don't ask for much. All I want is a power forward. If you can, get me a Horace Grant.

Mitch: OK, we're working on something. It's getting a little hairy right now. I don't know what's gonna happen.

Me: All right.

Mitch: But we were working on something else.

Me: Like who?

Mitch: Kendall Gill.

Me: Yeah. Kendall Gill's signing already, right?

Mitch: With who?

Me: With us. Isn't he?

Mitch: Well, that's why I'm calling you. He was here, you know, getting ready to sign. But I guess Jayson Williams and the owner from New Jersey called him. They offered him $7 million.

Me: Right.

Mitch: And all we can offer is the $2 million exception.

Me: Now, Mitch. Mitch? Let's be real here.

Mitch: Yeah?

Me: Realistically, with the new rule changes, do you think the guy is gonna take $7 million or $2.5?

Same with Brian Grant. They're offering Grant $9, $10 million. I know he wants to play for a championship contender, but you think he'll take $2.5 versus $9 million?

What about Horace? We can't get Horace at all?

Mitch: No, they don't want to move him right now. But we still have an option—we have a possibility with Christian Laettner.

Me: OK.

Mitch: Laettner would be good. He's a little surly, you know. But he would be good in the system.

Me: Yeah, he would.

Mitch: I think that's where our best chance is right now. But with Kendall, we could offer him a two-year deal.

Me: Right.

Mitch: The two years would equal almost $5 million.

Me: Right.

Mitch: And he's got a $7 million one-year offer from New Jersey. So it's almost $5 versus $7 million. And the kid really wants to be here.

Me: I know he does.

Mitch: They're trying to force us to do a sign-and-trade, but they don't want anyone that we would trade.

Me: Right.

Mitch: The thing is, I don't know how well you know Kendall, but he's been getting calls from Jayson Williams, you know, and the owner. I'm not sure they really want him. They went after [Ron] Mercer, [a free agent who ended up signing with Chicago].

Me: So what's his number? I'll call him.

Mitch: I don't want to put you in an uncomfortable situation.

Me: Listen, I'll do it, brother. 'Cause I want more than one ring.

Mitch: He would really give us great flexibility.

Me: Yeah.

Mitch: I mean, maybe part of him wants to feel wanted.

Me: All right.

Mitch: Because he asked about you, you know, yesterday— we had lunch together. He thinks you're incredible. So . . . But, you know, if he were to get hurt next year, he gets $5 million over two years.

Me: Right.

Mitch: If he gets hurt in New Jersey next year, he gets $7 million.

Me: Gotcha.

Mitch: I don't know if it's that big a difference. But all you can do, if you really love the guy, is say, "Listen, I want you here, I understand the money thing." Whatever you would say would obviously help.

Me: What about Glen? What you all gonna do with Glen?

Mitch: Well, we're working on that right now.

Me: OK.

Mitch: We can convert him into something, like a big player, like a Laettner or something like that, then I think we'd be happy.

Me: OK. I want Horace, man. Hey, you want me to get Horace to demand to be traded?

Mitch: Seattle wants a big guy in return.

Me: We'll give him Travis.

Mitch (laughing): I already talked to Wally Walker [the Seattle GM] last week.

Me: Horace is my man. I can make Horace talk to the media and say—demand, "I want to be out of here right now."

Mitch: Well, you know, I can't ask you to do that. I mean, if he wants to leave, he can do that on his own. You know, we would do anything we could to get him; but, you know, I can't conspire with you to have him do that.

Me: All right.

Mitch: That's not, you know—

Me: That's what? Tampering?

Mitch: Yeah.

Me: You honest guy, you. I like you, man. You're so aboveboard.

Mitch: That's who I am.

Me: OK. All right.

Mitch: I'll call Wally anyway again today, Wally Walker.

Me: All right. 'Cause I need a big man so we can match up against the Spurs. 'Cause I can't guard and go out on both those guys.

Mitch: I'm working on it.

Me: If you can get somebody to slow David down, I'll shut down Duncan.

Mitch: We're working on it.

Me: All right.

Mitch: If we can get Kendall Gill back on board and continue to work on this big guy, you know, that we're trying to get for you, I think we'll be OK.

Me: All right.

Mitch: All right, so if you get a chance and you feel like it, give him a call right away.

Me: OK, cool.

Two months later, Horace was back with me, where he belongs.

We'd been teammates in Orlando. He was a big part of our Eastern Conference championship season. Believe it or not, I also helped get him from Chicago to the Magic. I remember him being angry with the Bulls ownership. I called him and said, "Listen, man, you know we did OK last year. You know I need that power four."

"I love you, man," he said. "I want to come play with you."

"All right, I'll get you down there."

So I got him hooked up. He came down and signed a big deal, and we made it to the finals that year. In a lot of ways, I was the general manager of that team, too. I basically told them to go after Penny Hardaway with the first pick we had in the draft in 1993, figuring Scott Skiles, our starting point guard at the time and a true team dude, would be cool with moving aside.

But John Gabriel will never give me credit. We used to have the same relationship that Jerry and I had, and that Mitch and I have now. Leonard and me worked on a lot of that stuff behind the scenes, making things right.

But once we made it to the finals, John Gabriel, the Orlando GM, was walking around like he did it all. Pat Williams was walking around like he put the team together.

I'm not saying me and other players should be up for Executive of the Year awards or anything. But we're not the dummies we're often made out to be.

Being a student of the game—well, being a student of everything but free throws—I knew what a perfect team looked like. I used to hate Boston, but they had the perfect squad. They had Danny Ainge, who could hit the shot when it got kicked out. Dennis Johnson, hard-nosed point guard, got everybody involved. Kevin McHale, when he saw a mismatch, he'd damn near pump-fake you to death. Robert Parish got the ball out and scored. Larry Bird, the leader of the team, made sure everybody got theirs. The perfect team.

The Showtime Lakers had the perfect team. Magic, running the show, everybody knew their roles.

This team we got now in L.A., I helped put that together. Jerry West was the architect, but I helped.

Voice mail I left for Kendall Gill in the second week of August, 2000:

"Yo, Kendall, this is Shaq, dog. You know I'm gonna keep it real with you. They told me to call you. If I didn't want you, I wouldn't call. You know me for a long time; you know who I am. Yes, we need you. We want to have you. I understand about the money situation, but we can get a player like you and get a power four, we going back to the championship again and they will take care of you 'cause, you know, we know what type of player you are, we know you can hit that shot, we know you can slash, you gonna get your money.

"I know Jersey's offering you $7 million for one, only thing we can pay you is $2.5 million. We would love to have you. We want to make some moves, and we're trying to get back. You know we're the only team in the West that's really gonna get back. Everybody else stacking up their team, but they ain't got nothing. We need you. You call me back at my house or my pager. Oh, yeah, by the way, it was my idea to tell them to go get you.

"Peace."

We could use that cat, but I felt a little wrong leaving that message. Why? Because, as athletes, we have only a finite number of years to make money. It's not like a writer, who can write his whole life, or a dentist, who can do root canals till he's seventy.

The average number of years an NBA player draws a paycheck is 4.6. So by trying to encourage Kendall to take less money, I'm basically taking his retirement out of his pocket.

Fans and the media don't understand this. They hear about a guy who signed for the minimum salary instead of a big-time deal, and they go, "That's so touching, a guy who wanted to play for a championship instead of cashing in. That'll show all those greedy bastards."

But as players, for the most part, we look at those guys as not being financially responsible. Unless they got some under-the-table deal with the team—which happens more than the league wants to admit—they're hurting themselves.

You might say, "Why wouldn't you want to play with the best?" Why? Money, brother. I mean, $5 million or $7 million per year— that's almost the same. But $2 and $9 million is not the same.

Like if they ask me to call Brian Grant to convince him to play for our $2 million exception, I wouldn't do that. In good conscience, I couldn't. I think that guy's worth the $10 million that he's gonna get. We could pay him only $2.5 million. I'd tell him, "That would be a waste of time."

Charles Oakley took us for a ride in the summer of 1999. We could pay Oakley only $2 million, but he calls us up during our vacation and wants to meet with me and Kobe, pretending he wants to join us.

"I want to meet with you and Kobe, make sure . . ." Knowing damn well he wasn't gonna sign with us. He's in his late thirties. Toronto was offering him $6 to $7 million a year. No way he's gonna get a contract for $7 million again.

I knew damn well Oak wasn't coming. But I flew back anyway, just in case. He wants to see how hungry Kobe and I are about winning, whatever, whatever.

Then he signed with Toronto for $7 million a year. He was the guy everybody said wasn't about money. And look.

That's all right. Toronto went out in the first round. We won it all. And I didn't blame Oak for taking the money. I just didn't like the game playing.

Sometimes, though, I do take it personal. For example, John Amaechi, the starting center for the Orlando Magic? Idiot.

He made the dumbest decision in the world. I called him and talked to him. That cat could have come on our team, played, and even started. He could have started. Backed me up. Played some power forward. We offered him $17 million for six years. But Orlando feeds him some bullsh**. He signed for $600,000 for one season. That was the most idiotic deal I've ever seen in my life.

He probably had his reasons for staying.

I don't really care. All I know is, now Amaechi is on my list. When I come back to Orlando, I'm going to destroy him, put a big ol' Spalding tattoo on his head. He could have come and played on a world-championship team. We could have gone out there and done work. Some of these guys, I just don't know what they're thinking.

Recorded conversation with Kendall Gill, August 12, 2000. Kendall finally gets back to me.

(By the way, I don't know what the taping laws are in New Jersey, but I'm hoping Kendall won't press charges when he finds out I recorded him, too. After all, he might need a job next year, and we might need a slasher.)

Kendall: What's up, Shaq?
Me: What up, dog? How you doing?
Kendall: All right, man. How you doing?
Me: Chillin'. What's going on?
Kendall: Not much. Just calling to thank you, man, for calling. Just calling to let you know that I really wanted to come.
Me: OK. So?

Kendall: I wanted to come bad, man—you know what I'm saying? I mean, I waited till the last minute to see if they could do something, but, you know, nothing could be done. I was looking at that $7 million.

Me: Yeah.

Kendall: That's a lot of money.

Me: I know, brother. I feel you. But $7 million and $2.5 are two different things.

Kendall: Right. Exactly. So, you know, hopefully next year.

Me: All right. Cool. Good luck.

Kendall: If you all open to it, you know, I'll definitely come then. But, you know, I had to go get this money, man.

Me: All right, then. I feel you.

Kendall: All right.

Me: All right, cool.

Kendall took the money, and I can't blame him. That's what the league's about. Especially after the lockout. This money isn't coming around any more.

I don't want to put people to sleep with numbers, but prior to the 1998–99 season, the NBA and its players went to war over something like $2 billion in annual income. We ended up striking and missing the first three months of the season, and had to jam 50 games into, like, three months, which made for some sorry basketball.

People can say what they want about both sides getting a good deal, but in the end the owners won. Everyone knows it. And the reason they won is because they could sit back and wait while we lost paychecks.

They've got billions, we've got millions. And it's no secret that some players spend all they have. Foolishly. The owners know that. They see the cars we buy, the jewelry we buy. They know all the baby-mama stories, how many children some players are supporting.

That's why we finally buckled and took a deal we shouldn't have at the last minute. Alonzo Mourning and his boys were trying to mean-mug Paul Allen and those types, trying to intimidate billion-aires. They didn't understand: you don't do that to people with that kind of money.

I mean, you got Paul I-don't-give-a-damn-how-much-it-costs Allen, one of the richest men in the world. I don't really know a lot of the owners, but I like that dude. Mark Cuban, that Internet billionaire dude who owns the Dallas Mavericks, he's the type of owner that I like, too. Young. Doesn't care how much he spends, doesn't wear a suit.

Owners with that kind of money will wait you out. So we lost.

Our owner, Jerry Buss, has a lot of history behind him, too. With me and Kobe, he has another championship and isn't shell-ing out the crazy salaries like some owners. Meanwhile, he never gave me any grief about how I played, even when we failed in the play-offs. I remember in 1998, when we got swept by Utah. Right after the game, he was asking me, "You want to come over for a barbecue?"

You got to love an owner like that.

The night we won the championship, I walked up to the podium when Jerry was speaking. I pretended to cough the word, "Exten-sion," into the microphone a couple of times. I was trying to be funny, but also sending a little message.

Besides getting me an unreal, seven-year deal worth $121 million in 1996, Leonard, my agent, was smart enough to give me an option clause in my contract so I could keep pace with the rising salaries of the best players. Considering I'd just won the MVP and the title, I had some sweet leverage just then. But I didn't want to force the issue. I thought the coughing was a funny way to get a hint across. And that night, Jerry responded with, "Whatever you want, baby."

He wasn't joking. I signed a $88.5 million contract extension last October. Like I said, you got to love an owner like that.

After I helped bring Horace to L.A., I hooked up another one of my former teammates from Orlando: Brian Shaw, the cat who invented the ShawShaq Redemption. B. Shaw rejoined me with the Lakers last season and was a big part of our championship run. But after the season, he was a free agent, and a few teams were interested in him. One was Portland. I called him up and asked him what was up, how come he hadn't signed yet. "Mitch don't want to sign me," he said.

Now, without B. Shaw, I'm not wearing a championship ring.

He hit these clutch 3-pointers against Portland in Game 7 when the starters couldn't do a damn thing. We were down and out before he stepped up. I understood that L.A. wanted to save our $2.5 million exception for a really good player who could put us over the top again. But I felt B. Shaw was one of those players. And now he's going to sign with the enemy?

Gotta call Mitch.

"Listen, man," I said (I say, "Listen, man" a lot). "Let's show my brother some loyalty. He scored all of the points when the starters couldn't do nothing. Sign him up, please." I told Mitch if it means I'm not getting my extension, then go ahead. I think Brian Shaw signed a two-year deal the next day. It wasn't about the money for me.

Of course, that's easy for me to say. In nine years, I haven't touched any of my NBA money yet, meaning the contracts I signed with Orlando and the Lakers. My money is put away. I've got a few stocks, a couple of annuities. I got some property and stuff like that. I'm still living off Reebok, Pepsi and Taco Bell. All my NBA checks are in the bank, chillin', waiting for me.

I sometimes worry about young players getting all that money so early. They don't know. They have to be taught. My first year, me and a couple of my cousins ran up $90,000 a month in phone bills. I didn't learn until later that you could write off some of that stuff on your taxes. I didn't know about foreclosure. I think if I didn't know about foreclosure, I wouldn't have bought some of the property and homes I've bought.

My first million dollars? I spent that in about three days. I bought myself a Benz, my mother a Benz, my father a Benz, bought a couple suits. I gave my parents $200,000 each. Next thing I know, it was gone. I already had Leonard helping me out with finances, but I needed more. I asked him to line up the five best accountant firms in the world, told him to have them meet me in the office.

The last accountant was this little scrawny guy named Lester.

Lester Knispel
Orlando, Florida
August 13, 2000

Leonard Armato was looking to go into a business venture with one of my clients. Representing my client, I actually met with Leonard, negotiated against him. Well, we finished the negotiations, and it didn't go the way everyone had planned. I actually told both my client and Leonard that I didn't think the deal would work.

Leonard called me up subsequently and was impressed with the way I handled things. Even though the deal didn't work, it didn't work because it wouldn't have been good for him either. He said that he represented a basketball player at LSU, Shaquille O'Neal, and would I be interested in meeting him? They were looking for a new business manager.

Now, I didn't know anything about college basketball. And at that stage in my careeer, I wasn't taking in anybody new who was in college. So I said no. But when I went back to the office, I called my client on the phone and said, "Can you believe Leonard? He wants me to meet with a kid in college to do his work, Shaquille O'Neal."

Immediately, my client says, "Do you know who Shaquille O'Neal is? He's gonna be the next Michael Jordan. You call him now and you beg him for that meeting. You tell him you're sorry."

So I called Leonard immediately. "Could you reconsider? Can I have that meeting?"

"Sure, if you want it."

He told me I'd be one of eight people or groups meeting with Shaq. I was led to understand that all eight were pitching on the same day, and I would make the last presentation of the day.

Now, typically, there's an advantage to being either first or last. Sometimes if you're first and they like what you said, they won't even take the other meetings. And if they're interviewing two or three people, you like to be last because usually they remember everything you said—because you're the last one they talked to. But when you're the eighth one, you know they're gonna be tired. And that's what happened.

When I walked in, they were exhausted. I went into Leonard's conference room and Shaquille, his mother, father, Leonard, I believe Gary Uberstein—who at the time worked with Leonard—all of them were sitting around the table. They were obviously tired, had heard every possible pitch. There were piles of brochures from all the other big accounting firms, they had these beautiful color brochures.

"Just throw your brochure on the table," Shaquille's father told me.

Well, I didn't have a brochure. I don't do any advertising. I told them that and sat down. They asked me questions. Unbeknownst to me, one of the questions was something they asked everyone: how I felt about the family being involved, particularly Shaquille's mother. Would I mind Lucille looking at the checks, maybe signing some checks?

Now, I have handled a lot of people, especially actors, young actors, actresses, and I'm used to working with their parents all the time. So I had no problem with this. I never saw it as a threat or a problem.

But apparently all the others didn't want it. And they had all the reasons why, "No, we didn't think it would be good."

So then Shaq's family asked about the clients I represent, and I think they liked at the time that I represented some of the rappers they knew.

After this, they asked me about my investment philosophy, how I felt about real estate. Frankly, very knowledgeable questions, very sophisticated questions. Really, Shaquille's mom went over with me what she envisioned would be the way to handle the finances. She made it clear that even though the money was Shaquille's, their philosophy was that it was for the family—and not the immediate family, not from the standpoint of "What do we get?" They were very honest about the fact that Shaquille has a gift, and they wanted to take care of generations. They didn't want their descendants to go through what they went through, you know, driving a van with 200,000 miles on it because they couldn't afford a new car.

It's a very interesting thing—again, the way Lucille talked to me, she wanted to make sure. She said, "Shaquille should be happy and live the life he wants, but your obligation to this family is to make sure that for generations you take care of them."

Maybe a week later, Leonard called me and said that they had decided to pick me to work with them.

And that's what I've been doing, with trusts, with life insurance. That's been my job. Not just to see that Shaquille has enough to spend for his life, but to take care of his family forever.

A couple of firms told me what they thought I wanted to hear. "You give me $5 million, we can flip it and make it $50 million." I didn't want to take those risks. Coming from a household that never had a lot growing up, I wanted to hold onto my money. Lester told me who his clients were, that he had a small firm and how much money he manages for them. "I'm not high-risk at all," he said. "Low-risk, government bonds. Because I feel 6 percent is a better risk than getting 50 percent high-risk." So he's just a no-risk type of guy with cash. That's the guy I like. Leonard hooked me up financially more than anyone.

Some knucklehead agents may actually hurt their clients. When Scottie Pippen was in Chicago and Karl Malone had signed one of his deals in Utah, those guys were locked into long-term deals with no "out" clauses. Two of the best players of all time were underpaid during their primes. Two years went by, and they weren't getting market value. Leonard was one of the first agents to make sure he got escape clauses in my contracts after four years. That was why I was able to leave Orlando in 1996 and sign an extension with the Lakers last October. He made sure I always would make market value. From Day One.

Larry Johnson and Derrick Coleman—the two No. 1 draft picks before me—both signed big-time deals. To keep me at the scale, I got a big deal as a rookie.

I was thinking about this. I've signed a $41 million contract, a

$121 million contract, and last October an $88.5 million extension. If I play till I'm thirty-five, I'll make $152 million from the Lakers over the next six years. That's three unprecedented deals in one basketball-playing lifetime. That's unheard of. I feel like I won the lottery not once or twice, but three times. You remember that Nicolas Cage movie, *It Could Happen to You*? Well, it *did* happen to me.

I was checking out *Forbes* magazine's Celebrity 100 issue that came out in March 2000. I was listed at No. 35—my annual $31 million in salary and endorsements was more than David Letterman and Howard Stern. When I get on their shows, I have to give them grief about that.

Yo, Howard. You need a loan?

I don't know how long I'm going to play, but I'm under contract for six more seasons. If I play all six, I'll make $152 million. The last year of the deal in 2005–06, I'll get $32.5 million—more than Michael Jordan made in his last year with the Chicago Bulls.

I'm not going to go into why ballplayers make such crazy money and why people that do more important things for society do not. All I can say is, that's the economics of this business. We wouldn't be getting that kind of money if the owners didn't have it.

You always see players and their agents going at it with teams during contract time, and it's amazing how many times the player is also looked at as not being thankful enough, or wanting too much.

Meanwhile, sometimes, if a team goes about its negotiations in the wrong way, it can kiss all championship dreams good-bye. At least, that's what happened for me in Orlando.

One thing I am, I'm a reality-based man. For example, if they cut the NBA down today, I could work a nine-to-five job and be happy. I really could. If they wanted me to capsize my 15,000-square-foot house or sell it and get a smaller house, I could do that.

A lot of cats can't do that. Like during the lockout, a lot of cats were struggling. Kenny Anderson lived around the corner from me. He had thirteen cars. During the lockout, I don't know if those cars were repossessed or what, but they were gone. Zoom, zoom, zoom.

Kenny's my man, but I don't feel sorry for nobody because you got to manage that cash, brother. This is luxury. Take advantage of it.

This goes back to something my father told me a long time ago: "Even the sun don't shine forever." It will shine, shine real bright about from like 12:00 to 4:00. But from about 5:00 to 6:00 it will start setting. It will go down.

An athlete's life span isn't that long. A lot of cats think they're gonna be dunking on people forever. They think you're gonna get crossed-up forever. What you have to understand, while you're working your game and perfecting all your moves, the younger generation is taking your moves. The moves that you worked on, they're taking them, learning them in one day, mastering them.

I'll go to the Rucker courts in New York, where some of the best playground players in the world play. If some of these cats had their heads on straight, they'd be the best players ever in the history of the game. They would. They got the unbelievable handle, the passing skills; they love playing the game. That's what guys don't realize.

I realize that these younger big cats, they're trying to take me out. Tim Duncan and the guys like that, Kevin Garnett. They are. And that's what you have to do. The student has to kill the teacher eventually, can't show him no respect.

See, I turned twenty-nine on March 6, 2001. I probably got three or four more good dominant years left. Then I realize that when I'm thirty-one, thirty-two, I'm not gonna be the same Shaq I was in 1992. That's just life, and I will accept it. And when I feel it in my heart that I'm not the same Shaq, that I can't dominate no more, I'm gone. I'm gonna retire. I'm gonna retire peacefully, and that's gonna be it.

I don't want to be a general manager, I don't want to be a coach. I don't want to be a commentator. I'm gonna leave the game, and I'm gonna watch the game, and hope that the younger generation will make the game better, like we made the game better.

The only problem I have with a lot of the younger kids is they're materialistic at a young age. Don't get me wrong, I was, too. But I also realized I had to accomplish something before I went crazy with my money.

A lot of young kids are materialistic so young, they're talking about where the bling-bling is, where's my new car, and all that. I said to this one kid who had a chance to go pro: "Listen, man, you got to go to college, man. Got to go to college for two or three years. Then if you think you're good enough, you feel you can do it, then do it."

"No, I want to go right out of high school," he said. "Why? I need the money."

I said, "Listen, you been broke for eighteen years, you can be broke for two more years, for 730 more days." These kids got to learn how to manage that money. But a lot of them always go back to, "Yo, look at that girl," or "Yo, let me see that chain."

They want it so fast. I'm not saying there aren't situations where kids should come out early. Kobe is a good example. He was mature and ready for his age, a different breed. But I want to tell most of these kids they're not ready, that you have your whole life to work and only certain chances in life to go to school.

It's like John Wooden used to tell his players. "Before you learn the tricks of the trade, learn the trade." (Damn, I'm quoting John Wooden now. The Shaq Daddy's got religion.)

Anyway, this might sound crazy, but I want the young guys to say they're going to take it to me. Like I once asked a little boy, "Can you hoop?"

The young fella said, "I'll dunk on your head."

I like to see that because that's what it's gonna have to be for the game to be a better game. I want somebody, in a couple years, to just come and dog me out, just like I'm dogging out Dave Robinson and Hakeem. I want somebody to do that to me so when I retire, I could be like, "OK, that's good."

Then, while I'm kicking it on my couch, someone else can sign a $121 million contract and play GM in the off-season.

Time Out

My Sister

Ayesha Harrison
Orlando, Florida
August 11, 2000

When we were growing up in Germany, there were days where it snowed or rained real bad and we used to stay in the house. My mom and dad used to sleep in. So it would just be the four of us playing; Shaquille, me, my older sister, Lateefah, and my younger brother, Jamal. My Dad had these real thick sports socks that came all the way up to our knees. We played this game called "Taking Off the Socks."

Lateefah and I were a team, and Jamal and Shaquille were a team. The object of the game was simple: The first team to get the socks off won. You had to pull the socks off the other person. So my mom and dad were sleeping one morning, and Lateefah and I were winning. It took Jamal a while to get the socks off Shaquille. So when it was Shaquille's turn to get the socks off Jamal, he was pulling him so hard. He grabbed onto his leg. Jamal couldn't hold on because Shaquille was so strong and we were so little. He's pulling him real hard. I guess he yanked him too hard one time because Jamal just sailed right off the bed and hit the ground hard. They both ran into the closet. Made like a big noise, and then

Mom and Dad got up. Because Shaquille was older, he was either taking care of us or entertaining us.

One Christmas, we got Cabbage Patch dolls. Shaquille used to make the Cabbage Patch dolls break-dance. Shaquille taught us how to play basketball. He taught us how to swim. All four of us used to just hang together. When Shaquille went off to college, it was just me, Lateefah and Jamal.

He's still a big kid. Whenever I go to visit him in Los Angeles, he's always a kidder. He and his buddies would just be playing around, acting like Bruce Lee, doing karate and jumping all over the furniture. When he was growing up, Shaquille loved Dominique Wilkins and Michael Jordan. He was always talking about Dr. J. He'd have Michael Jordan posters hanging up on the closet in the room he and Jamal shared. They used to have rap posters on his wall, too. Eric B and Rakim, Run DMC, Curtis Blow, Heavy D. All the old-school rappers.

He always had a basketball with him. He actually slept with a basketball. He'd use it as a pillow sometimes. Shaquille also had a real talent for making motorized things out of cardboard. He made a fan once just from using a battery, some duct tape and some cardboard. He used to make little gadgets like that all the time.

We all came after Shaquille. Lateefah is twenty-two, I'm twenty-one, and Jamal is twenty. In basketball, I guess that's called good spacing.

When did I know my big brother would make it to the NBA? Well, it wasn't in Germany, that's for sure. He was clumsy when he was thirteen and fourteen. He would slip and fall. One time, I remember the ball hitting him right in the hands and he couldn't hold on.

But he was always stronger and more competitive than anyone. We would play kickball in Germany. Sometimes it was Shaquille against twenty other kids. And he would win all the time. We could never get him out. We'd play in a big field. Right behind us was a little playground, and past that was a brand-new school. Shaquille would kick the ball into the playground of the new school.

By the time whoever went to go get the ball came back, Shaquille would have been in the house, used the restroom, got a glass of water, and come back. And the kids still would be out there trying to find his ball. He would kick it that far.

He would always let us kick first. Once we got our three outs, we stayed in the outfield for the rest of the afternoon until he said, "I don't want to play no more."

I remember when he left Orlando in 1996. There were bumper stickers all over town: "Shaq ain't worth a Penny," or, "Take the money and run." One particular night, my cousin and I were at a Blockbuster video. It was real chilly that night, so I had on my NBA All-Star jacket and I checked out this videotape called, I think, Around the World with Shaq.

"Oh, you like Shaq?" this guy said.

"Yeah, he's good," I replied. I bent down to tie my shoe, act like it was nothing.

He made some smart remark.

Now, anyone who knows me knows I'm polite. I just don't get into it with people. But I couldn't help it on this night.

"What's wrong with him? How come you don't like Shaq?"

"Because he made this big announcement that Orlando was his home, he was gonna stay here, and, you know, now he's just gonna up and go to the Lakers,"

I told him it was a free country and it wasn't personal. "He is his own person. He can change his mind anytime he wants to, just like you can."

My mother was proud of me, but I was kind of shocked. That's not me.

Shaquille knows his family has his back; they're supporting him. Whenever he is feeling low, he'll always call and talk to my mom and dad. Sometimes after a bad game, he'll call and sound a little bit pitiful.

I'll say to him, "Hey, you played a good game."

"All right, thanks."

I'll tell him I love him and he'll say, "All right, I love you, too. Where's Daddy at?" or "Where's Mommy at?"

People call him "Shaq," but it just doesn't seem right to me. To me, he'll always be Shaquille. Shaq is almost like another person.

As far as Shaquille goes, my big claim to fame came when he decided to turn pro after his junior season at LSU. We were home and he was being interviewed by a reporter. He was about to sign his first contract, and it was the first time in his life he really had a lot of money.

As a joke, he said, "Noni (my nickname), go make me a peanut butter and jelly sandwich and give me a glass of milk, and I'll give you $300."

I said, "OK."

I came back with the sandwich and a big ol' glass of milk, and I gave it to him. He gave me $300. It was all over the newspaper. Some people took that as a big-time athlete getting whatever he wants. That's silly.

He was having fun with his sister, sharing his new wealth and making his family laugh. From the day he made those Cabbage Patch dolls break-dance for us, he's been good at that.

8

To Live and Strive in L.A.

and the NBA

When I turned pro in 1992, I was nineteen years old. Before playing one game in the NBA, I had an endorsement contract with Reebok, a $2 million bonus for signing that contract, and a deal for $41 million with the Orlando Magic. I celebrated by taking my mother to a Circuit City store. I wanted to have a sound system and electronic gadgets for my new home. I was racking up, shoving 70-inch speakers, 50-inch TVs and VCRs into my cart. While they're ringing up my purchases, Mom pulls the manager aside. When I get up to the counter, the guy breaks out a bunch of papers.

I'm like, "Layaway?"

"Yeah, your mom wanted to put this on the layaway program."

"Hold on for a second."

Looking at my mother, I said, "Mommy, layaway days are over. We'll never be on layaway again. I promise you. I'm writing a check for $60,000 right now. You hear me. It's over."

Over. No more Monday-Wednesday-Friday jeans, the pair you had to wear three days a week because the washer broke. No more boots that cramped your feet till your toes bent back and froze up in the winter. No more army rations in the refrigerator.

Like the Jeffersons, I was moving on up, living large and loving every minute of it. I went through my first million in three days. I'm not kidding. I don't know how I did it, but I just started buying cars for my family, cars for myself, all kind of expensive things. Couple nice suits. Next thing you know, I'm out a frickin' million dollars.

It wasn't all crazy spending though. I knew that with the money and fame came responsibilities and expectations. My father taught me to share the wealth. He showed me that money is currency. Like a current, it flows and sustains life. And if you give it away, it always comes back in ways you never imagined. I believe that.

Still, I had to be careful.

In Orlando, when the Magic players would go to the 'hood for some charity work, this guy kept coming around.

"Yo, you need to buy me a van so I could drive the kids around." That's all he kept saying.

I guess if I was an unintelligent brother, I would do it. But you just can't buy a van for somebody. Who's gonna pay the insurance? Who's gonna pay the notes? If I pay for all that and it's in my name and he hits somebody, am I responsible if he gets sued?

If I could save the world, change the world, I would do it. But you can't do it all at once. Little by little, I've tried to make my mark. A lot of times when I go in the 'hood, I try to do good and to keep the money flow as low as possible. 'Cause one thing I don't like, I just don't like writing checks. I like handling the money myself.

Here's what I mean.

Now, there was a playground in Newark where I used to play ball. It's all run-down, broken up. I don't know nothing about cement, but hey, I go to the cement company. I walk in there personally.

"Listen, man, this is the park I used to play in when I was in Newark. We're trying to fix it up. How much you gonna charge me to lay down some cement, paint the lines, whatever?"

The guy says, "Oh, Shaq, I love what you're doing. We ain't gonna charge you nothing."

All right, we got the cement company. Now we go to a fencing company.

"Listen, man, when I was coming up, the fence was ten foot. We used to jump it. Let's make a high fence so they don't want to jump it. You want to put some barbed wire at the top, that's cool. Let's just make it nice. How much you gonna charge me for 200 yards of fence?"

"Ahhh, I'm gonna show you how a fencing company works, how we got it at cost," the manager said. "I paid $2,000 for it."

"All right, I'll give you $2,500."

Newark, realizing it won't cost the city anything, jumps on the bandwagon.

All of a sudden, you've got an improved neighborhood.

In Florida, Jersey, and L.A., I've handled things in the 'hood. I'm hoping to start somewhat of a chain reaction. I'm hoping another big-time cat will take care of where he came from.

I think if every big-timer with business savvy could just take care of one city, the world would be a better place. Maybe it's a little unrealistic, but think about it. If we got one major athlete to take care of one city, that's fifty major cities that are getting better.

More than a run-down neighborhood, I hate to see people not have a place to stay. I hate to see homelessness. My father taught me that. When I was young, growing up in Newark, my father got some extra cash, went to a fast-food restaurant and ordered six double cheeseburgers and some sodas. And I was trying to outdo him, so I ordered six. We don't eat all twelve. We've got about five or six left over. So, you know, he sees this homeless guy, "Will work for food."

My father had $12 in his pocket. He gave the dude the burgers, he gave the dude the drinks and he gave him his last $12. He said, "Listen, don't buy no drugs. Go get a place to stay."

I can't tell you how much that influenced me at that age, to see my dad do that.

My father used to take some of his disgruntled troops and tell them, "Come with me, brother. You think you got it hard? Come with me." He'd take them down to the shelter, drop off extra sleeping bags and army boots. He would take me with him.

If something happened to a kid, if he broke his arm or was really sick, we would have to go to the hospital to see him. On the way, you'd see less-fortunate kids. And he'd say, "See, you always got to pray. You always got to pray that you're healthy."

So I don't like to just give people money on the street because you never know what their intentions are, but I try to see what their problem is.

I'll ask guys, "Yo, dog, you want to go to a restaurant?" When I say a restaurant, I don't mean Red Lobster. I mean McDonald's, Burger King.

We go to a place, the dude will say, "Shaq, I try to go in there every day. They won't give me no food, they won't let me in there."

"Come in with me, man. Go wash your hands, come in with me."

I'll go up to the front. "Yo, manager, this is my man. He's trying to get something to eat. I'm gonna pay for him. Here's $20. Get him whatever he wants. After he orders what he wants, give him his change."

I guess what I'm trying to say is, I'm not trying to keep a squeaky-clean image, or project myself to be somebody who learned how lucky I am to be this wealthy and healthy, or give you this pretty package, like I care about being seen as someone who is concerned about other people. My mother and father taught me. They showed me to do right.

If I have a message for people, this is it: If you don't enjoy doing it, don't do it. Image is reality.

I do a lot of charity work around the holidays, from Shaqa Claus, where I pass out toys to less-fortunate kids, to ShaqsGiving, where I give away turkeys each year, and there is a lot of publicity surrounding my generosity.

I even convinced Bill Gates to donate money for purchasing computers for inner-city schools, putting out the first $1 million during the lockout. That started a chain reaction that swept the country.

But it's the little, unpublicized moments that give me the most gratification.

I was driving around Orlando this summer and realized how the city has this beautiful arena blocks away from people who just can't get their lives together. I asked the question: How come all the arenas are in the 'hood? Now I know why. The land is cheaper. You can never build an arena in Beverly Hills because of the price of land. It makes sense, this is the way the world works. But I'd like to see the same owners who put arenas in inner-city communities take care of the surrounding areas, too, make some investments in the quality of life in those communities. Otherwise, to me, it looks greedy and unfair, and the NBA don't need that. Hell, the world don't need that.

I try to separate my life into have-tos and should-dos. Like I have to take care of my son and daughter and my mother and father and my younger siblings. I have to do that. Period. There's no questions asked. Things I should do are when I go on the court: I should work hard, should try to rebound. They're shoulds because I don't *have* to play basketball.

Most of my stress comes from basketball. I really don't have any family stress.

One of my favorite things to do in L.A. is just drive and think about what I have to do, what has to be done. Life. Also, in L.A., there's always something to do. So I just ride around and look. Like Monday night is the Improv. I'll cruise by, see friends.

"Oh, what's up, dog?"

"Good game yesterday."

"Thanks. All right, later." Just ride by. I'm just riding by, looking at the scenery.

But every now and then something will shake me up and I'll come back to reality.

We were in Indianapolis last January when they broke the news to the team that Bobby Phills had died in a car crash in Charlotte.

It was just sad. After a couple of guys made calls, we found out he and David Wesley were drag racing. One lost control.

The truth is, sometimes as a big-time athlete you feel indestructible, like nothing can hurt you. And then you get in a little sports car, step on the gas and you're flying, and there's nothing in the world telling you to slow down, think about your life and the people you could be hurting.

I'm not gonna lie to you, I like to drive fast. One time I made it to Pasadena in nine minutes from where I lived at. On the 101 to the 134, I made it in nine minutes. I was flying in my Ferrari M456. It was about 3:30 in the morning. No cars out there.

It was stupid of me. After Bobby passed away, I said, "That's it, I'm not doing this anymore." Because, you know, we all do the same thing. I wasn't thinking like that, that I was invincible.

I knew I wasn't gonna lose control; I knew that. But what if some little cat that I didn't see coming took me out?

The day after Phills died, I traded in my Ferrari.

I'm big on teammates. I'm big on thinking. I'm big on quotes. I get a lot of ideas from them. Once I read about this dude who interviewed Albert Einstein. At the end of the interview, he said, "OK, I want to send you what I'm writing. What's the address of your laboratory?"

Einstein said, "I don't know."

The guy said, "What do you mean you don't know? You're a genius."

Einstein said, "Things you can get access to, you should never memorize."

To me this makes a lot of sense. So I have a good team of people around me. Leonard handles all the contracts, all the numbers. I let him worry about that. I don't memorize my schedule at all. That's my personal assistant's job. Like I tell him, I don't think that far ahead. Someone takes care of my car, my house, my registration. I have no idea where my registration is. It's not my job to know. I want to keep my brain as loose as possible.

I always wake up with a new spring. I'll walk downstairs and Thomas, my personal chef, will have my schedule. During basketball season, there's not much to tell me: practice, interviews, Jay Leno, ride around, chill out. I'm a routine type of guy. At the same time, I'm also a businessman. I wake up, eat my breakfast, ask myself: "OK, what business you got to take care of? Oh, you got to call and talk to the editor of *Money* magazine."

In some ways, I guess I am like an actor, because I have a switch. If I got to talk to *Money* magazine, click. "Yes, sir; no, sir. Yes, I like the tech stocks. You know, I don't like the conventional Kmart or Wal-Mart stocks, I feel that the tech stocks are growing rapidly."

I can't call up and say, "Yeah, man, this chump called me up and he put a million dollars on damn Oracle 'cause he know Larry Ellison and he got me $2 million." You can't do that.

Professional. My mother always told me to be professional. You know, tuck your damn shirt in, button your thing up, be presentable.

So, you know, when I'm talking with certain people, I'm professional. But then, after my job is done, click, I get to be me. And this is me. Ride the Sea-Doos, watch TV, listen to rap music. I got rims on my trucks. I ghettoed out both of my Rolls-Royces. I hunt, I ride my bike, and I just have fun.

And, you know what? I think more people should live for themselves rather than try and live for everybody else. If I live for anybody else, it will be my family. And I think one of the reasons I'm not wild—like really wild—is because of my mother. My mother's a beautiful lady, beautiful, happy woman at peace right now. Very happy for me. Very happy that she raised me. So it would be idiotic for me to go out there and do something stupid, to get in trouble with the law. I would lose—you know, it would make her sad again. I don't want her ever to be sad.

When she used to have to work and bring home only $10,000 a year, it saddened her that her children couldn't have what all the other children had. I don't ever want her to go back there.

That was part of what drove me.

"I got to get my mom outta that sorry Toyota. Here, Mom, you got a Benz now."

Now I have children, so doing right by them drives me as well. I know I can't be doing crazy stuff, can't be doing anything that my kids are gonna be ashamed about.

All this heaviness does not mean I'm a monk. I'm an unorthodox type of guy, a funny guy—at least I think I'm funny. And one of the things I like to do is come up with nicknames for myself.

Some of my personal favorites:

"The Big Stock Exchange." I start off at one price. Every now and then I'll go down, but eventually I'll go back up.

"The Big IPO." Put your money on me. Because when I go public, we all gonna make money.

"The Big Aristotle" was coined the day I won the MVP last year. I stole a quote from that Greek philosopher cat: "Excellence is not a singular act, but a habit. You are what you repeatedly do."

Can't forget "The Big Antarctica" because I'm so cold.

Or "The Big Havlicek," which is what I called myself after making a bunch of foul shots one night.

How about "The Big Felon" for when I made a steal against Orlando and had a breakaway dunk with 15 seconds left, forcing overtime of what would become a Lakers victory?

And, of course, "The Almighty Conceitedness." That's the highest level of arrogance. I made that up, too.

In this world we live in, people like silliness and mischief. Or that's what I keep telling myself. I get paid big money and there's no way I'm going to pretend I have the problems of people who work 9-to-5. While sometimes I have to realize how fortunate I am before I go off about something that's not that big a deal, most of the time I'm not a complex guy. I like doing simple stuff. Fun stuff.

Like watching Vince Carter dunk. I have a thirty-minute Vince Carter dunk highlight tape. My people from the NBA send me footage and I put my own music on. I put it together. It's cold.

I got one that I made called *Vince versus Shaq*. It's like forty-five minutes. I show him doing a couple nasty dunks; then I show me doing a couple nice dunks. So when all my boys come to the house, they're constantly going "Oooohhhhh!"

The only problem is that Vince wins every time. Vince is doing that aerial act and my dunks are all the same—two-hand power dunks.

But don't think all I do is sit at home and watch videos. I have more than my share of wild times. So let Vince have his slam-dunk title. What would all my critics say if they knew that I was a champion years before the Lakers beat the Pacers? I was the slam-dance champion of England.

I should explain.

Like I said, I'm into having a good time, and I've been a big music fan all my life. So in 1994 I was in London, watching a psycho rap group called the Grave Diggaz perform in a club. The Grave Diggaz have this great jam called "Bang Your Head." And at the end of the concert, there was this slam-dance contest. This dude, Skullhead, was the champ. I don't know if Skullhead was his real name, probably not, but he was this big, pitbull-looking white boy with a tattoo on his head. Real mean. Cut up. I'd say he had about 4 percent body fat. Just body-slamming dudes.

All these kids started jumping up and down, so I start jumping up and down with them. My bodyguard Jerome and my Uncle Mike didn't know what was going on. Being from Newark and seeing a bunch of guys start slamming into each other, they thought a brawl was breaking out.

So Jerome and them get in their fighting position. They didn't know about the punk-rock scene and the crazy guys that hang out in these clubs.

I'm telling them, "Don't worry about it, we're just dancing." There's maybe thirty of us.

I'm dropping guys, left and right, slamming into everyone. Basically knock them all down. All of a sudden it's just me and one guy left.

Skullhead.

The crowd's going crazy, and he started sprinting at me, trying to jump into me. People are going, "Oh, no, Skullhead's hitting Shaq." I'm a little worried myself.

So I kind of moved, gave him a little nudge with my butt. He hit this brick wall. Just fell right over. Right on his back. Skullhead was out cold.

I won.

The place was rocking and after the Grave Diggaz finished playing, everybody hugged. "Yeah, Shaq, you cool, you down," people were saying. "I didn't know you was that cool, Shaq."

That's fun stuff, real-life fun. Not going out and posing at some big-time party.

Another time, in January 1996, the East Coast was hit with this monster blizzard. We were supposed to play New Jersey, but the game got canceled and they had to reroute the Orlando Magic's team plane to Allentown, Pennsylvania.

I'm thinking, "What the hell am I going to do in Allentown?"

It wasn't bad. We ended up at the Holiday Inn with—check out this crew—the cast from *Sesame Street Live* and Marilyn Manson. You had to check out the scene to believe it. Me, Marilyn, and Big Bird.

I guess lots of planes got rerouted because we were all in there, acting crazy, playing cards, gambling, laughing. They had like a little sports bar downstairs. We just stayed in the bar all night. We didn't have a game for four days. We couldn't leave. So I'm in there singing, "Can you tell me how to get, how to get to Sesame Street?"

Marilyn Manson wasn't as big as he is now. He came up to me afterward. "Remember my name," he said. "I'm gonna be famous." He was a nice guy. He wasn't the Marilyn Manson that he is now. I guess this is before he got his big record deal because he looked normal. Then the next time I seen him on TV: lipstick, makeup, crazy videos.

I guess it's like Dennis Rodman. Whatever works.

Being famous, I've gotten a lot of invitations to a lot of parties. Usually, I just chill out at home—especially during the season.

After last season, I brought my whole crew to Las Vegas. I ended up going to the Playboy party.

Not that I didn't have a good time, but it turned out to be a lot of girls taking pictures with a lot of horny old men.

They had the party at this water park. One side of the water park was closed, the one that had the best rides. So I had to pull some strings. I got the manager to get a lifeguard and open up a couple of the water slides, so me and my friends could goof off while everyone else was posing at the Playboy party.

I remember in San Antonio once in the off-season, I tried to give the owner of the water park $3,000 to open it up. He wouldn't do it. I had no power back then. Now I've got a little more juice.

The All-Star Game is always nonstop parties, and I must admit I have taken full advantage of a few. In 1993, Minnesota hosted the All-Star Game. At the same time, Prince was having "The Most Beautiful Girl in the World" contest. Prince is from Minneapolis, and was in this club called the Glam Slam, upstairs, hanging there like he owned the place, which I later found out, he does.

So I'm downstairs. This big guy taps me: "Prince want to see you."

I go upstairs. Prince got the finest girls I ever seen in my life, feeding him grapes, combing his hair, doing his toes. All of them were just looking at Prince. They weren't even looking at me. I guess Prince was saying he was gonna marry the most beautiful girl in the world, so he had girls from everywhere just trying to impress him. He even had some girls acting like mannequins, standing stiff the whole time. It was him and about twenty girls up there, feeding him grapes.

And you thought NBA players lived large.

Biggie Smalls (aka The Notorious B.I.G.) was one of my favorite rappers. I saw him three days before he was murdered, and actually was supposed to go to the party he was killed at.

Biggie and I had a little history. I flew him and his whole crew out to my house a few years ago. We hung out. We'd talk about a few things. We both had people in our professions who were jealous of us and wanted to take us down, so he wanted to know how I dealt with those kind of people. "How do I handle the haters?" he asked me.

I said, "Don't even worry about it. When you're the best, some people are gonna like you, some people are gonna hate you. Worry about what you do. Make your money and take care of your family."

He was an amazing rapper. I need to hear the beat, go into a room, and write something. Biggie could just hear the beat. No pencil, no paper. He'd just sit there and go, "All right, I'm ready." Then he went into my recording studio, said some crazy stuff.

I couldn't put what he said on my album at the time, it was so hot. Real hot. That was one cold cat.

The last time I saw him was at a tattoo parlor on Sunset Boulevard. It was my birthday, March 6. He was sitting in front of the place. I said, "What's up, man, what you doing?"

"Sitting out here, chillin'."

This was after Tupac Shakur had died, and the rivalry between East Coast and West Coast rappers was heating up. At the time, all of California was mad that Tupac was killed. Biggie was out in L.A., and his song had just come out, too. "Going Back to Cali."

I told Biggie, "Yo, man, be careful."

Three days later, they got him.

He was having a party at the Petersen Automotive Museum at Fairfax and Wilshire. Everybody wanted to go to that party. I thought my cousin Andre said he was gonna come get me. What happened, I left my pager in the room because I didn't want to take my pager that night. So I was sitting on the couch, watching TV. I was kind of tired, but was gonna go to the party anyway.

Andre never called because he was trying to page me.

At 3:30 A.M., my mother woke me.

"Did you go?"

I was like, "Go where? What are you talking about?"

She said, "Biggie's party. You know he was killed?"

March 9, that was a sad day.

If I would have been standing by his truck, would the killer still have shot? I've always asked that question. Asked a lot of people.

How close am I to the rap industry? I did five albums. For me, it wasn't about the money. Everyone in the record industry knows you don't make real big money unless you go on tour all the time. For me, it was about fulfilling my dream and rhyming with all my favorite emcees.

One album, *Shaq Diesel*, went platinum, selling almost 900,000 copies. My second album, *Shaq Fu, Da Return,* went gold, at about 269,000. *You Can't Stop the Reign* sold only 205,000 copies. I don't do a lot of heavy promotion. But I've got my own company now. That's where the money is.

I grew up with a lot of old-school rap influences. Run DMC. LL Cool J. My favorite Run DMC song was "Rock Box."

It was different. The drums in that song just worked, you know. I'm glad God invented rap music, 'cause before that it was Lionel Ritchie, The Commodores, and Earth, Wind and Fire.

Then it was Fat Boys, ("All You Could Eat," was the jam), Public Enemy, Flava Flav with the clock. Later on, I started to enjoy gangsta rap. When you hear it, it just makes you feel hard, like you're going back to the neighborhood.

But I should also say a few things about gangsta rap. I have four sisters, so I wouldn't use the word "bitches" in my own songs. Personally, as a rapper, I would never call a woman that. I also realize I've got little kids looking up to me. So that's not me; I don't live that life, I don't subscribe to those lyrics.

There's a lot of materialistic rappers now, talking about what they got. But it's all a dream. Only a few actually drive Benzes and live that kind of life. The others just glorify it, and I don't know if that's good.

I do know that a lot of people blame rap music for society's problems. And I don't agree with that. For example, a Lakers team official once told us that rap music was the reason he thought black kids have short attention spans. He said it in front of the whole team.

He gave us an example. He went into how black kids have too much going on when they're little. I'm paraphrasing, but the guy said something like, "You're listening to the rap music, your mommy and daddy are arguing, your boys outside are calling you, the TV is going on, Nintendo playing. Your brother is messing with you." He said that's why we have short attention spans. At first I thought it was kind of funny. Then I thought it was kind of messed up. But that's his opinion. Opinions are like belly buttons; everybody has one. I never knock a man for his opinion.

Do I believe that's true, that rap music is to blame? No. But I agree with him that black families do have a lot going on, especially when they're in the projects. You're inside, your cousin Andre wants you to come outside. You got to look out the window. Your mama is yelling at you to take the garbage out. Grandma arguing with one of your aunts. Your brother is wearing your shoes. You're about to mess him up. Grandpa gives you a dollar and told you to buy some beer; you try to buy the cheap brand so you can buy candy. Your dad's beating you up, your grandma's hitting him with a shoe. I don't know how the guys took what the Lakers official said. I mean, a lot of brothers, if they heard that, they would take that as racist. I looked at it like the dude is just speaking his mind.

One thing you have to understand about me, I'm not on that black-and-white kick. Even though I'm a hard-core brother in some ways, I'm not on that racist bandwagon. Never been. Never will be. My mother and father taught me to respect people as people. My father is Muslim. You could say he's down with Malcolm X. But just the same way Malcolm X found out that Muslims are other colors when he made a pilgrimage to Mecca, my father understands that people are people.

He taught me that, growing up around different nationalities and cultures on army bases. To this day, I'm not one of those brothers who surrounds himself with only friends from the 'hood—because I think those are the only people that understand where I came from.

My personal chef, who also happens to be my good friend, is white. One of my personal assistants and closest friends from high school is half-Thai, half-Italian. In short, color does not matter to me. You are who you are.

I've received more than my share of criticism for doing movies, and albums—so much, it's almost ridiculous. Maybe people wanted to see me win a championship before I had outside interests. But none of it ever interfered with my game. Never. It was always done during the off-season. The two movies I did, *Kazaam* and *Steel*, were not exactly critically acclaimed. I really didn't expect them to be. Truth is, I was just doing what I saw my heroes do. My favorite movie to this day is *The Fish That Saved Pittsburgh*, starring who? Starring Dr. J. Kareem got kicked by Bruce Lee and did *Airplane*. Wilt Chamberlain was in *Conan*. Is there a double standard in the criticism I received? I don't know. But it's worth bringing up.

I remember one time when Eddie Murphy was taking heat for a movie that got killed by the critics. He went on *Saturday Night Live* one night and said something like, "Hey, if they gave you a million dollars to do *Best Defense*, you would take the damn money, too."

One of the great things about being a famous athlete and going to Hollywood is that you get to cross over and live in that movie-star world. One of the worst things is, it opens you up to harder critics than just sportswriters.

People took a couple pokes at me for doing movies that weren't exactly blockbusters. I'm not sure if it was because they thought I should be working out instead of filming or because they thought the movies were just bad—or both. But I am not making apologies for my acting or my rap careers. They were activities I took advantage of in the off-season. Period. I never felt they affected my game. I never performed a rap show during the season, except in 1998 during the All-Star break because we had a couple of days off in New York. I have never filmed a movie during the season.

You can only work out so long and hard in the summer. When I was filming, I would work out every day from about 10:00 to 1:00 and then take care of my movie commitments. I realize I'm not Denzel Washington or Samuel L. Jackson. But, hey, when

Sherry Lansing, the CEO of Paramount says, "I'm going to do a movie about a bunch of college basketball players and what they do in college, and we think you're the perfect guy," what am I gonna say? No? I was twenty-one years old when I did *Blue Chips*. I was a kid having fun, taking advantage of opportunities same as any kid out of college my age would.

My second movie came about when Paul Michael Glaser—Starsky from *Starsky and Hutch*—approached me at an All-Star Game. His son, Jake, wanted to meet one guy at the All-Star Game: Me. I saw them in the lobby, made him laugh, hung out with him for a couple minutes. He had been through an awful experience, losing his mother and his sister to AIDS. I sent him some shoes, sent him some clothes. Paul said after I met his son, he had a dream I was a genie. He said I took Jake's mind off all the bad stuff that had happened in their lives. So I made *Kazaam*. A lot of older people tore it apart. Maybe it wasn't the best kids' movie ever, but it really didn't do too badly at the box office and the Disney channel played the heck out of it. Besides, when I can walk through the airport and a kid yells, "Kazaam!"—well, this might sound corny, but I feel like I did my job.

My last movie, Quincy Jones came to my house and asked if I would like to be the first black superhero. I told him I had been reading a black comic book about a guy named Steel. He said, "Perfect. Why don't you just be Steel?" And he put it together. Was *Steel* a great movie? No. Was it a nice, tame action movie for kids? I think so. Warner just didn't put much marketing behind it. Again, I feel like I did my job. Say what you want, but Hollywood came to me. And I know my performance on the court never suffered because of the movies. The only time my performance has ever suffered on the court was during the four years of my career that I had some kind of injury.

I knew that if I crossed over to those other things that my game had to be tight. They still try to kill me anyway, but my game was always there and the enthusiasm for basketball was always there.

Maybe it's a double-edged sword. But that's the world we live in. If I didn't play basketball, do you really think that Paramount would meet with me? They'd be like, "Who the hell is this big guy?" At best they're gonna use me for *Harry and the Hendersons,* make me play the big sasquatch thing—Shaquatch.

All I can say is, you take advantage of the opportunities while they are there. Plus, doubling as a movie star was a dream come true in some ways. I grew up watching superheroes and action flicks.

You know how directors and producers always talk about being "influenced" by another director or producer when they were coming up? I had my role models on the screen, too. Growing up, my cousins and I would watch karate movies, then go outside and try and do the same moves. James Bond was just amazing. He had all the gadgets I wish I had. And I used to watch *The Incredible Hulk* television show. When he turned from a person into a monster, I could identify with the Hulk when he wanted to tear stuff up.

No one made me pretend I was a superhero more than the Man of Steel. Superman was my favorite. The George Reeves *Superman.* The Christopher Reeve *Superman.* Whichever. I could watch those shows anytime and all the time. When the old black-and-white version came on and Clark Kent would come out in his little fedora, I would get all excited. When he'd step out the window of his *Daily Planet* twenty-story-high building and just start flying, I went crazy. That was my guy. I liked the Hulk almost as much. But because my name starts with an S, I thought I had a better chance of becoming Superman.

I don't want to give the critics more fuel, but did I mention I'm also a director? I directed a Nickelodeon series called *My Cousin Skeeter.* Now, that was work. I even co-produced and appeared in Nickelodeon's award-winning series, *Sports Theater.*

To be honest, I really couldn't tell the kids who starred it in anything; they were better actors than me. I was just sitting there going, "Cut! No, no, no, no. Action."

When you are directing episodic TV, those people at Nickelodeon want every angle. When I did a couple of rap videos, they wanted one or two shots. At Nickelodeon, you got to get the behind-the-head angle, get the wide-angle to show where we are, angle on the floor, the angle on the side. It takes all day.

I think I'm done with episodic TV, but as far as movies go, I want to start getting into action. I want to start shooting and kicking, do some Jackie Chan stuff, kick some ass. Not that I'm done with kids' movies, but I want to do something hard.

Like a *Matrix*-type movie, lots of special effects.

Any producers with season tickets listening out there?

During my sophomore year at LSU, this slick agent—I won't say his name—came from California and opened up a briefcase full of money. "Listen," he said, "if you sign with me, you're gonna be the No. 1 pick. I can get you this house, $80,000. Here, take the money. I'm not even gonna see you again. Here, I'll give you my card."

I looked at him. "Do you think I'm stupid?"

Dick Vitale, the college basketball announcer, and Marty Blake, the NBA scouting director, had already said whenever I decide to come out, I'm gonna be No. 1. So, no mistakes. I'm going to class. I'm staying out of trouble.

So there's this clean-cut Italian guy that I had met a long time ago; he used to play basketball for Stan Morrison in college. This guy represented only a few people: Ronnie Lott and Hakeem. After Kareem Abdul-Jabbar had gotten into some bad investment deals, this guy helped Kareem get some of his money back, so I respected him for that.

Leonard Armato, who would eventually become my agent, didn't say, "I'm gonna do this for you." He didn't promise anything. Actually, he said, "I can't do that." He said, "Look, I come from a good family, and I like to do things the right way."

And to this day, Leonard has never crossed anybody, never told anybody he's gonna do something he can't. He really is a clean-cut guy. Sometimes I have a problem with that. I tell him, "You're too nice sometimes."

We have a special relationship. Leonard always taught me how to talk and walk like a businessman. We have our battles. He wants me to be a perfect Goody Two-Shoes. But I can't be that all the time.

What you see is what you get. "Image is reality." Image is what you are and who you are. Leonard wants me to be perfect. When the NBC cameras catch me swearing on TV, he'll say, "Hey, watch your mouth. They can read your lips. Children are watching." But, again, I'm not a Goody Two-Shoes, I'm not gonna act like no Goody Two-Shoes all the time. There's part of me that's homeboy. That's all there is to it. In a lot of ways, Leonard is my safety net between me and the outside world. He is 100 percent corporate. He's a great agent and the things that we've done, we've done together. Leonard is the kind of guy you can talk to. So Leonard needed me; I needed him. We had to get to the top together. But that doesn't mean I don't make his life difficult. For example, take this past summer. Now, Leonard is trying to get me endorsement deals with all-American corporations. And I'm calling him up at his office in Santa Monica, California, on my cell phone while I'm cruising in my SUV truck.

I pitched Leonard the idea for my most recent flick. This summer, I wanted to make a short, gangster-fantasy movie. I wanted to call it, *Guess What Happened to Me Last Summer.*

It started out with me getting up in the morning. Only I'm no longer Goody Two-Shoes Shaq. I turn into a gangster and rob a bank. The best part is when I walk into the bank in a disguise, pull out a gun, and yell, "Everybody get down! Now!"

One of the security guards at the bank looks at me and asks, "Hey, Shaq, is that you?"

I look at him, all embarrassed. In a high-pitched voice, I reply, "This ain't Shaq."

Anyway, before I'm cornered and about to be killed, my friend wakes me up from the nightmare. I tell him the whole story. He says, "Gangster? Get your role-model ass up so you can go sign some autographs."

Leonard made some calls. The next thing you know, I had a director, producer and a weapons expert at my house the next day. We shot it in a couple of days. No, you won't see it on the Internet. I promised Leonard I wouldn't put it out.

Although if the Sundance Film Festival people call, I can't be held responsible.

A writer from *ESPN* magazine once described me as the world's largest eleven-year-old. That's true. I ride my Sea-Doo jet ski, play putt-putt golf, go to water parks and act silly. On the bottom floor of my house in Beverly Hills, I have video games, a pool table, a Pepsi machine and all the things they have in arcades. I drive go-karts, at least the ones I can fit in. I karate-chop my friends when they come over, like the Kato dude in the *Pink Panther* movies.

I painted my toenails before Dennis Rodman. One time at training camp, I stubbed my toe and the nail came loose. My mom gave me some toenail hardener and I painted over it. I scored 40-something that night, so it became a ritual. Paint my toenails, score 40 points.

Sometimes I feel like the Tom Hanks character in *Big*. But my life is not a movie. I never have to go back to Coney Island to find the fortune-teller machine so I have to grow up again.

When it's time to be serious and do my job on the court, I go into that mode. When it's time to talk to Bill Gates about raising money for charity, I go into that mode. Maybe it's my upbringing, but I do feel like a big chameleon. I can adapt to change because I grew up in different places. I've seen a lot of things. I know how I want to live my life.

Example: right now I'm in a barbershop. It's called Three in One, and it's located in one of the more dangerous neighborhoods in Orlando. The shop is owned by my good friend and former teammate, Dennis Scott. I've known everyone there since my playing days and they still cut my hair just like I like it.

There are tons of kids milling around, running up to me. One little girl has a cast on her right leg she wants me to sign. This is the inner city a lot of NBA players give hope to. It's also a place where everyone will tell you the truth and you don't just run into people always telling you what you want to hear. Let's put it this way: I can't let Charles Barkley beat me up, go in there and get a cut without getting some serious grief.

While I'm getting my hair cut, two kids walk up to me. One is Mark Moore, who is thirteen years old but has a little bit of an attitude for his age. The other is D-Shea Cooper, his eight-year-old friend.

"Can you hoop?" I ask Mark.

"I'll dunk on your head," he tells me.

He asks if I ever get dunked on.

"No. Never."

He asks if I've ever dunked on Tracy McGrady.

"I dunk on everybody."

After I get my haircut and visit with the barbershop crowd, I drive through the 'hood on the way back to my summer home. I see two young boys walking down the street, bouncing a basketball. I roll down my window. "Put that ball down, boy, you don't know how to work it." You should see their faces when they realize it's me. It's like, "It's Shaq!"

I guess I like making people smile, especially kids. When I see a bunch of kids playing ball on an outdoor court, sometimes I'll just roll up in the parking lot, walk up to them and say, "Give me that, man." Then I let them shake me, so the boys can go, "Oooohhh." I'll let them score on me. Sometimes I might even stop there and play with them for a while. I just like making them smile. I have a good time. It's the big kid in me coming out.

Like, I never try to big-time anybody. I can go to my places and wear my stuff and I'm cool. They know I'm approachable. I don't step on nobody's toes. And if I do, the first thing I say is, "My fault, dog." Somebody steps on my foot: "Don't worry about it, dog." I've seen other cats get angry, say things they shouldn't say. I don't do that. See, what many athletes don't realize is that a lot of people already hate what we represent. We're living how they want to live. So you can't belittle them. I never do that. I never create enemies. I could be in a club, a guy will give me the meanest look in the world and I'll look at him and say, "What's up, player? You all right?"

I'm nice to women, always saying hi, being respectful. When they ask for a hug, I usually oblige. "Nice to meet you," all that. It's called knowing your environment and respecting it. Too many athletes go to places and don't respect the people or the environment they're in. That's when the trouble starts.

I have worked with many charities, but one of my favorites is the Boys & Girls Clubs of America. It's still a grass-roots-level organization in a lot of ways, fixing up community centers and playgrounds. One of the most gratifying donations I ever made was the $1 million I gave to the Boys & Girls Club to start up technology centers. Bridging the gap between computers and inner-city kids is important to me.

I got Bill Gates involved, and all of a sudden it started a revolution. We found out Colin Powell was a member of the Boys Club, and we ended up having a big dinner in Washington, D.C., two years ago to raise money for the project. Bill Gates donated. Guys from Apple donated. I think we raised about $20 million. It wasn't something I did because I was told to or I thought it would be a tax write-off. It was important to me. I wish more athletes would use the game as a tool to help others instead of just themselves. Like I said, if one famous person pledged their money and time to taking care of their own neighborhood—the idea behind America's Promise, the Alliance for Youth organization—we could fix a lot in this world.

So how does a guy from Newark, New Jersey, talk the richest man in the world into contributing money to a cause? I dress up in a nice, clean suit and I talk to Bill Gates the way I talk to any businessman. I can't go to Bill and be like, "What's up, dog? I need some computers for the people in the 'hood, dog. I just gave a million dollars." You can't do that. It's, "Mr. Gates, hi. How are you doing? I feel there's a gap where technology is not equally avail-

My great-grandparents Cillar and Hilton O'Neal.

My grandmother Odessa.

Uncle Roy, Aunt Vivian, Aunt Velma, and my mother,
Lucille, as children.

Here I am at age one and, later, as a schoolboy.

Courtside with my mother, Lucille Harrison.
(Andrew D. Bernstein/NBA Photos)

My father, Phil Harrison, shares some time with me.
(Andrew D. Bernstein/NBA Photos)

Photos on next three pages:

Three tough rivals: (Left) Playing for Orlando, trying to get past
Patrick Ewing…(Nathaniel S. Butler/NBA Photos)

(Right) Laying one in over Hakeem Olajuwon…
(Bill Baptist/NBA Photos)

(Left) And dunking hard on Alonzo Mourning.
(Fernando Medina/NBA Photos)

Music is an important part of my life, whether I'm rapping with a band or just listening at home. (Andrew D. Bernstein/NBA Photos)

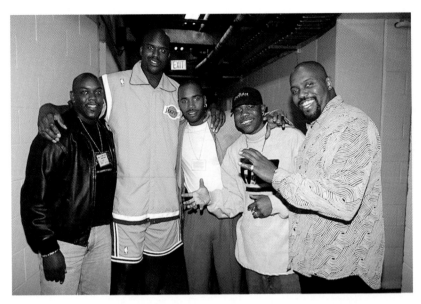

Some of the TWISM crew: Mike Parris, me, Andre Spellman,
Kenny Bailey, and Jerome Crawford.
(Andrew D. Bernstein/NBA Photos)

My agent, Leonard Armato, is my closest adviser.
(Andrew D. Bernstein/NBA Photos)

Powering up and reaching back for a dunk against the Golden State
Warriors. (Andrew D. Bernstein/NBA Photos)

Celebrating after the game when I scored 61 points.
(Andrew D. Bernstein/NBA Photos)

(Opposite page) Dunking on Arvydas Sabonis during Game 6 of the
playoff series against Portland. (Andrew D. Bernstein/NBA Photos)

Photos on next two pages:
(Left) Driving to the rim against three Pacers in the finals vs. Indiana.
(Right) Shooting over Rik Smits in Game 3.
(Andrew D. Bernstein/NBA Photos)

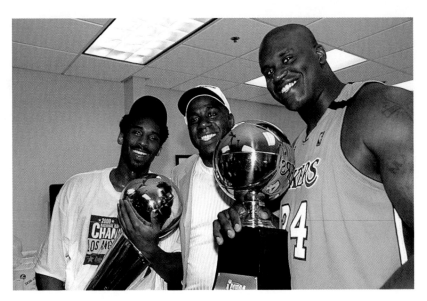

Celebrating with Magic Johnson and Kobe Bryant after
winning Game 6 and the NBA Championship.
(Andrew D. Bernstein/NBA Photos)

With the Lakers coach,
Phil Jackson, and the
championship
trophy.
(Andrew D.
Bernstein/NBA
Photos)

ible to all children, and we need to close the gap, especially with kids from the 'hood. So this is my proposal, sir. I'm putting up a million dollars. I want to build 100 technology centers. And if you want to donate computers, donate money, whatever you'd like to do, it would be great because you are the computer guru."

I'm a firm believer in getting involved with your community. But there is one thing I don't think all athletes should participate in: politics. A lot of people have given Michael Jordan grief about not being more active and supporting Democratic candidates in his home state of North Carolina, but I don't know if I agree. I had a bad experience in college that turned me off on attaching my celebrity to the political process. Someone asked me about David Duke, the former KKK member who was running for office in Louisiana. I said, "I don't care about David Duke." Those were my exact words.

David Duke gets on TV and says, "Shaquille O'Neal said he doesn't care if I run."

True story. I knew what David Duke did, who he was. And that's why I said I didn't care about him. But it was interpreted like I was giving him approval or something. So now I'm walking on campus, and people are giving me that what-was-that-about? glance. Like I sold out my race or something. That was my first and last adventure into politics.

One of the best things about being a celebrity is that you can get into any club free. Especially if they know you're nice and classy, they'll treat you the same. When my entourage and I go out in L.A., we roll up with ten people, and I'll send one guy out of the truck to check out the situation. We explain to the security guy at the club that we're all dressed up in suits—Uncle Jerome makes us get dressed up when we go out—we plan to act respectful, and we have no problem paying for everyone.

Now, if we came in with the bandannas, the jewelry, acting like knuckleheads, it would be a different story. But instead, we're dressed to kill. All of a sudden, it's "Look, Shaq . . ."

I try not to take advantage of my celebrity because nothing is truly free. A lot of times, the person doing you a favor expects something back, even if it means giving their restaurant a name because you ate there. Also, the more you accept special treatment, the more you think you're better than people around you. And I don't ever want to get like that.

I know I could have Leonard call somebody and get me out of a speeding ticket, but I'm a law-abiding citizen. I drive aggressive. If I speed, and get stopped, I'm not, "Yo, up yours. I'm Shaq on the way to the game." I'll just say, "My fault, sorry."

I respect the cops because those guys are hard workers, like my Uncle Mike and Jerome used to be in Newark. So if I get a ticket, whether it's a parking ticket or a speeding ticket, I'll send in my $30 or $50 just like everybody else.

One thing I really like about L.A. is that the city accepts you, no matter who you are. When I was in Orlando, I really felt like a big fish in a small, dried-up pond. No matter what I did, it got talked about, until I couldn't really live my life. But out in L.A., for everything you do, there's always some other star acting crazier.

Leonardo DiCaprio, Marky Wahlberg. I see them all hanging out. I don't really bond with any of the Hollywood types, but I like the actor Michael Rappaport. I like his work. Pierce Brosnan. Jack Nicholson and I say hi to each other. Denzel Washington is a good friend of mine. So I know all the actors, I know all the rappers.

I tried to hit on Tori Spelling once, but she wasn't havin' any of it. I asked for her phone number, and she didn't give it to me. She said, "Give me yours." Oh, well. Don't hurt to try.

I see Tyra Banks every day. She lives next door to the mother of my son. I've seen Tyra with and without makeup on. She seems nice, but if I saw her in a club I wouldn't try to talk to her. She's beautiful, but she ain't my type.

That's been a big plus about celebrity: the opportunities to meet interesting and exciting people. How else is a brother from the ghetto gonna meet Bill Gates? Every actress that I wanted to meet, I've met. I met Janet Jackson, Holly Robinson, Nia Long, Madonna. I met them all. I haven't met Anna Kournikova yet. Seriously. I like the way she rotates them shoulders. She's just beautiful. I know she's a kid in a lot of ways, but she is one of most beautiful women I have ever seen.

It's amazing how life can turn out. Here I am flirting and name dropping, and I didn't have a girlfriend until I was a sophomore in high school. Serious. She ran track at Cole in San Antonio. I met her after I had moved from Germany. She lived on one side of the army base and I lived on the other, so the only time I saw her was at school. She was a cutie. We went out for maybe eight weeks, but then the summer came and we went our separate ways. Nothing happened. I was a good boy.

My senior year of high school, I used to date a girl, and we even went out for a while my freshman year at LSU. She was at Xavier, so I used to drive up to New Orleans a lot and see her.

Fact is, I was a virgin until college. Oh, wait. My fault. Actually, I *did* get some action in high school. Prom night. ☺

Anyway, most of the time we used to sit in high school and lie about what happened with girls. But even then, if I liked someone, I was determined to see her.

I used to sneak over to my friend Joe's house. My girlfriend lived about a mile away. So I'd run to her house after I told Joe to tell my dad I was at his house. My dad would be calling, "Where's Shaquille and Joe?"

"Oh, they outside playing basketball."

"Well, go get him."

So Joe had to go run over to my girlfriend's house, tell me to get my ass home. I'd run back, huffing and puffing.

"What are you doing?" my father would ask.

"Playing ball."

I don't know if I have ever been in love, but I have had strong feelings for some of the women I have gone out with over the years. Have I broke some girls' hearts? Probably. But I got some scars myself.

I was boomeranged, so to speak, when I was in college.

From the ages of zero to seventeen, girls didn't care who I was. Freshman year at LSU, girls wasn't checking for me. Uh-oh, Chris and Stanley leave. Now *I'm* the man on campus. It's Shaq Daddy Time.

My last two years of college, I felt like I was paying back every girl who shot me down earlier my life. I'm telling them whatever they want to hear. Then I met this one girl I really started to like. Every one told me she was a freak and to be careful. But I was trying to make her my girlfriend. I bought her nice things, whatever I could afford at the time. I did the whole romance thing.

And she just dogged my ass out.

I'm walking on campus, holding her hand, and people are laughing at me. A couple of the football players were like, "Look at Shaq, I was with her last night."

I gave her money and found out she was giving it to some of the football players. She was riding them around in my car. I was hurt. Really and seriously hurt. I was into her. I was an All-American. I was the big man on that campus. And I was a big joke—because some girl I was crazy about was having sex with everybody else.

My mother always told me, "You better stop playing with girls like that. One gonna get you." She was right.

That girl could have easily hurt me worse. I think if I would have got her pregnant, she'd be telling the Shawn Kemp story right now. I was very bitter, and I don't know if I would have given her anything. She probably would have reported me, and we would have had to go to court.

But, yeah, she got me. After that, I believed in karma when it came to relationships. What goes around comes around.

I made a promise to myself that I would stop hurting girls' feelings. See, the thing is, I have a soft heart. So I thought I was doing women a favor when I would say nice things. But one of my sisters told me if you be honest with a girl, she'll love you even more, no matter what you do. If she knows you're doing it, then she has a decision to make on whether she's leaving or not.

Now, if I'm not in a relationship, I tell girls, "Look, you can't be my girlfriend, but we could hang out and go to the movies and have fun. And that's how it's gonna be. That's it. If you want to have something more serious, I can't do that in my life right now."

They love that honesty.

Every time someone messes you over, it's hard for you to trust the next person. That experience in college made it hard for me. But I got over it. And now I just try to be honest. It takes a lot of the problems away.

What's for sure is that NBA life can get crazy. You have to be careful.

At that same All-Star Game in Minnesota where I met Prince, someone's mom called an emergency meeting of all the players. The story was, one of the All-Stars got caught with a transvestite. Everybody started looking around, trying to figure out who it was.

One of the security people told us the transvestite was working for Dr. You-Know-Who. That meant Dr. Boudreaux. Anyway, that was his street name. He was this con artist who used to send girls down to the bars to meet pro athletes. They would put something in your drink and try and get you back to your room before you got completely knocked out. The next thing you knew, two weeks went by, and you would receive pictures in the mail of yourself with another man. Supposedly, this Dr. Boudreaux would tell you to send him $200,000, or he would send those pictures to a magazine. Rumor was, he had scammed a couple guys in the NBA and a couple guys in the NFL.

I'm not sure if I believed the stories, but they scared everyone at that meeting. The NBA security guy came flat out and said, "You know who you are. Don't make a scene. You need to come see me now. This person works for Dr. Boudreaux and you could be in danger." Most of us were looking around and laughing. But I'll tell you what. The rest of All-Star weekend, I don't think you saw one guy walking around with a girl other than his wife or girlfriend.

That's the world we live in. It also helps explain why a lot of players go to adult-entertainment clubs. I'm not going lie about going to strip clubs. I've been to a few. (Actually, only two since I've been in L.A.) It's not something I do regularly, but I'm human.

Like I said at the beginning of this book, yes, I am a role model. My job is to stay out of trouble, to set good examples for kids. I don't disrespect people. I don't disrespect women. I don't do drugs. But I'm also a real model. I don't wear suits all the time, and I don't talk with a Harvard education. I'm not a saint. It's just me, Shaquille O'Neal, from the projects of Newark, New Jersey, good basketball player and nice guy. I'm also a red-blooded American man who loves to look at beautiful women.

I never understood why people said, "Be like Mike." You want kids to be better than Jordan. Better than me. We're not saints. Players in the NBA curse, smoke, have kids out of wedlock, stay up all night and party. Some of us make a lot of money, and we spend it unwisely. What kind of life is *that* for a kid to look up to?

One of the main problems I have with a lot of athletes is they get diplomatic immunity for almost everything they do. They end up thinking they're above the world. They know they can get into a fight and it's, "So what? I'm so-and-so. I'll call my lawyer, pay some money and it will be over." And that's not right. Once they start making examples of these athletes, I think the world would be a better place.

Anyway, about strip clubs and athletes. The best way I can explain why a lot of players end up there is because it's one of the safest places a high-profile person can spend time in a boring city. You get on the road, half the time you're flying out of one city soon as you get done playing. You get to the next city, maybe you've got a spare night before the next game. When you're in a place like Milwaukee or Indiana, what's there to do? How much time can you spend sitting in your hotel room, watching TV? After a while, the hotels are all the same; they all got the same pay-per-view movies. And it's almost impossible to walk around a mall, go to a popular restaurant, or check out a flick without people wanting a lot of your time and attention—personally, I don't mind that so much, but a lot of players want their privacy. The attention gets to them.

At a strip club, there is lots of security, everybody is quiet about you coming and going, and it's not like you're trying to get involved with a woman or anything. A lot of players I know go to look at the women dance, tip them very well, and go back to their hotel rooms. Have some players I know tried to bring them home? I've seen that. But that doesn't happen often. Most of us realize we have an image to uphold, even in a place where a lot of people look down on us for even stepping inside.

The times I've been to strip bars, I've usually gone almost as a chaperon to other players. Since I'm the type of guy who doesn't drink, I'll go in and make sure everything is all right, that no one is acting crazy. I do not drink in public. Only in the confines of my own home, mostly on New Year's Eve, and even then it's not hard liquor, maybe a little wine. When I'm out, it's water and Sprite. I never drink in a club. I have never, ever got drunk in public and I would never drink and drive.

I know this life is a fairy tale. But there's certain things a person still has to do to maintain the fairy tale. A lot of athletes, they get here, get caught up in it, and think the money and the fame will last forever. I know that basketball and fame are going to end. I feel like it's my responsibility to make sure they don't end because I go and do something stupid.

It's funny. I remember being like sixteen or seventeen, saying to myself, "You know what, I want to be like the Kennedys." I wasn't thinking about being from a powerful political family or anything. It was more basic. They lived like kings and queens, and I wanted to be like these white boys who got money and keep their money and keep making more money. That's how I wanted my family to be.

I'm from the projects of Newark. Nobody in my family had ever attended college and graduated. Now we're living as good as anyone on the planet. And on December 15, 2000, I made my mother proud. I kept my promise, graduated from Louisiana State University.

I'd left college early to go into the NBA and have been taking correspondence courses for a while. As of last summer, I needed only two credits to finish. When I went back to see my professors, they told me what I had to make up. Just so I could attend graduation, I missed our game against Vancouver on December 15. It meant that much to me. It means a lot to be a college graduate even though experience has been the best teacher for me.

See, I left college early because you can always go back to school. Meanwhile, if you mess your knee up, you can't always get that contract offer. Athletes say it all the time because it's true. At the same time, I've always felt strange about participating in the NBA's Stay-in-School program. Now that I've got my degree, when I tell kids that education is important, I feel like I've walked the walk a little more. And like I said on graduation day, LSU now stands for "Love Shaq University."

A lot of NBA players get grief for having their friends they grew up with around. On one hand, I don't have a problem with it. You always need your boys because your boys were there before you made it. But if you've got friends who you don't have anything in common with anymore, and you're just keeping them around because you used to hang out in high school or the 'hood, then it's time to grow up and get rid of them, find some people who can contribute to your life.

Most of the male friends I have in my life are older than I am and help keep me in check. The youngest is about twenty-five years old. Every one of them is productive. If they're not working for me, they've got their own careers going. All of them are people who I've been fortunate enough to be around, people who have helped me through some rough times.

I don't like the words "posse" or "entourage," because then people think you just took your boys from the neighborhood, bought them gold chains, and told them to ride around in a limousine with you. I'm beyond those days.

So let me introduce some of my crew:

Two of the most important people are Uncle Mike and Uncle Jerome. Uncle Mike is actually Mike Parris, my personal assistant in L.A. who makes sure a lot of my charity events run smoothly. And Uncle Jerome is Jerome Crawford, who works security for the Lakers.

They're not my real uncles, but they seem like it. Aunt Velma, my mother's sister, was Mike's girlfriend for a long time. So we just starting calling him "uncle" even though they never got married. Jerome was Uncle Mike's partner. They worked on the robbery squad together. They used to come through the projects, and cats on the block used to scatter.

My father was the strongest male influence in my life, but Uncle Mike and Uncle Jerome were also very important. They've been taking care of me for a long time. When I came back from Germany as a teenager in 1986, I wanted the life that a couple of drug dealers in our neighborhood had. There were two of them. One was named Wadoo and the other was a cat named Mustafa. When you don't have nothing and you see somebody with something living a life you want to live, it's a very powerful image in the inner city. No matter what your parents taught you, you see these cats driving Mercedeses with leather jackets on and gold watches. Well, when I came home from Germany, that's how I wanted to live. Those cats were large. They were living in the projects and one had a money-green Benz, the other had a money-green Volvo. Right there in the middle of the 17th Street projects.

I was told not to go near them by Mike, Jerome, and everyone else around me. I was told to stay away. By the time I was at LSU for a year, they found out who I was. By the time I got back to the neighborhood, they knew not to hang around me. Mike and Jerome put the word out.

Still, Mustafa and Wadoo would say things like, "What's up, man, how you doing tonight? Nice to meet you. Later."

It's like they wanted us to make it. They wanted us to get out. They wanted us to do the right thing, even though they didn't.

From about 1985 to 1998, Mustafa was large, running the neighborhood. I think he was put away two years ago. I don't know what happened to Wadoo.

See, a lot of young brothers growing up in the 'hood learn only to live in a materialistic society. When you have nothing and TV is telling you everyone else has the glamour and glitz, you find a way to get it. Any way. That's what happens to these kids who pursue the thug life. They see someone they know having a better life than them, and they try and grab onto it. Like how I wanted to be like Dr. J because he had his own poster and he was on TV a lot. I didn't know anything about the guy. But because he was famous, I wanted to be him.

Same thing with Mustafa and Wadoo and their Benzes. I saw them, that's what I wanted to drive. I didn't know or care what they did to get that Benz.

When I moved out to L.A., I asked Mike and Jerome if they wanted to leave the force and make better money. I've always felt cops are some of the most underpaid people in the world for what they do. It was time to get them out. Newark was just getting worse and worse.

Even though I live in Beverly Hills now, I still go through the world I used to know in Newark, just to remind myself how far I've come and to let the people in the inner city know I haven't forgot what that's about. Sometimes I drive through Compton late at night, in South Central Los Angeles. People know who I am. I'm approachable. I'm not flossing, showing off. I'm just passing through.

Here's the deal. Everyone thinks once you become a millionaire and have the house in Beverly Hills and the NBA life, that you immediately leave the old world behind. In my case, it's a little different because I've had a different upbringing. I grew up in the projects first, then moved around to army bases. But the truth is, for many players in the league, they're still not that far from the 'hood. Guys are always fighting inside with themselves. On one hand, we're saying, "I have to remember where I came from and who helped me get here." On the other, "Project the image the NBA wants so people will like you."

My crew is productive. They keep me balanced, and they also all have motivations and reasons not to mess my name over, or ruin my image. I learned at an early age that you have to use what you got to get what you want.

Joe Cavallero is my personal assistant in Florida. We played together in high school. He was our point guard. We always stayed
close. He makes sure all my stuff goes right in Florida and has his
own construction business down there.

Thomas Gosney is my personal chef. He was working at the
Hyatt in Orlando as one of their top chefs when I hired him away
one day.

He'll cook anything, but usually I have him stick to the basics. I
eat the same thing every day. The usual game day, for breakfast, I
have my own version of a sausage McMuffin and cheese made by
Thomas. I come home for lunch after shoot-around practice and
have a turkey club and fries. I take a nap, wake up about 4:00 P.M.
I'll have a sip of some ginseng and maybe a couple bites of prime
rib before leaving the house by 4:30 P.M. and getting to the Staples
Center about 6:00 P.M. for the game.

Anyway, then there's D-Mac Charlie, Chicago, and Black Ron.
Chicago does his own thing. He's acting. He's got Charlie running
my company. Black Ron is a family friend. He is in the army in San
Antonio. And my cousin Kenny. Kenny loves the music industry,
so I let him produce my album. He handles that part of my life.

Now, I admit, I have let some of my guys use me, somewhat, to
get where they want to go in life. I've told them, "When it's all
over, it's gonna be all over. You all are going to make a lot of
money. You're going to know some of the people I know and have
great opportunities in life." If they want to start up a business, I
might help them. But by the time I retire, they should all be set in
a lot of ways. I don't consider anyone in my crew hangers-on, people
who just take things from you. There was an article in *Sports Illustrated* once that kind of made fun of them, calling them "The Men
of Unclear Purpose." It made it look like these cats were riding
around with me, doing nothing with their lives.

It was funny, but it wasn't fair. They all have jobs and they all
earn a living. Andre Spellman, another one of my crew, is my first
cousin, my father's sister's son. The guys who Uncle Mike tried to
keep me away from, Andre got caught up in that life. I took him

away from that. He works security for me, too. While Jerome is more corporate, Andre is more street. He watches my back, period. When I go to homeboy events, I take Andre with me. When I go to the clubs with all my bling-bling on, when I'm just riding around, I take Andre with me. Jerome is more corporate. Like at the games, or when I go to events with Bill Gates.

You can't have people jeopardizing your empire. My crew would never do that. Most of them have a tattoo with the initials "T.W.I.S.M" on it. It's almost like a fraternity thing. It stands for "The World Is Mine." This is going to sound kind of silly, but I got the idea after watching *Scarface* in college.

Tony Montana, the character played by Al Pacino, had that great, big globe of the world.

On it was the message: "The world is ours."

So, now that I'm living large, making the world mine, and have achieved the ultimate in my profession, the marketing and endorsement people are coming back around and being nice again. Pepsi called. I've got a couple deals with technology companies, including Sportsline and Digex. I'm not sure if I want to be corporate anymore, so Leonard and I are going to pick and choose and make sure we do the right things. One thing I'll never complain about is if a business does not renew their contract with me—Reebok ending their deal with me in 1998, or someone else pulling out—because I've already got more than enough money to live on for the rest of my life.

But I gotta tell you: being let go by Taco Bell hurt.

I created that chihuahua on the commercials, and the damn dog took my job. I'm gonna tell you how it happened.

My movies might have not been blockbusters, but I've always done pretty good commercials. Remember the one with me and the little boy who wouldn't give up his Pepsi? *"Don't even think about it?"* Remember? Yeah, well, that actually won an award.

So anyway, Taco Bell is trying to come up with something new.

This was when Budweiser started using "Bud . . . weis . . . er." They were killing us with the frogs.

"Listen," I said. "You want to go to animals? Think back. Who's the number-one-selling animal ever? Who's the hottest animal ever?"

Lassie? No. Spuds Mackenzie. Beer. Spuds never said anything, just rode around in a truck with beautiful girls and looked stupid. But he got paid.

"Use a dog," I said. "Everybody know the Mexican dog is a chihuahua. Do something with that."

Their marketing people are like, "OK, we'll talk to our people, we'll look at it."

So then they come out with the first commercial. What does the dog say?

"Who did you expect, Shaquille O'Neal?"

That's how it started.

Now the chihuahua's in and I'm out. And his guild scale is much cheaper than mine, maybe $100 an hour and they just put something in his mouth between takes. They were paying me $5 million a year, and we weren't winning awards. I came up with the dog. I'm serious.

I should write a book called, *How I Killed My Career at Taco Bell.* That little dog cold took me out.

SHAQSPEAK A Shaq-to-English Translation for Those Not Schooled in the Language of Homeboy

Bling-bling   The gleam that occurs when the sun hits a diamond just right. When I say, "I got my bling-bling on," it means I've got my nice jewelry on and I'm showing it off, living large for all the world to see. A couple of magazines had fun with it, calling me and Kobe, "The Bling-Bling Dynasty."

Flossin'   Just as you floss your pearly-white teeth in the mirror, this is showing off to the extreme, rubbing your wealth and success in people's faces. Flossin' is when you think you're bigger than everybody else.

Foul shaving   Kind of like point shaving, except this occurs when a big man who is afraid of me intentionally gets three fouls in about thirty seconds. That way, he can sit on the bench, blame the referees, and not get dunked on. Is Arvydas Sabonis of the Portland Trail Blazers a big-time foul shaver? Well, you be the judge. He almost cries to the officials in a little-baby voice, "Shaq is fouling me. He's hurting me. Ow." I don't even get mad. I just kind of laugh. A 7'3", 300-pound guy, crying like that?

Living large   *See* Bling-bling.

S.H.A.M.   In most dictionaries, "sham" means phony or a fraud. In ShaqSpeak, S.H.A.M. stands for Short Answer Method. When I'm uncomfortable around reporters I don't know, I get tired of someone asking the same question, or I think someone is just being too negative, I resort to the S.H.A.M. method. For example, if a reporter asks, "What do you think of Patrick Ewing?" enough times, I start shamming them. "He's a great player," I'll say. Or, "He's the franchise center." I'm not saying this is the best way to handle the media, but I felt like I got burned early in my career in Orlando, where a lot of things I said were switched up. So while I goof around and joke with anyone, on some things I'm not very open around people I don't know or trust. I could go on and on about Patrick for an hour, tell the reporter all the things about Patrick that I've said in this book. But if only one of those things gets used in a story, is that explaining how I really feel about Patrick? So that's why I invented the S.H.A.M. It's like putting my guard up.

I.D.G.A.F.   That's the nameplate above my locker in the Staples Center. It stands for I Don't Give a F%$@! Maybe I should explain. A few years ago, before I moved to L.A., it seems like all I was trying to do was please everybody but myself. I was living for everyone but me. And so, that's where the attitude comes from. It's more of a joke, but since so many people started talking about it I just left it up there. It's my playful way of saying: You can't get to me, no matter what you do. The Parental Guidance version is: I Dominate Games Always and Forever.

9

Nuthin' But Actors; Around the NBA

They say the NBA stands for National Basketball Association, but it really means Nothing But Actors. These days, it's all about marketing: the posing after dunking, acting crazy, talking noise to the fans, talking noise to the opposing players and opposing coach, acting stupid off the court.

Hey, we all like certain players for certain reasons. I'm sure people like me because I'm big and mean and play like my size. I'm one of the few guys in a long time who really does that. They say Wilt played like that; they say Russell played like that. Kareem may have played like that, but I never really saw Kareem bang that much.

Sometimes I wonder if all the flash has hurt the game. Like a lot of kids now don't try to make the simple lay-up. If they even see a hand, they double-clutch it. Michael Jordan even blamed himself for this a few years ago, saying all the kids tried to be like him and forgot the fundamentals. Mike, Dominique Wilkins, Doctor J never really did that. Doc would just have one or two moves in there and dunk. Julius Erving was all about class.

I guess I'm the one to blame for dunking and hanging on the rim, getting the knees up. Talking up, pounding the chest, looking funny. 'Bowing. Yeah, I'm a knucklehead. I admit it. But I'm a low-level knucklehead. And when it comes time to taking care of business, I'm not a knucklehead at all.

Now, to me, high-level knuckleheads are guys who don't care about what they do and how it affects other people. They do it their way, no matter what. You can't be like that around Phil Jackson. After practice, though, it's my day. And if we don't practice, I'll ride around, hang out, stay up, watch some highlights, be a knucklehead, do what I want to do and not worry about everyone else.

The other stuff I was talking about—the posing after dunking, acting crazy, talking noise to the fans, talking noise to the opposing players and opposing coach, acting stupid off the court, that's being a high-level knucklehead.

Top five knuckleheads: Dennis Rodman takes the top spot on my list, easy. Then you've got my new teammate, J. R. Rider. Anthony Mason. Vernon Maxwell. And Oliver Miller.

Why the Marketing of the NBA is Slipping

Michael Jordan was a great, phenomenal player. He did more to sell the league than anyone over the last ten years. But now the NBA is looking for that next Mike, and they're going about it all wrong. Instead of trying to find something new, they want what worked five years ago, latch on to that and keep the profits rolling in.

They should market big guys more often. Like, uh, me. ☺

I like to talk. I do movies. I rap. I'm a clown. But they're kind of scared to go in that direction.

They've been going with the Magics, the Birds, the Isiahs, the Mikes, the Jerry Wests. Guards. Forwards. I understand it. They're hyping up Vince and Kobe now, guys like that. They want the next highlight.

But it wouldn't hurt to take some chances now and then.

For example, the uniforms they sell.

If I worked in that uniform division, I'd make them $5 billion a year.

Drop the shorts a few extra inches to where they come over the knee. UNLV style. Kids like that. Kids don't like the John Stockton shorts any more. Sometimes I think the NBA wants to keep a squeaky-clean image, and they don't understand that business is business. You either want the image or you want the money; you can't have both. The league isn't squeaky-clean. Everyone knows that. So instead of acting like that, use marketing to your advantage.

Imagine if everybody was like Hulk Hogan in wrestling. It would be awful if everybody was a good guy. You need the Undertakers, Goldberg, guys like that, because it makes the sport exciting. That's why they're the No. 1–watched sport and not us. That's why they make all the money.

It's fake, but they're selling entertainment.

The NBA also hasn't gotten much help from some players lately. A lot of guys are so obsessed with "keeping it real," they cost themselves and their families a lot of financial security.

Marketing is a game that you've got to know how to play. My man Allen Iverson, I like the way he plays; he's fearless on the court. I just wish he would not worry about being so hard, and would understand the marketing game a little more. Iverson's one of those guys who thinks if you play the marketing game, you're selling out. When you're trying to take care of your family, there is no such thing as selling out. Me, I'm real. I'm hard. But I also know how to play the marketing game. That puts an extra $20 million in my pocket.

See, people want to like Iverson. They do. Even despite the controversy with his rap CD, they want to like Allen Iverson. But they don't like all the scarves and the do-rags and all that.

When I came into the league, I wanted to be famous and all that. And I wanted to keep it real: the term a lot of us brothers use for not selling out to what everybody says is White America. I also wanted to get paid, get my family out of the 'hood. That's no secret. I wasn't going to be a doctor. So basketball—and the marketing opportunities around it—became a good way for me to get this money and live the life that I always dreamed about.

I don't want to call Iverson a knucklehead because I think he has too much game to say he doesn't care. I mean, I understand what these new-jack cats are doing, and I know why they are doing it. We don't want everybody to be the same, because if everybody was clean-cut, the game would be boring.

Personally, I thought Iverson was treated unfairly by the league when his rap CD came out with all those explicit lyrics. David Stern had a meeting with him, and Iverson agreed to change some of the lyrics that people thought were offensive.

Now, I know we work for the NBA and have to maintain a certain image, but we don't have to change who we are to play in the league. Some guys were raised hearing language and talking a certain way that bothers some people. Some guys like tattoos. This is the life they know outside of the NBA. Why should they conform to what the NBA wants when they're done with their work?

I'm not talking about criminal acts and things that violate the morality clause of your contract. I'm talking about being who you are without worrying about offending someone.

The players can help the situation, too.

What these cats have to realize, this is a beautiful thing we have here. You have to respect the game. You have to respect the people who came before you, and who made the NBA what it is. It's no secret. A lot of knuckleheads are messing up the game right now. They are messing up the integrity of the game. They see the NBA as their birthright, like "I'm getting mines now." Not enough of them look at it as a privilege.

Me, I've tried to stay true to who I am. For the past two summers I didn't do any movies. No albums. I just wanted to get away from doing that. And I endorse only products I actually use. Like Wheaties keeps offering me money, but I don't eat Wheaties, so I can't do it. Now, if Rice Krispies or Frosted Flakes offered me a deal, I'd take it right away. Apple Jacks, I'd be on the box in a heartbeat. Apple Shaqs. Yeah.

Meanwhile, throw out all the commercials and movies and endorsements, and I could walk back in Newark and hang out where I used to go and play; I could do that. In fact, I do.

You know how I get my satisfaction some days? Whenever I see a kid wearing my jersey, I pull up and say, "Take my jersey off, fool."

Then I just roll the window up and drive off.

I look in the rearview and they're going, "Oh, my God. That was Shaq."

I just like to hit them every now and then, have fun with them.

When I talk to the kids, I talk in their language. I'm from the 'hood. I'm not from Harvard. I didn't go to Boston College. I did not attend a five-star university. (I've made fun of LSU, calling it Learn Slowly University, although I actually did learn a lot of stuff there.)

Maybe because I spent my early childhood years in Newark, then moved to Germany, Georgia and Texas, I ended up learning how to talk to anyone, to just deal with people. Like a chameleon, I can change up at any time to fit whatever social situation I'm in.

People can look at that as being phony and selling out all they want. That's surviving in your environment; that's what that is. And too many players in this league are afraid to open up and let other people and cultures into their world.

They look at it like they're being down with their boys, hanging out with the guys they grew up with, keeping it real. Meanwhile, they're missing out on a lot of life experiences.

Grant Hill is suburban. His mom used to work for the White House; his father was a Dallas Cowboy. He had grass when he was growing up. I had glass when I was growing up; broken glass. That's not a knock. That's who he is. Suburban. No ghetto or thug in him at all. He's also one of the greatest competitors in the game. Other players should respect him for that, instead of being like, "Grant ain't one of us." It's not his fault his father made it out of the 'hood.

Or Larry Bird. Bird ain't street, but Bird used to bust guys' asses. "Doesn't matter where you're from," my father told me a long time ago. "If you're good, you're good."

Same with Karl Malone. Always accused of being a sellout. Like, what brother do you know rides a Harley-Davidson and wears jeans and boots?

But he's from the country in Louisiana. Country brothers are different from city brothers. Country brothers wear jeans and they farm and they hunt and they fish. City brothers don't do that. City brothers ride around; we got to have the dopest clothes, we got to have the gold chains. They're different.

But that's just how Karl grew up. He never changed. He liked driving that big eighteen-wheeler truck.

Another reason I like Karl is because he lives for himself. When I was first living in Orlando, I tried to do things to make everybody else happy. You can't live like that. You got to stick with what made you successful. I started living for myself.

I can say now I was a hypocrite when it came to how I felt about Karl early in his career. See, like when you're a competitor, in order for me to dominate you, I have to not like you. So I forced myself not to like him because he was on the other team.

But when we played on the Olympic team together in Atlanta, I realized he worked hard and he was a family man. His kids love him.

I told him, "You know, I didn't like you at first."

He said, "*I* didn't like *you*. I thought you were arrogant, you didn't care. But now I see that you're a nice person, I see that you're silly."

So I admit I was a hypocrite with Karl, a guy who I thought was a sellout but turned out to be a real, good person, true to himself.

That's the only way to play the marketing game.

Centers of Attention: The Georgetown Fraternity and Other Cats I Have to Dominate

When I first found out Alonzo Mourning had a kidney disorder and was going to have to miss the whole season, I was stunned. Not just because I thought Miami had a good shot of getting to the finals. That's the basketball part of it.

But when another big man goes down to injury, you start thinking about your own career and all the things that can happen to take you away from the game you love.

I hope he gets healthy, and I hope he comes back because he's one of the great competitors in the game. Something like that shows you how fragile we are. If one of the strongest, biggest, most intimidating guys in the league can be sidelined for health reasons, anyone can.

'Zo and I have had our differences on the court. For some reason, those Georgetown guys think they're the baddest things on the Earth. 'Zo likes to mean-mug people and try to intimidate and dominate them. But he'll never do that to me. Alonzo tries to be a big Superman. In reality, *I'm* big Superman. That's why I go off on him.

Still, 'Zo is cool. I've got to know him a little bit the last few years. I asked him at the All-Star Game last year, "Why you have to always look so mean and serious all the time?"

He was like, "That's just me. That's who I am."

Down deep, I know what kind of person he is.

Now, the only Georgetown big man I really like is John Thompson, who coached all those guys and now is an announcer. Everybody else, I don't care too much for on the court. Ewing, Dikembe and 'Zo, too, they just think they're bad as hell. Guess what? So does this LSU guy. So of course we're going to clash.

A lot of people don't know why I don't like Ewing. I would have been a Ewing fan. In fact, after Dr. J, he was one of my idols growing up. That's why I wore No. 33 in high school. But the first time I played the Knicks, I went up to Patrick and said, "Nice to meet you, man."

He looked at me kind of strange. Then, instead of giving me a pregame handshake, he just pounded my fists down, like he was getting ready for a boxing match or something. Like, "Shut up."

All I wanted was one of my favorite players just to say, "Nice to meet you, too." But Patrick couldn't bring himself to do that.

So that's why I have to give him the business when I play him.

I just think Pat's talent passed him up. And Pat thinks he's a young Pat. I was watching some old highlights last summer, skinny Pat with the flattop. He was deadly. Pat isn't like that anymore. He needs to change his role. Someone needs to tell him, "You're not the same player you were when you were twenty-nine, thirty." Saying all that, Pat has accepted a new role in Seattle and made the change. Most guys don't realize it, but Pat's old-school. See, I'm new school, new era. I know when cats start dogging me out, then it will be time to start admitting to myself, "Hey, I'm not the same cat."

I was still shocked when the Knicks traded him. Patrick was the Knicks for all those years. I know he wanted things to change, but I just felt New York dishonored him. They never truly appreciated Patrick for how great a player he was.

I never thought I'd see my idol in another jersey, and a part of me is like, "If Patrick can get traded, anyone can."

The Knicks have a pretty solid team, but now they have to show they can play without Patrick. After they dishonored him, I'm waiting to see it happen.

Dikembe? I like Dikembe. He's a funny guy, especially when he starts up in that baritone voice of his. Like a big frog or something. But he gets me angry when he starts waving his finger after he blocks shots, that "No! No! No!" stuff he does. So that's why I have to dominate him.

I like Tim Duncan. He reminds me of Brad Daugherty, who could have been a Hall of Famer if injuries hadn't cut short his career. Tim is very fundamentally sound. In fact, my nickname for him is The Big Fundamental. He faces you up and puts those 18-footers off the glass like he's Walt Frazier. He's got all the tools.

But having David Robinson helps a lot. You take one of them seven-footers away, and I don't know. I think if Duncan had to do what I had to do . . . I'm not taking away from his game, I'm just saying if I had another seven-footer, I'd have an even nicer game.

Maybe I'm too mean and competitive. But it's better than the alternative. I look at Michael Olowokandi and Shawn Bradley. They're big, they have skills. But they're just not mean. They don't play hard. That's why they're two of the softer centers in the league.

One time Bradley fouled me, and I fell. You know what he said?

"You all right, man? You all right? You all right?" He said it about six times going down the court. "My fault, man. I didn't mean to do it."

Finally I said, "I'm all right, Shawn. Don't worry about it."

One game I put up 40, 50 points, dunking on him. After the game, he brought his family over. He says, "This is my wife. She wants to take a picture."

I'm like, "Nice to meet you." I smile into the camera, take the picture, and then felt guilty about dunking on him so many times.

You're probably wondering about Greg Ostertag, the Utah Jazz center I knocked to the ground with an openhanded slap about two years ago. All I can say is, it's Joe Cavallero's fault.

Joe is one of my personal assistants and the former point guard on our Cole High School championship team in San Antonio. He's like a lot of players' friends in the league: he checks the Internet and make sure he has your back.

A lot of players in the NBA never read the stories written about them, but they do hear about them. Their friends will read something and report back to them, like little spies.

Anyway, Joe is always checking out stuff on ESPN.com and all those other sites, and he found something Ostertag said about me in a Utah paper. I don't even remember what it was—something about, "Shaq can be contained, he's not dominant," something like that. Anyway, after Joe pulled it off the Web and showed it to me, I was in a bad mood.

Utah had just beaten us in the play-offs the year before, and my knee was screwed up. Ostertag was scoring, blocking a couple of my shots. I guess it gave him confidence. Lord knows, after seeing his game, he needs it. I went to talk to him after a practice before the game and let him know he needs to just play and not talk.

"Man, you need to watch what you say," I said.

"Fuck you, watch what *you* say," he said.

"Oh, you bad now?"

I wasn't even really mad. It was just like a reflex. My openhanded right hand somehow came up and smacked him upside his crew-cut head. He went down. Fetal positon. Whining, "My contact, my contact lens."

If Ostertag had known that I had taken Tae-Bo with Billy Blanks for about four years, he wouldn't have said that.

Legends I Like and Legends I'm Still Waiting to Say, "You're Not Bad, Shaq"

When I came to the Lakers in 1996, one of the first things I did was look at all the retired jerseys up on the wall of the Forum. I said to my friend, "I want to get my name up there."

When I had the injuries the first few years, I started to worry if that would ever happen. But now it's something I think is possible if I keep working hard.

In the last few years, people have started to make noise about putting me in the category of Wilt Chamberlain, Bill Russell and Kareem Abdul-Jabbar. They are the holy trinity of centers in basketball, the greatest big men to play the game.

If I could ever be included in that category, I would be honored. People like to compare eras a lot, like how would I have done against Russell, Chamberlain or Abdul-Jabbar. I like to answer that like this: you can't compare a 1960 Mercedes-Benz to a 2000 Mercedes-Benz. I don't want to disrespect history, but when Russell played, they only had about eleven teams. And there were only one or two seven-footers. If I would have played in the league with eleven teams and one seven-footer, instead of twenty-eight teams and a seven-footer on every squad, then I'd have ten championships, too. Period. That's nothing against Bill Russell.

When I was coming up and my father was teaching me, he always used to say, "I want you to be strong and powerful like Wilt, play defense like Russell, and develop a skyhook like Kareem." Those are his guys.

I never knew Wilt. One time we were in the same restaurant, sitting almost next to each other and he didn't say anything to me. This was about a year before he died.

I'm sitting with my back turned, and he didn't say anything. He didn't look at me. It was kind of weird. Two of the top centers—one from the past, one from the present—don't say anything to each other? There was a little tension. You could feel it.

Maybe he thought, "I'm Wilt, and Shaq should come to me and pay his respects."

I think that's what he thought. It was almost like a big-man pride battle.

To this day, I regret that I never talked to him. He was with a lady, and a friend of mine once told me that the right way to handle it would have been to go up to her, as a way of breaking the ice, and introduce myself. Maybe so.

It's interesting, though. I've heard how when Kareem was coming up, Wilt wouldn't give him proper respect, that the papers would print articles with Wilt bad-mouthing Kareem all the time. And maybe that's why Kareem is always killing me.

Of those three guys, I'm more of a Bill Russell man. He did a photo shoot with me once, spent all day with me, gave me some hints. Wilt never said anything to me. Kareem never said anything to me.

When we were struggling, Kareem would always criticize me. "Shaq doesn't concentrate. He doesn't focus. The younger players don't have the discipline I used to have."

The only two guys from the Laker organization who stuck with me behind everything—never went at me—were Jerry West and Magic Johnson. Those are the only two who always had my back.

Bill Sharman, a Hall of Famer and former Laker great, said to me during the finals, "You're the greatest big man I've ever seen." But before that, he was, "Shaq, I'll teach you how to shoot free throws. I shot 80 percent. Shaq doesn't work hard."

I just looked at him like, "Please." You know, this is the same guy who put articles in the paper, "What Shaq should do."

I can't help it. Sometimes, I carry grudges.

When I scored 61 points during a game against the Clippers last year, I felt like I was scoring on Kareem, one of the Clippers' assistant coaches. He was over on their bench, telling Michael Olowokandi and Keith Closs, "Put your hands on him. Do this, don't let him cut to the middle." I put his face on Olowokandi. Every time I scored, I was looking at their bench, looking at him. "All that stuff you teaching them, it don't work." At one point, I even said to him, "I'm a 2000 Benz; you a '69."

I know if you bring Kareem into my era now, I'd bust his ass. The 1960s Benz would be too slow. Ain't even got a navigational system on it. He would get lost on the way to the arena.

Maybe that's harsh. Maybe he's not ready to pass the torch, or maybe he knows that I'm the type of person that responds well to criticism and he wants me to do well. But it would have been nice if just once he said, "Shaq's a good player." That's all I want him to say.

One of the greatest compliments of my career was paid to me by Larry Bird last season. First I heard about something he wrote about me in his book. *Bird Watching*. "People ask me all the time who I think will be the next superstar, now that Michael has retired," he said. "To me, the next great player is Shaquille O'Neal. I truly believe his time is going to come. I don't know him at all, but I've got him marked down for four or five championships. He's sort of like Michael was early on. He hasn't figured it out yet, but he will."

Then, he came out and said during the finals, "We can't stop Shaq. He's just too good."

When a legend breaks down and gives you props like that, which he didn't have to do, that's big. That's like a heart-touching thing. Bird is one of the greatest players of all time, a guy I truly respect. And for him to say that about a guy outside of his generation—and let's face it, he played in the greatest generation of players—meant so much.

For the most part, I respect the game's greatest players and coaches. But that doesn't mean I have to like everything they do.

For example, I would never play for Pat Riley. Part of the reason was because he played me only twenty-five minutes at my first All-Star Game in Salt Lake City in 1992. I know I shouldn't hold a grudge and it's been eight years. But he was so upset that I was voted on as the starter over his center at the time, Patrick Ewing, that he felt like he had to put the young fella in his place and give the veteran his due.

Maybe an even bigger reason is those five-hour practices he puts his teams through. Riley is known as a workaholic, and during the season he runs his team until they drop. I'm coming up on thirty years old. I don't need more than two hard hours. Watch some film. Tell me what you need me to do. That's it. Unless the team is falling apart, that's all a real professional needs to get ready for an NBA game. Trust me.

I think Riley burns out his teams. All those suicide drills, where you run and run. It just takes too much out of you. Look at his Knicks and Heat teams and see how fresh they were at the end of the regular season. I'm not saying the man is not one of the greatest coaches to ever coach the game. I'm just saying as a hardworking NBA player, I don't know how much more my body can take.

I'll shake his hand, say hello. But I also always give his teams big numbers.

I need a coach who, after a hard game, would say the next day, "You did a good job last night. You're banged up, you're not prac-ticing. Go sit in a hot tub." I didn't have a coach like that until last season, a big man who understood the game and how beat up an-other big man can get.

Just to prove I have long-term memory and don't forget any slight, one more shaft from my career.

Lenny Wilkens, the all-time winningest coach, played me forty-three seconds in the gold-medal game at the Summer Olympics in Atlanta in 1996. He put David Robinson in the whole game. I have no idea why. He never told me why. All those other games when Dave and them were screwing around, I was the one leading them back, getting the crowd going.

Then he played me only forty-three seconds in the gold-medal game. I don't like him for that. He's a great coach and all, but I'm still upset.

Winning Combinations

Orlando did pretty good last year, almost making the play-offs with a bunch of nobodies. They played hard. They played together. But now those nobodies have Grant Hill and Tracy McGrady, and everyone is going, "Oooohh, Orlando, they're back. Watch out."

Having those two guys could be the best thing to ever happen or the worst thing. Those guys play the same position. They both want the ball; they both like to shoot. But one has to eventually bow down. One has to know, "I'm a star, I've got to come down and throw the ball to him first."

For example, if I played with Jordan, I would know that Jordan's taking most of the shots, and I would have to change my role. I would accept that. Dennis Rodman was good at this. He never shot, but he shined. He knew his role. Same with Scottie Pippen.

See, in order for two superstars to coexist, one has to bow down. Like James Worthy. He was a great player, but he knew it was about Magic and Kareem. He knew that in certain games, he wasn't going to be much of an option. But when he did get the shots, he took over.

That's what more guys need to do in this league, figure out their role. I've been around guys who want to be the man, who want to get their plays called. Then, when you call the plays for them, they don't do anything. Like Nick Anderson in Orlando.

Grant and Tracy may be good, but I kind of look at it like another two All-Stars playing together. Can they? Will jealousy get in the way. Will guys start getting mad who used to get shots?

Because those two aren't about being selfish, I think they'll be OK. But they still don't have much of a supporting cast.

Which brings me to the Eastern Conference. I don't want to sound like I'm not giving the East respect, but I don't worry about it. Miami made some nice moves, and New York is always going to be there. You got Milwaukee. You can't look past Vince Carter in Toronto or Allen Iverson in Philadelphia.

But the teams in the East, they're just going to beat each other up. Pacers gonna beat up the Knicks. Miami gonna beat up Orlando. Philly beat somebody up. Jersey's gonna try to beat somebody up. So by the time they come out West, we're gonna run them to death.

Then I'm gonna beat them up.

The harsh truth: There's only 2.5 dominant teams in the NBA. The Lakers and Portland. I don't count nobody else. I'll give San Antonio the .5; but now that we have Horace Grant to help me with the Twin Towers, I can't consider them a dominant team. Horace will guard David and I'll guard Tim.

By the way, Phil got a lot of grief when he said that the Spurs' winning the championship in 1999 was an asterisk season because of the lockout. I agree. I'm not saying they didn't work hard. They did what they had to do to win the title.

Everyone knows how many cats came into the season out of shape that year, wondering if we were even going to play. You play 50 games in three-something months, and that's a regular season? Nuh-uh. That's an asterisk season, plain and simple. They didn't have to go through the grind of an 82-game year that starts in October during training camp. The season didn't even start until February, and they play only 65 total games, 40 less than we played last year. Nobody respects that title. That's not real blood, sweat, and tears like mine, Magic's, Mike's, and Bird's. Put an asterisk by that championship.

The fact is, until the Spurs play a full season and win it all, I can't respect their title.

I'm not bitter because David Robinson won a ring before me. It's just the truth. If they don't want to admit it to themselves, that's their business.

To All the Girls We've Loved Before (Including the Ones Who Broke Up Our Teams)

I was dating this girl who I really liked during the lockout. I don't know if I was in love, but I really liked her. She lived in L.A., and

I was in Texas with my daughter. She heard I was getting married. I guess her friend said, "Why are you messing with him? He's about to get married."

It wasn't true, but that was it. The relationship was over. She tried calling me, but I didn't have my pager on.

Did my heart get broken? My heart doesn't get broken. That's cool. That's life.

After that, she started dating a guy from the Knicks.

I hate to say this, but it was probably more of a challenge for him than it was for her. You know, "Let me get Shaq's girl." A lot of NBA guys are like that, although I don't think that's the case with this guy. He doesn't seem like that type of cat.

But women can tear NBA teams apart. Every one has heard of the story involving Jason Kidd and Jimmy Jackson. While they were teammates in Dallas, both were interested in the singer Toni Braxton, and they supposedly ended up feuding over her.

When I was in Orlando, a couple of guys on my team were seeing the same woman. They started talking about each other and fighting in the locker room. It wasn't good.

I've never told anyone this, but in my rookie year, a woman banged on my hotel-room door in Detroit. I opened it to see a nice-looking woman. Beautiful, gorgeous. Fine, real fine.

I'm like, "Hel-lo."

She opened up her coat. She was buck naked.

I slammed the door in her face, told her to leave me alone. If I was a weak kid, I probably would have brought her into the room or whatever.

To this day, I'm convinced it was either a prank or somebody was trying to set me up.

Every now and then, a girl will say, "Sign my breast." Sometimes I sign it; sometimes I don't. But that stuff happens when you're an NBA player. You're famous. You get noticed. You get girls throwing themselves at you everywhere you go. But let me tell you something. When I get done playing, I'll settle down a lot. I could just focus on my family, focus on my wife.

Me and the Media

Since I came into the league, I've had a pretty good relationship with the media. For the most part, I've also steered away from controversy. But I do want to get one incident off my chest.

NBC's Bob Costas, who I like and respect, was announcing one of our games against Portland last season. He was talking about Arvydas Sabonis trying to play me and said something like, "Well how can you move a 10,000-pound gorilla?"

Now, Dan Rather has been referred to as an 800-hundred pound gorilla, so I know it could be construed as a corporate term. And Costas insisted his remark wasn't racist. I also know that wasn't his intention. But his remark bothered me. The brothers don't see using the word "gorilla" as no corporate nuthin'.

I could have made a big deal out of it, but my mother said to let it go. I mean, I didn't want to be in the middle of a controversy during the play-offs.

Costas came to me and apologized. I told him, "You're lucky my father didn't hear that. He's Muslim. He would have come here and said something to you."

Bob said, "You don't understand. When I see him, I'll explain it to him."

I said, "No, don't say nothing. Just forget about it."

I have a great relationship with most of the media but some are bandwagon jumpers. They love you when things are going well, and they can't wait to take you apart when things aren't.

Bill Walton comes into the locker room, tries to give me tips. Every now and then he says smack on TV just to be saying it. I'm like, "What the hell are you talking about?" It kind of makes me wonder about him. Is everything he's telling me in the locker room sincere, or is he just saying it to say it? Then, when he gets on TV next to all the other guys, "You know, he's just blah, blah, blah. . . ."

Peter Vecsey? I don't trust him. Doesn't care about people's feelings or people's families. That crazy cat will write anything. Talking about people getting traded and what they did and their baby mamas. He'll just write anything. He's tricky. Very tricky.

I'm comfortable with the decisions I've made in my life, but that doesn't mean I haven't said some things I regret. I think it goes back to when I was younger and was trying to overcome a stuttering problem. I used to give short, funny answers to questions people asked me. It made me more confident about how I sounded in person.

But there's been times when the strategy has backfired.

When I was in Greece a few years ago, someone asked me if I had a chance to visit the Parthenon. To be honest, I didn't know what the Parthenon was. Some broken-down-ass building on top of a mountain? I had no idea it was a temple built in 438 B.C.

So I said, "I haven't been to that club yet."

Hey, I'm from Newark, New Jersey. The only thing I know about Greek history is Zeus and mythology and the toga party from that *Animal House* flick.

One of my other quotes was, "I've won on every level except college and the pros."

That got me a lot of criticism. People made fun of me for not winning a championship. I know people won't get this, but I was trying to tell them I'm a winner. Olympics, high school, youth programs, summer league. I win. I know what it takes to win. I've won before.

Anyway, now my new quote goes, "I've won on every level except college." I can say that, right?

Does Race Matter in the NBA

Race is overrated in the NBA in some ways. But I will admit this: If you're from the 'hood, you don't want to get dunked on by a white guy. That's just how it is.

Then again, not many white guys in the league will flush on you. Keith Van Horn will flush on you. Tom Gugliotta will flush on you. Vitaly Potapenko will try to flush on you. Andrew DeClercq will try to flush on you. But that's about it.

Again, if you get dunked on by a white boy, you got to come home to your friends and hear it. I'm not enough of a sociology major to explain the whys and hows, but that's the reality of the NBA.

Here's my top five white players in the league: Jason "White Chocolate" Williams. John Stockton, Tom Gugliotta and, let's see, I'll go with Dallas' Dirk Nowitzky and Minnesota's Wally Szczerbiak.

Keith Van Horn? I like Van Horn, but he don't play mean enough for me. He's sometimey.

White Chocolate is my favorite point guard. I'd rather watch him than even Gary Payton and Jason Kidd, although those two are the best in the game. Why? Because the game is about winning, but it's also about excitement. Ultimately, people want to win. But I think during the regular season, they want to see excitement, too. They don't want to come down and see called plays all the time.

Imagine if I had White Chocolate on my team. We'd have people spitting up nachos. I would be throwing down the nastiest dunks of all time. We would have the greatest highlights in NBA history.

Now, my top five black players.

Me, Kobe, Vince Carter, Kevin Garnett and Tim Duncan.

Top power forward in the league: I would go with Malone. Nice body. Shoots the jumper well. Hard-nosed, knows how to get to the line, knows how to get in your head.

Top small forward in the game today? I got to go with Grant Hill.

Shooting guard? I'd say Kobe because I play with Kobe and I've seen what Kobe can do. And Kobe has a lot of heart for a youngster. He's like the only youngster who wants it. Down by one, "Give me the ball, I'll shoot it."

Drugs and the NBA

Is marijuana prevalent in the NBA? Have I seen any of my players do it? No. Do I know what it smells like? Yeah. Have I ever smelled it on players I've played with? Yeah.

I'm not going to ruin any careers. I mean, I know for a fact there's a lot of guys who smoke weed. I've never done it and I've never wanted to.

The league came up with a new drug test last season, but it's not the greatest drug test for catching people who use them. They basically tell you when they're gonna drug-test you.

They'll call you on Tuesday and say, "We're going to test you next Monday." Rather than just showing up, "Hey, Shaq, why don't you piss in this cup for me?" they let you know when it's coming down.

I think if the league and union would agree to the element of surprise, it would almost eliminate drug use in the NBA. Every player gets tested during training camp. Rookies get tested three times a year. The only time they do random testing is when they think you've got a problem.

For example, when I ripped the backboard down in New Jersey my second year in the league, the league gave me a urine test two days later. I'm serious. Maybe they thought I was on steroids or something.

I tried Creatine when it first came out and androstendione, the pill that Mark McGwire has used. But I didn't feel anything. I think I used it for one summer, and then they started testing for it. So I gave it up.

At least the new drug policy is better than the old one. The old one tested only for heroin and PCP and that kind of stuff, things players don't even do anymore.

Time Out

The Original Shaq Daddy

It was few years back, around Christmastime. This lady asked me, "Shaq, how do you feel?" I told her I was tired. Said I had to buy toys for my seventeen kids by eighty-eight different women. She was like, "Huh?" Then she saw me laughing, and realized it was a joke. She cracked up, too.

I do have two children from two different women. Taahirah, my four-year-old daughter, lives with her mother. Shareef, my one-year-old son, lives with his mother. I see both of them often. No matter what kinds of jokes I might make, the fact is this: Both of my kids will always know who their father is. They will always love me. I'm very involved in both of their lives and see them as often as I can. I take care of both my kids.

During the summer, I spend a lot of time with my children. One of the best days of my summer was when I took Taahirah to the zoo with eight of her friends on July 19, her birthday. I also took them to the Ringling Brothers Barnum & Bailey Circus. I could hear my daughter in the background saying, "My daddy's Superman, so that makes me Supergirl." And all the kids went, "Yeah, you are Supergirl. Your daddy is Superman."

I was with Taahirah's mother for almost six years until we

broke up. It wasn't ugly. I'm a nice, peaceful guy. And like I said, I take care of my business. When my kids get older, they'll understand about relationships. They'll see that you get together with someone you care about, and you hope it lasts forever. Eventually, if things don't work out, then you break up.

Now, that joke I made, my mom hates it when I say stuff like that. It especially bothers her because of the perception about NBA players having kids out of wedlock. Remember that *Sports Illustrated* cover story, the one about NBA players not taking care of their kids? The truth is complicated. While some of the examples were legitimate, some were just women and their sob stories. At the same time, some guys have been very stingy with their money. But there also are a lot of NBA players who have children out of wedlock, and are not deadbeat dads. Then, throw into the mix the women who are out there trying to profit off the fathers, saying, "You make $4 million? I want $60,000 a month."

It can get ugly. One thing I will say about that *Sports Illustrated* article: at least you got to hear the women's side of the story.

Money will never be an issue for me, because I do the right thing. It's my children. I give them whatever they want. That's my rule, that's my responsibility.

There's a few stories that I can recall where NBA players don't know their dad or don't want to communicate with their dad. I was in Gonzales, Louisiana, last summer. This big guy, 6'9", kind of looked like a construction worker, came up to me. He said, "My son's in the NBA." I thought he was joking or whatever. Then he said, "Rashard Lewis." When I stopped for a second and looked at his face, he looked just like Rashard, the Seattle SuperSonics shooting guard.

He said, "Yeah, he just signed that new, big contract. I'm proud of him."

Now, this is probably the first Rashard sees or hears of this story. I never told him that I saw his old man, and it's pretty obvious that Rashard doesn't talk to the guy. It's probably one of those cases where he never knew his dad, didn't want to know his dad, or his dad left. Meanwhile, meeting the guy, him looking like that, it was a powerful image. It definitely made an impression.

I'm sure there's a lot of stories like that in the NBA with guys who don't know their father. Luckily, I had Phil Harrison. He taught me how to be a father in the same way. I also look after Shareef's brother, Miles. I call Miles, "The Next," because I met his mother like the Sarge met my mother. Even though he is not my biological child, I treat him as my son, just like Sarge treated me as his son.

I have nicknames for all my children. Shareef is "The Saga Continues," for obvious reasons.

Taahirah? I call her "Chexy" and "The Princess." I know what you're thinking. Chexy? One of my nieces is Chuty, which is baby talk for "cutey." Chexy is baby talk for "sexy." Trust me on this.

When I was growing up, I changed the diapers of my youngest siblings, Ayesha, Lateefah, and Jamal. If my father came home and things weren't right, I got a bip-bip-bip upside my head. I wasn't having that, man. So my mom taught me to change diapers, powder them, everything.

I change diapers for my kids. I baby-sit. I like the fact that they call me "Daddy." I understand that I can quit basketball right now, but I can't quit fatherhood. A lot of people try to play basketball forever. But it's a fairy tale. I have to be a daddy. I have to be there for my kids, and I will be. I know that.

I don't consider myself a bachelor, but I do think marriage is a job. I've seen a lot of marriages start off great, but end up bad. I'm an observer. So I try to watch and see what's done right and what's done wrong. Like, I just watched Kobe Bryant get engaged. Now, a lot of people have been giving him grief for getting hitched at such a young age, but I don't have a problem with it. He doesn't really flirt with women, anyway, so hopefully he'll be all right. With all the money he has, though, I would advise him to be careful. I mean, California law, if things don't work out, she's getting half.

Hopefully it will work. Kobe seems to have a strong mentality. I've never seen him out carousing. I never seen him talk about girls. So hopefully he'll be a committed husband and not have to worry about marital problems. If anybody can pull it off that young, Kobe can.

As for me, my view on marriage is that you can't have two cars when you're supposed to have only one. Marriage is supposed to be about being with one person. That's what I'm going to try to have it be when I tie the knot.

In a perfect world, would it be great to be married and see my children every single day? Yes.

And slowly but surely, I'm working on it.

10

The 1999–2000 Regular Season

Or, When We Learned How Good We Could Be

For two of my first three seasons in Los Angeles, we were swept from the play-offs. Utah destroyed us in 1998, and San Antonio took us apart in 1999. After each loss, I kept saying the same things: "Before you succeed, you have to fail" and "We're still learning how to be a great team." But inside, ending each season like that was eating at me.

I would go into hiding. I'd secretly fly to my summer home in Orlando, don't call nobody, don't talk to anyone, and don't let nobody know where I am. After taking a week off, eating whatever I wanted to eat, sitting around and trying not to think about basketball, I would wake up one morning and go back at it. Pumping weights. Eating better. Making sure I took care of my body.

The criticism reached an all-time high in the summer of 1999. Tim Duncan and the Spurs were the new hot thing. They swept us in the second round of the Western Conference semifinals, swept Portland in the West finals, and beat the Knicks in five games to win the championship. The Shaq-and-Kobe Show? Preempted. I guess people just got tired of picking us to win the championship. They figured, "Man, these knuckleheads are never going to grow up."

I usually don't dwell on what happened last year. Most of the time, I don't even dwell on yesterday. Instead, I always try to move forward: "It's over, it's done with," I would tell myself. "After this year, nobody's gonna care about last year."

But I knew people were talking. They were forming opinions about what we had done in the past. Every now and then you'd turn on ESPN: "Oh, Utah. The Lakers will be OK, but Shaq isn't a leader, Kobe isn't a leader. They need a leader on that team. Shaq can't hit free throws. Shaq's worried about doing movies. I saw him at the Grammys. I saw him at the Source Awards with all the homeboys, all his bling-bling. Acting all crazy. Shaq isn't ready to win."

In the back of my head, I'm remembering what people said, remembering all the hurtful things that people wrote. I'm not a whiner. And if the criticism is fair, I can take it. But it just kept coming, magazine after magazine, preview show after preview show: "Shaq can't win."

The criticism helped me grow. I was always hungry to win. Because I got close but didn't get close enough just made me more hungry. By the time the summer of 1999 was over, I was starving to win. I knew the only way I would get people to change what they write is to prove them wrong.

Going into the 1999–2000 season, I felt good about a lot of things. We had the general, Phil Jackson, in charge. I was completely healthy. We weren't as talented or athletic as some of the Lakers teams of the past, but we'd added some nice veterans and role players around Kobe and me. You got Ron Harper doing his thing in the backcourt. A.C. Green at power forward. A.C. didn't have a lot left, but he had enough to put a body on the big guys and help me out.

Three reasons I knew we were going to have a good season: Derek Fisher, Robert Horry and Rick Fox. Those three players were starters on the 1997, 62-win Laker team. Two years later, they were coming off the bench, taking lesser roles and sacrificing. When you get guys who could start on any team in the league to do that, you're already on the right road.

Did I think we were gonna win the whole thing? Like I said

before, no. But I'm feeling OK. Phil set up a couple goals for us on the board, about getting home-court advantage and other things. Me, I just wanted to take one goal at a time.

At first, playing for Phil was weird. He would have us doing drills without a basketball, going through a layup line and pretending we were laying the ball up. We did a lot of stretching, running, envisioning ourselves playing. I'm thinking: "OK, where's the ball? I'm ready to break the backboard."

The NBA preseason is a joke in a lot of ways. Teams schedule these games in crazy places. They try to make more money off fans, who end up watching a lot of guys not even worried about winning. But last year, the exhibition games helped the Lakers. It made us realize how bad we could be. It also took us a while to pick up the triangle offense. Phil's Chicago teams had perfected that offense. They would always have three guys—a lot of times it was Michael Jordan, Scottie Pippen, and Toni Kukoc—in spots on the floor where they could take advantage of their individual talents.

The Lakers? We were running into each other, turning the ball over and looking awful. Bad news turned to worse. Kobe broke his hand in an exhibition game. He would be out for the first month of the season.

About that time, Phil said something that made sense to a lot of us: "It's not how hard you play, it's how *smart* you play."

After that, we started picking up the offense. Guys started to trust their teammates, the new coaching staff and themselves. I was in a system that made my teammates better, passing more, playing smarter. After Phil told me to drop some pounds in the summer and quit trying to be a muscleman, I got in better physical shape. My mentality was better. I don't know if I was more mature, but I felt like it.

Kobe's getting hurt made a lot of people outside the organization panic, like, "Oh, my God, they don't have Kobe."

That made me a little angry. I was thinking, "The Daddy's still here." All of a sudden it's all about Kobe again, which I have no problem with. But don't forget about Shaq Daddy.

For the first fifteen games, we had just one star and four role players. The ball is coming down to me every time, deep inside the post, just where I like it. Even when I don't want it, it's coming down. That rock is moving, it's flinging, bling-bling. We were sharing, getting layups, getting easy shots. Harp and A.C. are fitting in as new starters. When I'm getting double-teamed, I'm kicking it out. Guys are having fun, shooting jumpers.

In the first month, we beat Utah twice, Houston, Phoenix and Seattle. Without Kobe, we started off 12–3. People were shocked. "Shaq's having a great year. It looks like he's in shape for the first time. Phil's the only coach who can get Shaq to play that way."

It's never good to have one of your best players injured, but that might have been the best thing for Kobe. All of a sudden, he could watch the game a little bit, see what we're doing without him. Truth is, when Kobe was ready to return, a lot of the guys were worried. We already had our little team system, moving the ball. Glen Rice was kind of down because his shots were going to cut down, times three. And Kobe is not that happy because Phil has to sit him down every now and then.

What could have been a tough adjustment period was made easy by Phil. Kobe wanted to be a part of things right away. But he was still doing that one-on-one stuff. Phil brought Kobe along in a nice, constructive way. He never raised his voice. Every single practice, Phil sat Kobe down, blows his whistle. We're going over the triangle every day, learning how to run it.

And we're winning. We won 20 of our first 21 games after Kobe came back. From December 11 to January 14, we didn't lose one game. Sixteen straight.

Now the NBC games are kicking in. The hype is on us. We're playing on NBC every Sunday. Everything's going good. Phil likes what he sees. I'm already having an MVP-type year. Kobe is back. In my mind, I'm thinking, "This is what I wanted all these years."

Midway through January, we were 31–5. Kobe had taken it to Vince Carter in Toronto, I gave David Robinson and the Spurs 32 and 11 on Christmas Day, and we hardly had any problems.

I missed only one game the first half of the season, and that was because I got into a fight with Charles Barkley during the sixth game. We got tangled up under the basket, he shoved the ball in my chest, and I took a swing at him. Nothing serious. But it was a one-game suspension, and we lost to Houston two nights later in the game I missed.

Phil has individual goals for me, stuff all the other players don't know about. I'm trying to accomplish that, too. They think I can't rebound. They think I can't block shots. So now I got to show them. This is what the general said to do, so I have to do it. If not, I get yelled at.

A lot of the reason why we got off to a quick start was because Kobe, me and my teammates were already veterans. The whole Lakers-as-kids story line was tired. We were more mature than the first few years we played together.

But Phil also had a lot to do with our success.

All the little things added up. The time he spent with Kobe watching tape and explaining where one-on-one ball didn't work. The personal challenges and messages he gave me. For example: In a magazine article before the season, he said I couldn't be considered a leader if I wasn't on the floor in the fourth quarter. The idea there was, if I kept missing free throws, it was dangerous to have me out there.

Knowing the type of guy I am, Phil understood that I was gonna have to listen, say "OK," and step up my game.

He also opened us up to a whole new world. By December 1999, we were meeting with George Mumford, this New-Age spiritual cat. He's coming in with the incense while we're stretching, talking about dreams.

The incense smelled like weed. He said it came from the same family as weed, but it's not weed. I don't know what it was, but it smelled like weed. All the brothers are in there going, "What the hell is this?"

Whatever it was, all those things made practice seem less like work.

Even though Phil could go off, he wasn't about yelling and cursing you out. There's a lot of player-coach in him, too. You could joke with Phil. I was one of the few players he yelled at and it only happened three times last year. He could talk to me like a man.

He used to play shooting games at practice. Phil would say, "OK, you hit this half-court shot, we're not practicing today. You take this shot, Travis." If Travis Knight missed the shot, we had to practice.

Guys would say, "Come on, Phil, you promised."

If Phil was in a good mood and we were winning, he'd say, "All right, we're gonna practice only 40 minutes. But make it a good 40 minutes." We never lost respect for him, even when he was acting like one of the guys.

If a guy did something wrong, Phil would fine him. Not big money, like ten, twenty bucks. If someone came in late, he wouldn't say, "Where the hell you been?" He would just look over at assistant coach Frank Hamblen and say, "All right. Frank, fine him." Then, at the end of every week, if the pot was around $1,000, we'd split up the team and play a shooting game for the $1,000.

Unless you did something serious, that was his way of disciplining you.

From the start of the season, the Lakers' mood was good. Me, I'm injury-free. No more abdominal pain. I could reach. I could rotate. I was step-sliding. The whole team's getting along, taking right away to what Phil wanted. We had just moved into a new arena, too. The Staples Center, in downtown Los Angeles, took the place of the old Great Western Forum in Inglewood, California. Luxury boxes, big-ole food court, all futuristic. It looked like the inside of a spaceship.

It was a long way from the courts they called "The Hole" in Newark.

Playing pro basketball is a dream life in a lot of ways. The money. The fame. The fact that you're basically playing a kid's game for a living is also cool. But like every job, it can get old.

When you play 82 games during the regular season, traveling from airport to airport, hotel to hotel and arena to arena, you have to find ways to motivate yourself for each challenge.

Michael Jordan was the best of all time at that. Mike would just take any little thing someone said and create a challenge for himself to beat that person or team. He kept his edge 'cause he just made stuff up in his mind. You did not want to make Mike mad.

I've got a little of that in me.

Playing a big-time team on national television requires no motivation. You know you and your teammates are going to come out and play because everyone is watching. But when you're in the middle of a long season and you're going up against somebody you know you're supposed to beat, that's when you got to play little mind games with yourself.

For example, we played Atlanta at home in November. The Hawks used to be strong, but now they're weak. I need to get hyped. Let's see. Dikembe Mutombo is one of the best centers, and he's going to wave his finger at me if he blocks my shot. Oh, and Lenny Wilkens dogged me out at the Olympics, played me only 43 seconds in the gold-medal game. So I'm pissed. Now I've got a challenge.

We played at Phoenix a few days later. Penny Hardaway is hurt, so I can't beat him down personally. So, let's see. Luc Longley, their center from Australia. I'm thinking, "Luc has three rings and I have none. So I need to demolish him." Now I've got another challenge.

Last November 19, we end up in Chicago against the worst team in the league (after the Clippers). But it's Phil's homecoming. He hasn't been back to Chicago as coach since the Bulls won six championships with him as coach. I decide I'm going to do it for Phil. I give the Bulls 41 points and 17 rebounds.

It doesn't always work out that way. The night before we played the Bulls, we were in Denver. I wanted so bad to bust Nick Van Exel. But he had a hot game. The altitude messed us up, too. All right, that's a bad excuse. I would have had 48 points and we would have won if I didn't miss 12 free throws. We lost by 11 points.

But getting up for games during the NBA grind is important. You do what you have to do.

Last January we played the Clippers in back-to-back games. Other than making sure you're the best team in L.A. and Billy Crystal gets a nice show, there is not much to play for. I remember Michael Olowokandi getting killed in the paper the day before the second game. Even though the Clippers center was in only his second year, they were comparing his numbers against mine. They were saying he isn't ready and he has no heart. Just killing him. I kind of felt sorry for him. It was unfair. But, hey, I had a job to do.

So instead of trying to dominate Olowokandi, I'm focusing on the fact that the Clippers haven't beaten L.A. in, like, the last fourteen tries. I'm thinking, "Gotta make it fifteen. Can't let these clowns win."

Usually, I make it a personal challenge. See, for me to really dominate you, I have to not like you. Sometimes I'll be looking for a reason not to like you. Like Karl Malone. I just didn't like the way he played. That feeling carried over off the court until I met him and realized he was a good, family guy.

One thing you find out about the regular season is how great some of the other players in the league are. I mean, you see the highlights and you always talk trash with the guys at the All-Star Game. But, for example, Detroit came to L.A. in early December. Now, everyone knows Grant Hill is one of the best players in the world. But he just blew me away how good he was when he was healthy last year. When he was going upcourt, he was moving.

I always knew he had a nice game, but when we played him it was like trying to catch a damn greyhound. He never got tired. He just got that long stride. Get the ball and push it in front. He was nice. He doesn't make faces. He doesn't talk trash. He's truly a class act. If more guys could be like him in the league, then this league would be a better league.

But it isn't. The league just has to accept what they got and market certain guys for what they're worth. You can't market everybody the same.

After we won sixteen straight, we traveled to Indiana to face the Pacers on Friday, January 14. Dale Davis was playing me one-on-

one, and so I'm about to explode on the Pacers. I'm getting in deep position, throwing up my jump hook. But nothing was falling: I think I went 2 for 25 that game. We ended up losing, 111–102.

You know why? Because of the *Sports Illustrated* jinx. Yep. The magazine came out that Thursday with us on the cover, and all of a sudden we lose. It happened to me in college. It happened in Orlando. It's happened to a lot of greater athletes than me. Anytime *Sports Illustrated* puts a picture of you or your team on the cover, watch out. You're probably going to lose the next game. Hey, I gotta come up with some reason why we lost. It can't be we just didn't play well.

After the game, I even said, "Listen, Dale's good. But he ain't that good. It's a *Sports Illustrated* jinx."

Guys were mad we lost because Indiana was looking like the best team in the East, a team we might meet up with in the finals.

Phil just looked around the locker room and shook his head.

"Hey, pick your head up; we're not going to go 82–0," he said. "We're gonna lose some games."

Then he would start messing with us. "You're not my Chicago team that went 72–10," he said. "We're early in the season, and you already have 16 straight wins. But you're not going to beat that record, so forget about it. And we're not going to go 82–0, so forget about that. Let's get on the plane."

The Indiana game started a bad trend. We ended up losing six of our next nine, and had our first crisis—if you want to call it that.

At the end of a game against Seattle in L.A. on January 17, Phil told Ron to go over a screen to pick up Gary Payton so he doesn't beat us with a 3-pointer. We were up by 2 points and the game was on the line. So what happens? Harp goes under the screen. Gary gets free. Shoots a 3-pointer. Seattle wins.

Two days later, we played a bad game against Cleveland. That's the game where Kobe was trying to outdo Bobby Sura and got stripped. We won, but Phil yelled at Kobe after the game, told him to "cut out the one-on-one crap."

Our problems weren't over. Portland beat us for the second time in three games, and they did it on our home court, 95–91. Then we went to San Antonio, and the Twin Towers drilled us. We lost to the Spurs, 105–81. The crowd got into the game. David and Tim were looking like they were going to the finals again.

After that loss, we were 34–11 and falling behind Portland in the Pacific Divison. People are starting to talk. "Here go the Lakers again."

We had a few team meetings, but I don't think they did any good. I don't believe in them myself. I don't like when guys talk and don't show up. If you know what you got to do, just go out and do it. I always know what I have to do. I don't need anybody to tell me.

I also knew why we lost six of nine games. Because we weren't a mentally tough team. When we went on our winning streak, we thought "Sixteen in a row? Season's over. We're gonna win it now." Everybody's talking, getting cocky. We're in first place.

Going into the All-Star break, we needed a challenge.

Alonzo Mourning helped out. About that time, he started complaining about the Lakers being on TV too much, something like, "The Lakers are on TV every Sunday. How come we aren't?" I think he said he was mad at NBC Sports president Dick Ebersol for not putting more Miami Heat games on TV.

I'm thinking, "Please."

After we beat Utah, Denver and Minnesota, we went into the All-Star break with a 37–11 record.

All-Star Weekend is about two things: money and more money. You got all these corporate sponsors of the NBA coming into a city, flossin', acting all big-time. You got every knucklehead MTV cat running around with a microphone and a camera, asking you things like, "Yo, Shaq, what's up with the bling-bling?"

All these middle-aged sportswriter cats are looking around, going, "Uh, Phil, what exactly is the bling-bling? Is that a part of the triangle offense?"

All-Star Weekend is about everything but real basketball. It's about parties, relaxing, dunk contests, trying out your craziest move in the game.

It's wild, but it's about business, too. I conducted some of my own in San Francisco last year. Leonard and I helped put together a technology summit, a big Internet conference that included all the top-dog people in the business. I actually rented out a whole hotel for all these bigwigs to stay. It was a write-off. ☺

Everybody flexed their technology muscles. I was more interested in trying to put more computers in the 'hood for children who need to be challenged.

After the summit, I went and took my video camera to the New Arena in Oakland, where they were holding the slam-dunk contest on Saturday and the All-Star Game on Sunday.

Now, if you're an NBA fan, you know what Vince Carter did. I came up with the line about him; "Half-man, half-amazing." When he threw that one dunk down, where his whole arm went in the rim, I was just shocked. I had to rewind my little camera, see if it really happened.

When you make other NBA players go, "Oooohhhh," you know you've done something great. See, even though I was the leading candidate for the MVP award at that point, Vince was getting most of the hype. I didn't mind. Not only did it take media pressure off me and some of the other players, but Vince deserved it. Last year, he became the kind of player that kids pretend they are on the playground. Watching him brought back a lot of memories, memories about my first basketball idol.

Julius Erving surprised me at the All-Star Game last year when he came up and spoke to me in the locker room. When you're famous, you don't really get excited when you meet other famous people. But Doc was different. We had history.

In my sophomore year at LSU, I was sleeping in my dorm room one morning. I'd been out all night, so I didn't go to my early class. I'm sleeping like a mug when all of a sudden I feel this tap on my face. I look up. It's Dr. J.

He was going to speak at some Converse event with Dale Brown and told my coach he wanted to meet me. So Dale brought him to the dorm room, and somehow they got in. Maybe they knocked and I never heard them.

Anyway, I was shocked. "Get dressed," Dr. J said. "Let's go eat some lunch."

I looked up and thought I was dreaming. Until Dale Brown said, "Yeah, it's Dr. J. Get dressed."

He's always been nice to me. Even when I tried to take his daughter out on a date a few years ago, he was still nice to me. Yes, I asked Dr. J's daughter out on a date. I know the family. I got permission from him at the time. She was a manager at a store in Atlanta. No, we never got a chance to go out. She had a boyfriend at the time. So she told me, "No."

When Dr. J spoke to me at the All-Star Game, it felt really good. One of the first things he said was how he was so proud of me for using the criticism to get better. "It's about time that they give you respect," he said. "Whatever they said you couldn't do, you've done." That meant a lot. My idol, my legend, a guy who's always been good to me, spending that kind of time and letting me know how he feels.

After the Portland Trail Blazers, the two teams that gave us the most problems during the regular season were San Antonio and Sacramento. We just couldn't match up inside with the Spurs; either Tim or David was going to have a big game because I couldn't guard both. And the Kings played this freak-it, herky-jerky game that we got caught up in.

It wasn't just Chris Webber and Jason Williams. They had guys coming off the bench like Jon Barry, who played the year before with me on the Lakers. Now, when Jon was a Laker, he couldn't hit a freakin' shot. But against us, he's shooting threes, making them, rubbing it in our faces.

Portland was our real challenge, but the way things were going, it was going to be us, the Blazers, or San Antonio coming out of the West.

After the All-Star break, people had already said Portland was a force to be reckoned with. We found out firsthand when they beat us two out of three times.

Steve Smith and Bonzi Wells were talking trash after the first win. And Greg Anthony and Scottie Pippen were trying to act all hard. Their owner, Paul Allen, had spent all this money trying to win a championship. Their starters alone made more than $50 million for a single season.

If we were ever going to make a stand, we had to do it in Portland on February 29, the date of the most crucial regular-season game of the 1999–2000 season.

The Lakers and the Blazers were tied for the best record in the NBA at 45–11. We had won eleven straight games, and Portland was on fire, taking out everybody.

Before the game, we were already being counted out. I'm watching TV, and ESPN's Dr. Jack Ramsay is going on about Portland having too much depth. "Shaq may have problems when Portland's big men take him outside. All they have to do is pull Shaq out, spread the defense, and put Rasheed Wallace on A.C."

That night, I was on a mission. I was focused. I had that look in my eye. The guys were bringing me the ball down low and I was scoring. Portland was playing well, too, in front of their home crowd at the Rose Garden.

We're going back and forth the whole game until we lead by 3 points with about a minute left. Scottie shoots this wild 3-pointer to tie it up. We go up one and then Kobe comes down, gets fouled, and makes two free throws. The Trail Blazers are down to their last possession.

Steve Smith gets in the corner and throws up a prayer on the left baseline. It hit the top of the backboard.

The Lakers win, 90–87.

I don't like the term "statement games," but that was a message.

After the buzzer, we celebrated. We're not acting like we won the championship, but more with relief, like, "Phew, we're still in first."

In the locker room afterward, Phil was happy.

"All right, good job," he said. "Good job. I knew you could do it. Good job. Let's get back on track. Now that we're in first, let's make some space for ourselves."

Joe Kleine, Portland's backup center, called it the most hyped regular-season game that he'd ever seen. And he played in Boston with Larry Bird and in Chicago with Michael Jordan.

Portland was crushed after they lost that game. They went in a funk and we took off, winning our next seven games. We had a 19-game win streak to go with our earlier 16-game streak.

All cylinders were clicking. Everybody's playing well, everybody's playing hard. Everybody's hitting shots, nobody's complaining. Glen is playing well. Kobe is doing all right. And I'm dominating. I'm putting up numbers, and the chant "MVP! MVP!" is starting to make its way around the Staples Center.

I heard it loud and clear on March 6, my birthday game. Ever since the second year of my career, I've been an MVP candidate. But now people were starting to talk about it, say it loud and say it proud. I'm saying to myself, "I don't even want it; I don't even care."

I felt I was close to winning three other times in my career. In my second year, Hakeem Olajuwon won the award but I felt I was right there. The year that I came back after my first injury in Orlando—in 1995–96—Michael Jordan won the award. Then in the lockout year, I thought I might have had a shot, but Karl Malone won. All three seasons, I never averaged less than 26 points and almost 11 rebounds.

But there was always an excuse, just like the All-Star Game in San Antonio, when they gave the award to Michael.

At this point, I'm thinking, "Forget the trophy. I'm playing for a title." That's the one thing that's going to validate my status in the game. I'm not trying to win a popularity contest.

When I took the floor for the Clippers game, I had broken all my game-day rituals. I had a party set up for that night. I didn't get a nap. Shareef, my son, just born on January 11, was crying in the background. Everybody is at the house. It's noisy.

So I put on this fly-ass suit, clothes nobody ever seen before; it was a gray suit with the matching hat. I'm tired, but I'm ready to go to the game.

By the time I got to the Staples Center, I was thinking more about the party than about the Clippers. I was hoping other players were going to shine, that I could be more of a role player.

Magic Johnson used to have the title as the best party-thrower in L.A., but I was also hoping to take that over.

Now it's game time, and the Clippers are hanging tough. As I said before, I'm angry because their organization wouldn't give me eight tickets for my friends and family. Both L.A. teams play at the Staples Center, but since it was the Clippers' night to host, I had to go through them for tickets.

"No, Shaq, sorry. Can't do it."

All right, you watch how I treat your basketball team.

I tried to get Kareem's attention before the game. "Hey, what's up?"

He doesn't even acknowledge me. He just looks at me, stares me down.

The Clippers came out tough. At one point, Phil yelled at me. "Come on, stop screwing around," he said. "You're not playing. What, you got a party tonight?"

Uh-oh. The General found out. He's yelling at me. And the Clippers are insulting me. They're not double-teaming me. That's an insult. I always said to the media, "If a team doesn't double me, I'm breaking out."

I broke out. I don't want to go over the details again, but after I had 26 points at halftime and 42 at the end of the third quarter, Uncle Jerome, my bodyguard and the Lakers security man, joked about how it would be a good thing if I get 50 on my birthday.

"Okay, I'm gonna get 50," I said.

Pete Chilcutt was trying to guard me, Anthony Avent, the same cat who's from my hometown and who couldn't guard me when I was twelve, thirteen, well, he is not gonna guard me now. So I kept going. By the time it was over, I had my career high of 61 points.

On top of that, Kobe Bryant and I had our nice connection that night.

It was a great birthday, and it wasn't over. With the money my mother had after she traded in my Ferrari, she bought me a new Bentley.

I pulled up in my black Rolls-Royce to the Voodoo Lounge on Olympic and Crenshaw in L.A. Me and Jerome. Girls were everywhere.

The comedian Alex Thomas has a camera, so I do a skit for him. I go up to the VIP section. Women everywhere. People just hanging out. Everybody had watched the game. There were a lot of actresses and superstars. Leonardo DiCaprio, Jada Pinkett, Will Smith, Snoop Dog, Dr. Dre. They're all upstairs in VIP, just chillin'.

After some birthday cake, I go home and see Shareef.

Life was good. My team was the best in the NBA, I was up for MVP, Kobe and I were getting along real well and most of my family and friends celebrated my birthday.

Every now and then, when I ride around in my car, I point to the sky and I say, "Thank you, God." Because I have made it. Just getting out, being successful, knowing a lot of people, making good money, I made it. Despite not having a championship, not having an MVP trophy, I feel I made it. I always do that.

And I did it that night.

I read something John Salley once said about an NBA team not really being made up of twelve basketball players, but instead being made up of twelve CEOs who own their own countries. It's not like high school or college, where there's more pressure to fit in and do what the coach tells you. In the NBA, contracts are guaranteed. You can't get cut from the team. Sometimes the players are more powerful than the coaches supposedly in charge of them. (Like me. ☺) We're all rich, just some more rich than others. By the time you're in the league for a few years, you're set in your ways, just like one-half of an old married couple. You know your routine and you don't need anybody coming in and changing it. Players spend hours with each other, hooked up to machines in the training room. In that locker room—in the hotels, on those buses and on those planes—we see more of each other from October to June than most families. People always say, "Why couldn't they just get along?" It's not like that. Chemistry is a fragile thing in the NBA. You can have it one minute and lose it forever the next. I've been on some talented, winning teams where players just didn't like each other. I've been on other teams that weren't as talented and didn't have as much chance to win a championship, but everybody got along and liked and trusted each other.

The Lakers of last season were one of those teams. No matter what happened on the court, it never affected our personal relationships off it. Kobe and I had basketball issues to work through and Glen Rice had trouble fitting in on offense sometimes, but we rose above all that. If we saw each other in the hallway in the hotel, riding in the bus, or on the plane, we always talked with each other. We were much closer than any other Laker team I remember. I'm not saying you have to have great chemistry and like all your teammates, but it makes the game much easier. We just had a nice mix. You had veterans like Ron Harper, John Salley, Robert Horry, and A.C. Green, players who had all won championships; hard-working, smart veterans like Rick Fox, Glen Rice, Derek Fisher, and Brian Shaw and those end-of-the-bench role players like Travis Knight and Tyronn Lue, who kept the mood light. Ron was one of our most valuable players. He wasn't just a good guy, he was a good floor leader. His career tells you more about sacrifice than anything.

When Harp came in with Cleveland in 1986—I was fourteen years old—people were saying he could have been a dominant legend. He could shoot, jump and dunk like Jordan, and he could pick you clean on defense. But then he blew out his knee, and he never averaged as many points as he did when he was a rookie.

Instead of just sulking and wondering what might have been, he became one of the great role players of all time, playing alongside Michael and Scottie on those Bulls championship teams. He played defense harder than anyone. He came in with a couple of rings, and he's telling us what to do and how it's gonna be. He really kept it real for all the young players on the team. When Phil wasn't saying anything, Ron was in charge of keeping Kobe in check. "Listen, you can't do that sh**," he would tell him sometimes. "You got to get everybody involved, start passing."

Ron also overcame something harder than a knee injury. He had a stuttering problem. I had that small problem, too, as a child, and to this day say things fast so I don't get hung up on words. But Ron really stuttered when he came into the league. He worked hard over the past fifteen years to try and overcome it. Now he's one of the best guys with the media, joking, laughing, telling them anything they want to know.

The Lakers cracked on each other all the time. Nothing was off-limits. Physical appearances, anything. The best thing about the locker room is, you don't have to grow up. You can act like a juvenile delinquent. One of the funniest moments of the season came when someone was actually talking about Ron's stuttering problem. I don't know who said it, but somebody just piped up, "Yo, what's up, Damon Stuttermire?" Even Ron was busting up laughing.

The real pranksters on the team were Glen and B. Shaw. One time I got out of the shower and my skin was real dry. I was all ashy. So after I put some baby powder on, Glen said, "Yo, what happened to you? Someone shoot you with powdered darts?" Those guys would just talk trash about people. Like if Glen had bumps on the back of his neck, B. Shaw would call him "Ant-pile neck." And B. Shaw had a lightbulb head, his hairline was receding. We would call him either "Microphone Head" or "Uncircumcised 8-ball Head."

Like I said, nothing was off-limits. Rick Fox looked Arab and he had a temper. We would talk about him blowing up the bus, like he was a terrorist. We called him "bin Laden." Rick also got teased because he had just married Vanessa Williams, the actress and singer who already had children from a previous marriage. After she and Rick had a baby together, we were like, "Damn, five kids in one summer. We couldn't even pull that off."

Rick is a nice guy, real emotional. He hated Portland. He wanted to mess Scottie up for some reason, especially when Pippen started talking smack to Phil. He would even joke with us, "Let me do it. Please." Only in Hollywood can a pretty-boy actor be considered a thug. He was like Charles Oakley, but better looking. He read a lot of books, read a lot of screenplays. He thinks he's a stockbroker, he and John Salley. Salley was Mr. Comedian sometimes. But mostly, he would just sit there and tell me like old war stories about what Isiah Thomas used to do in Detroit when the Pistons won their two championships. He was like a walking history lesson. Especially like during the play-offs. We were screwing around against Sacramento, letting them back in the series, and he'd say, "Don't worry, this sh** happened to me when I first played with Detroit against Dallas. We played Dallas and they had Mark Aguirre. They came back on us. Then we came back and blew them out."

Harp's the type of guard that knows how a big man wants the ball, knows where to put it. He knows when a guy's leaning on me. You got to feel how a guy's playing. When I first came into the league, I used to try to waste my energy fighting and pushing. Finally I said no to all that pushing. Just spin off. When they push you, spin off them. It's t'ai chi every time. I'm using your positive energy, and I'm blowing off it. See, most guys can't push, they got to lean. When they lean, I spin.

Travis Knight was a guy who beat the system, a guy who Rick Pitino destroyed. Travis's rookie year, he listened. I'd say, "Cut to the basket." He used to catch it, dunk it, shoot the little jumper. He was playing free. He was having fun. Rick Pitino sees him, thinks he can be a bona fide center, offers him a lot of money—$21 million for seven seasons. He gets him in Boston and destroys his confidence. Yelling at him every day, cursing at him every day. He finally traded him back to L.A. When Travis was here before, all his energy was up in his head. We get him back, it's all in his ankles. He's scared to get yelled at. Whenever he gets yelled at, it just messes him up. I liked Travis, even though we traded him to the Knicks last summer. When I say he beat the system, he took good money and ran. Very smart.

Derek Fisher was another very good role player. Hard worker. He doesn't have the most talent, but he would dive on the floor for anything. Great with kids, does a lot of community service.

Tyronn Lue—now, there's a guy who has a lot of talent, has all that little Iverson stuff. But at 6'0", you wonder if he will ever get a chance to show it because Phil likes big guards. When Tyronn Lue got in the game, he spread the floor more; he brought some excitement to the game because he knows how to get in the middle, like Muggsy Bogues used to do and dish it off.

We didn't re-sign A.C. Green, but he really had my back last season at power forward. He is one of those saved guys, born-again Christians. He didn't use curse words and his biggest claim to fame—other than being the league's iron man for consecutive games played—was that he was a virgin at thirty-six years old. Talk about discipline.

But anyone who thought he was a choirboy is wrong. A.C. would do anything to get a rebound. He was a great guy to have on your team, but he was dirty. I guess when some guys don't have a lot of talent, they got to do what they got to do to survive.

All I know is, my shoulder is still messed up to this day because of A.C. We were in a rebounding drill during practice. I was getting ready to go up, jump with all my might and grab it. But A.C. was locked up on my arm. He knocked my shoulder out of place. Good guy, but dirty.

By the last two months of the regular season, between guys shoving on me in games, and A.C. nailing me in practices, I was starting to feel beat up and worn down. We hadn't lost a game for more than a month—from February 4 to March 16. But the winning was taking its toll on my body.

I told Phil I had a hamstring pull when we played Denver on March 13.

Phil's reply: "So?"

I kept playing. The Lakers didn't think I'm hurting that much because I scored more than 40 points three times over the next eight days. But I needed help, and not just massage and ice.

I went to Dr. Shen Hsu, the acupuncturist. He does more than that. He's one of those Eastern medicine guys, with all the herbs and ancient techniques.

Whenever I had a big bruise, he would give me a cupping treatment: I would drive to his office, jump on his treatment table, and put my head in the headrest. Shen would put oil on my back, rub small plastic suction cups around the injury.

It's not a pretty sight. The surface of the skin gets sucked by the pressure in the cup. It opens my blood vessels until the blood comes out. It feels like someone giving you a tattoo, hurts like hell. Some Western medicine people don't agree that it's a good treatment.

But without Shen, I couldn't have played two years ago. Besides, Western medicine is too analog. I'm digital, brother. Every time I went to Shen, he fixed me up—from my thumb to my knee to my abdomen. The American guys, they want to give you pills. And I've already got too much Indocin and anti-inflammatory drugs in my body.

I've already taken so many pills, my kidneys are probably going to be messed up. That's a big issue in the league right now. My partying days are long over. I mean, I'll enjoy life now and then, but I've gotten serious about taking care of my body. See, I don't get tired. I get beat up. You keep chopping on a tree, you need to give the tree some rest so the chlorophyll will fill back up and the tree gets its energy back. Shen helped me get ready for the homestretch and the play-offs.

A few days after he worked on me, we played the Knicks at home. It was April 2, the anniversary of my grandmother's death. So I have that on my mind and I'm playing against Patrick Ewing. I'm going to work. I score 34 points and grab 12 rebounds, and we blow out New York, 106–82.

There was a little bit of drama at the end of the season, especially on April 19, in the last game against San Antonio. That was the game when my father ran onto the court and tried to get in Phil's face.

That's also the game Phil and Spurs coach Gregg Popovich got into it. When one would call a time-out at the end of the game, the other guy would call a time-out just to piss him off and stop the game. Then Pop would do it. Then Phil would do it again. Phil pissed off a lot of people that day.

Even though that was the seventh time in the past eight games they beat us, I never felt the Spurs were really into the season. They had a bunch of old guys. They don't have any new-wave homeboys on their team.

Like Jaren Jackson—he can play. But I'm sure he's just glad to be there, on the team. His role is just get it and shoot and not get dunked on hard by Kobe, which he did last season. Avery Johnson just wants to get everybody involved as the point guard. David is just happy to be there. All the pressure's off him now; he gave up the mantle to Tim. Sean Elliott was coming back from a kidney transplant. I've never said this before, but I was scared to play against him.

I was worried that if put my big body on him and he got hit and it did something to his surgery, something bad might happen. To this day, I'm scared to play him. He came through the lane one time, I had to let him go. I just had to.

After they swept us in 1999, I wanted to see the Spurs in the play-offs last year. I really felt we could beat them. By the time we lost that last, meaningless game, we had already locked up home-court advantage throughout the play-offs.

With winning streaks of 11, 16, and 19 games, we ended up 67–15 for the regular season, best in the league. We'd answered all the questions, except the most important: Could we win the championship?

With the play-offs around the corner, it was finally time to see if we could live up to our potential.

11

The Playoffs

Before our first-round series, the Sacramento Kings were talking a lot of noise. They had split the season series with us and were feeling good about themselves. "We match up with the Lakers," Chris Webber said. "This is the team we wanted. All we have to do is pull Shaq away from the basket."

I'm thinking to myself: "Be careful what you ask for."

The only problem Sacramento really gave us was Webber, one of the top power forwards in the game. C. Webb could run the floor like a guard, post you up like a center, and dunk on you like a small forward. We knew he would get his points. We had to stop everybody else.

We also needed to keep Jason Williams in front of us, because if he started going by guys and getting everybody else involved, anything could happen. White Chocolate may have been inconsistent, but when he was in that zone where the game just came to him, that little cat could find his teammates with his eyes closed. (Sometimes, his eyes *were* closed.)

We weren't worried about Nick Anderson, my old teammate from Orlando. He was just too streaky. You never knew what he was going to do, from game to game. Sacramento also had some nice role players, from the Croatian dude named Peja (Predrag Sto-jakovic) to Vlade Divac, the Serbian center who was the Lakers center before I came to town. There was Corliss Williamson at one forward; he could bang some. And they had a nice bench.

But the Kings also had a big problem to worry about:

Me.

Phil had stressed how important it was be dominant at the Staples Center all season, so in our first home play-off game under the General, our squad came to play. Myself, I had gotten tired of the "Shaq-can't-do-this" crowd and was ready to explode. I went straight to the blocks, put my be-hind in the gut of whoever was guarding me. Bumping, grinding, I was going to force the referees to call a three-second violation on me before I moved away from the basket. Finger-roll here, two-hand power dunk there. A putback on Kobe's miss. All of a sudden, we're running away with the game. The crowd's going wild. We take the game 117–107, to jump out to a 1–0 lead in the best-three-of-five series. I had 46 points, 17 rebounds.

I didn't say anything to the Sacramento players, but inside I'm thinking to myself, "OK, is this what you wanted? Is this the team you really thought you could match up against?

"Forty-six and seventeen. Is that what you wanted?"

We were too strong, too poised. I was ready to go at Vlade. He's one of those finesse-type centers, like Arvydas Sabonis. He doesn't want to bang down low and get too physical. I told him in the first game, straight up, "I'm getting 50." If it weren't for a couple of free throws that I missed, I would have had it. You know that saying Stuart Scott has on ESPN, "Vla-day Da-day, Rock Your Par-tay?" Yeah? Well, Vlade got rocked, all right.

In Game 2, we looked even better. Kobe scored 32 points and I chipped in with 17 rebounds. We blew the Kings out, 113–89. I threw this alley-oop to Kobe in that game. When he took the ball and dunked it, the Staples Center was just shaking. The crowd started chanting, "Sweep! Sweep!"

Now, the Lakers have always won their opening-round play-off series since I've been there, but as we went up 2–0 on Sacramento, there was a feeling about this team that I knew was different from other seasons. Maybe it was the structure. Everybody got tapes to watch of every player before every game. Everybody was coming in at a certain time of the day. We were staying an hour or two after practice, going over things. Whether we were working on our drills or playing little shooting games after practice, there was a bond carrying over from the regular season.

At this point, we were feeling invincible. Me, I not only had to live up to Phil's expectations, but also to my own. In other seasons, the league MVP award was given out right after the regular season. This year, they still hadn't named anybody. I was waiting, wondering if there was a slim chance I had somehow lost out again.

People think, "Aw, Shaq, you knew you had it." But in sports, the one thing you learn is to take nothing for granted. I thought I had gotten robbed at the All-Star Game once because of favoritism for Michael Jordan. While I know I had had the best 1999–2000 season, I didn't know if all the media members were going to give me the benefit of the doubt. Remember, I've mumbled my way through my share of press conferences. So not everyone was on the Shaq bandwagon.

That's why I felt I had to dominate the first game of every series, to make sure everyone knew. I had to let them know: Superman is here.

Before I go into Games 3 and 4 and how those Sacramento dudes hit every shot you could think of, let me just say one thing about the Kings' home, Arco Arena: Crazy. Absolutely, frickin' crazy. I mean, those fans get into the game like no other fans I've ever seen. They've got little alarms for old ladies to hold. They've got cowbells and horns. It's like playing somewhere in Europe, where they throw money at you. Arco Arena is as loud as I've heard a building since Kentucky, when Rick Pitino was coaching.

Sacramento fans are loud, they're consistent. Some were rude, but for the most part, they just support their team like nobody supports their team. A couple times I was at the free-throw line, and I couldn't even hear the referee's whistle.

We didn't help ourselves. We had gotten too comfortable after the wins in L.A., and were already up to our old cocky, Laker ways. Guys are talking smack, saying things like, "We're packing for only one day."

That stuff made its way to the Kings' locker room, which meant one thing: We have a series on our hands.

I know I didn't pack for one day. I brought two sweatsuits, two pairs of underwear, my toiletry bag, all the usual stuff. In my mind, this wasn't a day trip. I knew they would play hard at home.

We had a chance to win Game 3 late before going down, 99–91. Because the league was dragging out the first round over two weekends to help NBC's ratings, we were stuck in Sacramento the next three days, trapped at the Hyatt Regency in downtown Sacramento. Everything closed early. There's nothing to do. I think I had already watched every movie there was to watch on TV. It was like being on an island, with nowhere to go. Me and Jerome finally got a rental car and drove to Friday's and Ruth's Chris Steakhouse.

Most of the people we're running into in restaurants are nice, but a couple of young guys got kind of belligerent, started going off on the Lakers. "You guys are done. It's all over, Shaq." I kind of felt sorry for them. I knew I was going to have to demolish their team, even if it took two more games.

I don't know if hanging out in Sacramento that long got to us, or the Kings were much better than we thought. But they came out loose in Game 4—so loose they were hitting shots out of nowhere. Hot, hot, hot. Unbelievably hot. And on top of things, they were defending me illegally, dropping guys down below the free-throw line. The referees were not calling any fouls.

A lot of our fans were using conspiracy theories, saying the league wanted the series to go five games because of better NBC ratings. If the Kings weren't killing us, I could believe that.

Meanwhile, Randy Moss, the Minnesota wide receiver who went to high school in West Virginia with Jason Williams, was in the stands. Every time Jason throws some funky pass, he's looking at Randy. Webber is playing out of his mind, rebounding, scoring, doing it all.

I was missing free throws, not concentrating. One of the things I remember was near the end of the game. Ron Harper showed off his championship ring to a bunch of rowdy fans behind the bench. They started chanting, "Not with Shaq! Not with Shaq!" That hurt.

The Kings won, 101–88. Right before the game ended, C. Webb started the fast break, gave it up, got it back, and scored on a nasty dunk that turned up the noise at Arco. Now it's 2–2, and the Lakers aren't unbeatable any longer. We're one game from being eliminated. Again.

I called my dad and let him know I wasn't feeling too good about my game. "Dad, I can't get a good game in Sacramento," I said.

"Have you ever played well in Sacramento?"

"No."

"All right, then," he said. "Don't worry about it."

We also had home-court advantage, something we had worked for the whole season. Between that advantage and the conversation with my pops, I felt a little bit better about Game 5. Our fans were worried, but they're not panicking. When I go to the barber shop, the guys are like, "Come on, man, let's go. Why can't you guys put it away?"

The team may have been flat, but we knew what we had to do. Phil Jackson knew, too. He was so confident we were going to take care of business against the Kings in Game 5 at the Staples Center that we didn't even practice. He told us, "You don't need to practice. Rest your bodies. We're going to beat this team. They're playing illegal defense. The first three to five plays, stand in this position, point to the referees, and let them know that what Sacramento is doing is illegal."

Rick Adelman, the Kings' coach, had been saying all week that I was getting away with murder under the basket. I didn't take it personally because every coach becomes a politician during the playoffs. That's just the way it is in the NBA. But with the series 2–2 and the Kings talking, guys are mad.

My dad is not panicking. The General ain't panicking. I'm not gonna panic. In my first elimination game as the league's MVP, I know what I have to do. Put on a show or go home. And I'm not going home. Not this early.

Phil's strategy about pointing out the illegal defenses works perfectly. Dudes on Sacramento pick up early fouls and start bitching to the officials. They're not hitting the shots they hit at home. By the opening minutes, they're off their game, and meanwhile Kobe is playing well, Glen Rice is feeling it from the outside; everything is clicking. We take control. I give the Kings 32 points and 18 rebounds, and we storm into the second round with a 113–86 win. We take apart the team everybody called the playground Kings, the razzmatazz team of the NBA that plays like they're running and gunning at the park.

Now, who's got next?

Before the second round began, it was official: I won my first Most Valuable Player award. I had just come off my best season, leading the league in scoring with 29.7 points per game and grabbing an average of 13.6 rebounds. I was finding my teammates like never before, too. (In the 1999 lockout season, I averaged only 2.3 assists per game. In 1999–2000, I averaged a career-high 3.8 assists to go with three blocked shots per game.) This made me No. 1 in the league in scoring, No. 2 in rebounds, No. 3 in blocked shots. Only three people played more minutes than me in the 1999–2000 season.

There was a big press conference, and everything was just feeling right. Afterwards, I went up to the microphone and had one more message.

"For all my friends in the media who like quotes, mark this quote down," I said. "From this day on, I would like to be known as the Big Aristotle. Because it was Aristotle who said, 'Excellence is not a singular act, but a habit. You are what you repeatedly do.' "

The defending champion San Antonio Spurs were matched up with Phoenix in the first round. Tim Duncan missed the series with a knee injury he suffered at the end of the regular season, but if David Robinson could hold the fort until he came back, it looked like we were going to play the Spurs.

214

San Antonio went down 2–1 in the series. But I was thinking, "They're going to come back." They were the defending champions. I told some of the Lakers video people to get me as many Duncan tapes as possible.

I started watching all Tim's moves. San Antonio had our number like no other team. They swept us in the play-offs the year before and won seven of the last eight games between us leading up to the play-offs—including the game my father almost got into it with Phil.

So I'm boning up on my Duncan homework, watching how fundamentally sound he is, using the glass from the outside, drop-stepping inside. And as I'm watching one of the tapes, I'm realizing Phoenix is going to win the series. Tim is not coming back.

I hadn't even bothered to watch any tape on Luc Longley, Phoenix's center. I'm thinking: "If Phoenix wins, I'm taking him out. Luc is a nice guy with some pretty good offensive skills. But he's just not strong enough to stop me. And there is no way I'm losing to Penny Hardaway, my former teammate in Orlando."

Penny had left the Magic in 1998, and it was almost as ugly as me leaving in 1996. Nearly everyone in town had turned on him. So he knew the feeling of a fresh start, and was playing fast and free.

Phoenix may not have been as entertaining as the Kings, or as powerful as a healthy San Antonio, but they were solid. Their coach, Scott Skiles, was the first point guard I played with in Orlando. Six years had gone by since we were teammates, but he probably felt he knew my game. Phoenix had Penny, plus Jason Kidd, their best player, and one of the quickest and most talented cats in the game. With a basketball in his hand, Kidd could probably beat anybody in the league dribbling downcourt. He's the truth. Gets everyone involved, plays defense as hard as anyone and can break you down and score when he wants. The only weakness in his game is his jumper, and at times even that was starting to come around.

But the Suns just didn't have weapons for us. They were the first team in the play-offs to resort to the Hack-a-Shaq defense. I knew players were going to start fouling me intentionally and sending me to the free-throw line, but a part of me was thinking, "Do people really want to watch this stuff?" I thought I was playing the best ball I ever played, and that people wouldn't just take the easy way out and foul me. But I guess that's the only way some teams felt they could defend me.

The ball would get dumped to me in the low post, someone would come to double-team. I'd just hold the ball up high and wait for someone to cut to the basket. Kobe and I were hooking up on a lot of nice give-and-go plays, where he would throw it in to me and I would give it back to him for a layup. It didn't look as easy as Magic Johnson and Kareem Abdul-Jabbar, but we were trying.

Honestly, I'd go so far as to say that in a lot of ways, dealing with Penny helped me learn how to deal with and relate to Kobe. Penny and I may have ended up feuding and not winning a title together when we were young; but the truth is, I learned a lot about the game and about teammates from my relationship with him. That might have even helped the Lakers beat the Suns the way we did.

Game 1, I made sure I sent a message: 37 points, 14 rebounds. We blew the Suns out, 105–77.

But in Game 2 at the Staples Center, Phoenix came back and played us hard for four quarters. On our last possession, we were trailing by one point and staring at something we didn't want: an even series heading back to America West Arena in Phoenix, going into the teeth of a crowd that was going to be hyped as all hell.

I was having another monster game—38 points, 20 rebounds— but in the final seconds, everyone and their mom surrounded me. With Phoenix leading 96–95, someone else was going to have to play Superman.

Kobe.

He had the ball out on the perimeter with the clock ticking down and everyone in the Staples Center holding their breath. Remember, Kobe shot those play-off air balls in Utah in '97. And up to that point, I couldn't remember a last-second basket he made to win a game.

Wait. There was a tip-in against Golden State in a regular-season game in 1998, a play that sent the game into overtime and helped us win. But that was the regular season. That was Golden State.

Now we're talking the Western Conference semifinals, game on the line, going to Phoenix 1–1 if Kobe doesn't do something quick. Ten seconds left, he starts crossing over, working the clock down. He's on the left side a few feet in back of the free-throw line. Five . . . Four . . . Kidd is all over him, like Velcro.

You've seen the highlight. Kobe rises in the air, double-clutches, and shoots with 2.6 seconds left.

While the ball was in the air, all you could hear was noise.

All net.

It was the most important shot of the series because it basically took the life out of Phoenix. Kobe saved the day. We held on to win, 97–96, and went up 2–0. Afterwards, in the locker room, Phil lectured us, telling us we can't be messing around, that we have to protect home-court advantage. We found out later in the play-offs what he meant.

Heading to Phoenix, we were feeling good. In Game 3, I put together another double-double (37 points, 17 rebounds), and we held on for a 105–99 win.

Now we're thinking a 4–0 sweep, off to the conference finals for the first time since Utah swept us in 1998.

Meanwhile, Portland is taking care of the Jazz in the other semifinal, going up 2–0.

We had a day off in Phoenix, and I got a chance to relax. This business partner of mine invited me to his son's hockey game in some little neighborhood outside of Phoenix. So I went, checked his kid out. He was knocking other kids down, people were laughing, having a good time. It was a nice break.

I guess the Lakers forgot that Phoenix had some veterans on its team because in Game 4, the Suns came out on fire. Kidd made a half-court shot. Penny was dominating. Even their role players, like Corie Blount, was hitting jumpers. Luc Longley was sticking it to me with little hooks and jumpers inside. They blew us out, 117–98.

"You guys got cheap, that's OK," Phil said. He's laughing and joking. "We'll just get them next time." We had been in this position the whole season. Dominate, mess around, and then come back and show everyone how much heart and talent we had.

I guess every good, young team goes through that, but it just seemed like even when things weren't going well, no one really worried about getting knocked out of the play-offs. We felt we were that good.

Phil's light practices helped. He knew our bodies were banged up from a long season and wanted to save our energy. Some days he just made me ride the bike, do my stomach exercises, drink some water and get my sports massages from the team masseuse.

Actually, I shouldn't speak for Phil. But if he reads this in the 2000–2001 season, maybe he'll think, "Yeah, Shaq is right. I need to give him some more days off."

The only thing that started to bother me during the Phoenix series was the media. After one loss, the tired, old stories starting coming up again. *Lakers Don't Have Killer Instinct, Can't Put Teams Away.*

Now, we were up 3 games to 1 in a best-of-seven series. We were coming off a 67–15 season, one of the greatest regular seasons in franchise history. Yeah we had let the Kings back in the first-round series, but at the same time, we'd blown the doors off Sacramento in Game 5. And it's not like those other teams didn't have talent. Why were we expected to blow every team out of the water every game?

Bunch of bandwagon jumpers, the media. You go on a 19-game winning streak, lose one game, and it's, "Uh-oh, the Lakers aren't focused, they don't have the killer instinct."

So when they started asking about whether Phoenix was going to turn into Sacramento all over again, I started shamming them, giving them the Short Answer Method.

Between games, NBC's Doug Collins asked me what the Hack-a-Shaq defense would do to my confidence at the foul line. I was thinking, "Doug, haven't I proved that it doesn't bother me, that I can win games even when teams come at me with that strategy?"

I don't want to say that on the air because I've got to be positive, and I'm not supposed to add fuel to the fire. And I knew NBC needs to pump up the stories for their weekend games. And also that we have a habit of letting teams back into series. But that's what I was thinking.

I couldn't wait to knock Phoenix out—just so we could quiet the media for a day.

Since Scott Skiles didn't want me to beat the Suns by myself, the Phoenix players start doubling and tripling me like I knew they would. And Kobe came through again, leading us in scoring and penetrating the heart of the Suns defense. Penny Hardaway didn't turn out to be much of a factor. Kobe went right at his onetime idol. Took care of him. We ran them off the court 87–65.

For the third time in my career, I was going to the conference finals.

Portland, our rivals all season long, had done its part by beating Utah in five games. We were ready for the series everyone wanted. And thanks to that huge win over the Trail Blazers in February and our 67-win season, the Lakers had home-court advantage.

We never understood how crucial that would become.

I've said this before, but I still mean it:

Too much heat isn't good. I learned this in college at LSU. Chris Jackson (Mahmoud Abdul-Rauf), Stanley Roberts. Maurice Williamson. Me. Too many guys wanting the ball, wanting to score. Meanwhile, my 36–0 Cole High School team was the best team I've been on in my life. We had me, a couple of other guys who could score, and a lot of great role players. We never even thought about losing. The best teams I've been on, we only had one or two star players.

The Trail Blazers? Scottie Pippen wants the ball. Damon Stoudamire wants the ball. Rasheed Wallace. Steve Smith. You can go down the roster. Too many cats who want the ball. Meanwhile they don't have a go-to guy. That's what hurt them in Game 7. They were hitting shots the whole game but in the last eight minutes, they couldn't make anything. They didn't have that go-to guy who said, "Give me the damn ball. We're up by 6 points, give me the ball. Move."

Scottie didn't want to take over. Stoudamire was pissed off because he didn't get the shot. Rasheed, too busy talking trash. Steve Smith, worried about getting fouled.

And Arvydas Sabonis, Portland's 7'3", 295-pound center? I own Sabonis. It's not like I dislike him.

In 1984 at the Summer Olympics, he was the truth, maybe one of the top four or five players in the world—including NBA players. He was big, strong, skilled. One of the great shames in basketball is that he never got to play in the league during his prime, when no one could stop him. Fine. But he's thirty-six years old now. He can't move like he used to. I just have to back him down, then dog him out. That's the law of the playground. Sabonis doesn't like that.

It's kind of funny to me how a guy 7'3" who weighs almost as much as me starts crying to the officials. "Help, he's pushing," he would say in a little whiny voice. Whoever thinks they can play me, I back them down lightly. I'm going up with all my might and trying to tear the rim off.

My father always told me, "Take it to them first before they take it to you." If you take it to them first, you get them thinking first. Most guys can't think and play.

The regular-season win over Portland in February gave the Lakers the confidence we needed to pull away from the pack. By the time we had met up in the Western Conference finals, the Trail Blazers were no longer regarded as the best team in the NBA. They were the best team their owner, Paul Allen, could buy.

But they had something to prove after struggling at times the last half of the season. They were hungry. And we really had no answer for them at power forward, where Rasheed Wallace had a big advantage over A.C. Green.

A couple of guys on the team hate Portland, so they're ready by the time Game 1 rolls around. My personal assignment is to dominate Sabonis. I'm not really worried about Brian Grant, their big-brute forward off the bench. He can't hold me down.

I studied tapes of Sabonis leading up to that series and figured out a way to block his rolling hook shot in the lane. I learned how to get in the way of the skyhook. Instead of coming at him straight up and trying to block it with my right hand, which I usually do, I started to use the other hand.

When Sabonis would start to make his move, he held the ball down low. I started getting him with my left hand. I'm just step-sliding, anticipating and catching a couple of his shots. It threw him off in those early games. Plus, Phil presents a challenge: "Don't let him score," he said.

In typical Game 1 fashion, I dominate. Scored 41 points and grabbed 11 rebounds. We played well, winning 109–94. Surprisingly, I didn't get double-teamed that much, and some of my points came easy. But I knew Game 2 would be different.

Portland Coach Mike Dunleavy tried the Hack-a-Shaq defense, and I was helping the Trail Blazers. I don't know how many free throws I missed, but I missed a bunch. We had one of those un-believable droughts in the third quarter where we could not put the ball in the basket. We forgot about our inside-outside game. Every-body wanted to shoot threes, trade jumpers with the Blazers. I don't think we got an inside basket for about ten minutes.

For some reason, Phil would not call a time-out. He refused to do it. You could even hear the announcers on the side talking about it, saying, "What is Phil Jackson doing? What is he trying to prove?"

Later on, he told us he wanted us to play through it. He said this would be a good experience for us.

Some people took it as Phil playing mind games with his team. I kind of agreed with him. We got ourselves into this mess; now we had to work ourselves out of it. We had to play.

Portland pulled off a big win on our home floor, embarrassing us 106–77, and talking all kinds of trash to us on our home floor. When Phil came into the locker room, he said, "You know what? I knew this was going to happen. This is a good experience for us. We've been winning at home. Now we've got to win on the road. See you at practice tomorrow."

Giving back home-court advantage after winning that game in

February made guys angry. We went up to Portland cocky and mad. We were not going to lose Game 3.

It bothered me that I had missed some free throws. The whole season, I had spent time every night working on my free throws. It's not that I wasn't comfortable. I was trying too hard to figure out the percentages. That's why I missed. But anyway, once the Hack-a-Shaq works once, you know I'm going to see it again. (The only thing worse for basketball than that defense is the *Lack*-a-Shaq offense, where I have to go to the bench because of foul trouble. There is no fun in that.)

So, there were four days between Game 2 in L.A. and Game 3 in Portland. We didn't go straight to Portland. Instead, we practiced at our training facility in El Segundo, California, about a five-minute drive from LAX airport in an industrial part of town. We weren't tight at all, thinking maybe we were going to have problems in Portland. In fact, at the last practice before we left, guys were throwing a football in the gym. As a captain, I was thinking about saying, "Put that down, fellas. Let's get serious."

But I'm also thinking, it's basketball. We know what we have to do. "Screw it, I'm gonna be loose, too." I picked up the football and started messing around. Phil was OK with it because we had had a good practice.

Game 3 was a war. They're hitting tough shots; we're pounding it inside and trying to get our perimeter game going. The crowd at the Rose Garden is getting loud—maybe not Sacramento loud, but noisy enough where you could barely hear the referees' whistle in the final minutes. We showed big heart coming back from fourteen down in the third quarter. Ron Harper showed how cool he is under pressure. He dropped in this sweet baseline jumper in the final minute, quieting the crowd.

And then Kobe finished them off. He made a great defensive play on Sabonis, who had got by me with a pump fake. Kobe got a hand on the ball when Sabonis tried to duck inside the key and shoot a little runner.

Everybody was crying foul—especially Sabonis. But you can't get that call at that time. I'm sorry. 93–91, Good Guys.

Then, on Sunday, we took control of the series. Dunleavy was trying the Hack-a-Shaq crap again, but I wasn't having any of it. I made 9 of 9 free throws and we won, 103–91. In the two wins in Portland, I had a combined 51 points and 23 rebounds.

Doug Collins was getting carried away on NBC, saying I'd be more happy with making my foul shots "than any dunk, any score, anything that he's ever done." Let's see: I graduated from LSU in December, fathered two beautiful children, lived the life I've always wanted.

C'mon, Dougie, it wasn't that huge. I'd been working on my throws.

After destroying his Shaq-proof strategy, I'm secretly laughing at Dunleavy. I'd prepared myself for the Hack-a-Shaq and we'd taken care of business, winning both games at the Rose Garden, basically taking the life out of the Trail Blazers. Now everybody's hyped for Game 5. The Lakers are rolling, heading on a runaway train toward the finals. Indiana and New York are going at it hard in the Eastern Conference. And I just can't wait to get my paws on the Knicks' Patrick Ewing or the Pacers' Rik Smits.

Even Phil got into it. He upped the ante of the series even more by saying the Trail Blazers were "at death's door."

Now I don't know what to tell you about what happened in the next seven days. Even now, it feels like a bad dream, one big night-mare. All I can say is, Mr. Death wasn't home.

We lost Game 5 at the Staples Center, 96–88. I gave Sabonis 31 and 12, but it didn't matter. Instead of coming inside, trying to demolish these guys, our guys got cute. All year we had been playing the inside-outside game. Post up, kick it out, using all our weapons. Game 5, we tried 27 3-pointers and ruined a perfectly good chance to close the Trail Blazers out and give ourselves some rest before the finals. Afterwards, I was pissed.

A lot of conspiracy theories get thrown around by players in this league. One of them is, when NBC has a Sunday game penciled in during the playoffs, somehow, some way, you always end up playing that game. Minutes before we started Game 6 in Portland, the Indiana Pacers had already beaten New York in six games. The finals weren't supposed to start until the following Wednesday. So if we won, NBC would not have a Sunday game.

Do I think that's why we didn't get any calls in Game 6? No. But that kind of stuff makes you wonder. We played hard, we worked, and we battled. We also got fouled the hell out of and had nothing to show for it. To this day, I can't understand it. They were hacking and scratching, playing what I called their Outbreak-Rick-Pitino-monkey defense. I think Phil knew what was going on. So we just had to play through it.

Maybe we got caught up in not getting those calls, or maybe we just didn't expect Portland to have that much heart. But that night in the Rose Garden, all our worst nightmares about going home early were starting to come back to us.

Their crowd was finally getting into the game, going all crazy. Scottie had this sly smile, like he knew something you didn't. We just lost control of the series. I threw up one wild shot with my left hand, trying to be Bird or something. The damn ball went over the backboard. I wasn't being Shaq, I was trying to get cute. I should have just powered inside for a dunk.

It's virtually impossible to beat a team that good three times in a row on their home court. We couldn't do it. Portland took Game 6, 103–93. Now it's 3–3. Game 7 would be in L.A. on Sunday. So NBC got its wish: Shaq and Kobe with their backs to the wall.

Walking off the court after Game 6, I didn't feel good at all. I wasn't thinking we're going to blow the whole season, but I was remembering all those people who kept badgering me about the Lakers not having a killer instinct.

As much as I hated to admit it, they were right. It was the truth. We couldn't put the nail in the coffin.

It was time to grow up or shut up.

With all of America watching on Sunday afternoon, June 4, Bill Walton came on the NBC pregame show with Bob Costas and put me on the spot. "If Shaq doesn't do it today, everything he's accomplished this year goes up in smoke," he said. "That's what the MVP is all about."

Before the game, Phil Jackson walked into the locker room. "You guys messed around," he said. "You either win and keep going or lose and go home."

And then he walked out.

We just sat there, looking at each other, thinking about what happened and what we had to do.

The L.A. media had been going crazy, writing about how we were about to become the seventh team in NBA history to blow a 3–1 lead. You could almost imagine the headlines: *Shaq and the Lakers Choke in the Spotlight Again.*

But for all the doubts, the people of L.A. never really got down on us. I was riding around the day before the game, and some guy would just roll down his window and say, "Go get 'em." Before the light would change, another guy would pull up and say, "You gonna get Pippen and those sorry-ass Blazers tomorrow?"

"Yeah, we got 'em," I said. "Don't worry about it. We got 'em."

I don't know where those two dudes were for the first three quarters of Game 7, but they couldn't have been feeling good. Nothing was going right. Steve Smith was hitting shots from all over. Portland's playing loose, showing off. They completely took me out of my game, made sure I was double- and triple-teamed every time the ball came inside. If I tried to put the ball on the floor, they had three guys swiping at it, trying to knock it away. I couldn't find room to use my moves. All I could do was kick it out each time it came into me.

After a mediocre first half, we came out flat in the third quarter and somehow fell behind by 16 points. I don't know how it happened, but I looked up at the scoreboard, and it's 75–59.

For the first time all season, I was worried. Real worried.

I was thinking the obvious: "We're not gonna make it to the

finals. Portland is gonna beat us and laugh on our home court." It was almost the end of the third quarter and I was still in single digits. I knew I was gonna hear it. Another off-season of "Why? What happened, Shaq? You just can't win the big one."

The worst nightmare was watching Smith making unreal shots. He was just pulling up as soon as he crossed half-court.

I'm out on the court thinking, "How did everything get so bad? How did we put ourselves in a position where it could all be over?" And I wasn't alone. They might not admit it, but everybody on the team was panicking in some way. We were down, forcing shots, the crowd was booing, and we couldn't get ourselves back in the game. We needed something—anything—to wake us up.

Brian Shaw gave us a little spark when he hit a bank shot, a crazy 3-pointer at the buzzer which ended the third quarter, a shot which brought us to within 13 points.

Then it was Phil Jackson's turn. In the huddle, he poured gasoline on us and lit the match. I can't remember everything he said, but I'll give you both the R and the PG version. The part they showed on NBC was when he walked into the huddle and talked about strategy. "Forget about Shaq. If he's open, throw it in. If he's not, don't change your game just to go into him. We've got to loosen up."

There was also another message: "You fuckers play all year for this? This is what you want to do; you want to lose like that?"

Coming out of the huddle, Kobe and everybody was yelling, "Let's go. Let's go!" I felt like I needed to say something. I took a few guys aside.

"We've come too far to let this thing just end like this," I said. "Let's fight, let's scratch, let's claw, and let's play. Let's play."

We fell behind by 15 points in the first minute of the quarter, but then the game changed. Kobe ended up having a huge game, but without B. Shaw, Robert Horry and Rick Fox, we were done. Those three cats hit some of the biggest jumpers of their careers. Suddenly, it wasn't a 15-point lead anymore. We were hitting shots. We started rebounding. The crowd was getting into the game. A 13-point lead shrank to 10, then 9. And all the shots that Steve Smith and Bonzi Wells were shooting out of their asses, that stuff is not going in.

We're down 5 points. Then 3 points.

B. Shaw hits another big three, a bomb from the left baseline. With four minutes and two seconds left, the game is tied at 75–75. Portland's stunned.

Now the team is starting to play. And I'm starting to wake up. I realized that I had only 9 points, which is a disgrace. After doing all this, coming this far, one of the biggest games of my career and 9, 10 points?

Time to wake up.

Oh, no, I've got a little room, let me go to this fade away. Whap! Down by one.

Uh-oh, Shaq gets fouled. 2:44 left and—can you believe it?—he hits two important free throws. Tie game.

Then Kobe takes it up a notch. He makes two free throws with 1:34 left and then, twenty seconds later, knocks down a 16-footer. We're up by 4 points, starting to feel like this crazy comeback is gonna happen.

After 'Sheed missed two free throws with 1:25 left, we're smelling it.

What happened next, I really can't do justice in describing. All I can say is, I've never felt higher on a basketball court in my life.

During the whole game, the Portland players were collapsing on whoever drove to the middle of the key. I had been telling Kobe all game, "Yo, whenever you go to the lane, throw it up, throw it up."

He said, "All right, I got you."

So the shot clock is ticking down, and Portland needs a stop. Kobe crosses up and shakes Scottie at the top of the key. I'm lurking along the baseline, seeing what he's going to do.

Brian Grant left me to come at Kobe. Rasheed was defending the post, but he wasn't sure what to do; commit to Kobe or rotate over to me.

Scottie started to recover from getting beat off the dribble and came from behind Kobe. All of a sudden, Kobe's got three dudes on him in the lane and I'm just waiting on the right baseline—about five feet from the basket.

It was like the sea opened up or something. No one was around me. At the last second, Kobe lobs the ball up. High. Way up high. Almost behind the backboard on the right side.

I had gotten behind Rasheed and found myself taking off, going after the ball, catching the thing like a wide receiver pulls in a pass that's been thrown behind his head. In one powerful motion, I cocked that ball back with my right hand. *Wha-pah!*

The greatest dunk and highlight of my career.

By the time I came down, the noise in the building was echoing in my head. It was like I dropped out of the ceiling or something. Lakers 85. Blazers 79. Forty-one seconds left. I started running up-court like a man possessed, eyes wide open, looking crazy. I pointed to my six-month-old son, Shareef, in the stands. Now I'm hyped. I'm amped. The Portland players know it's over. You can see it in their faces. The tables just turned. We've seen the light, exorcised the demons. The Lakers are going to the NBA finals.

I had scored 9 of my 18 points in the final quarter and made 8 of 12 free throws—which is pretty damn good for me. Kobe finished with 25 points, 11 rebounds, 7 assists, and 4 blocked shots.

I remember Rick Fox saying something about "growing up and conquering demons in one twelve-minute swoop." He was right.

I started thinking back to being swept by Utah in the 1998 conference finals. I said then, "Before you succeed, you've got to fail." We knew what failure was about, and we'd almost messed it up a couple times in these play-offs. But we'd adjusted, learned our lesson, reached a point where we grew through those failures and found a way to fight through the adversity. We still didn't have the killer instinct like that 72–10 Chicago team. And even though we made the greatest fourth-quarter comeback in Western Conference finals history, we knew Portland lost that game as much as we won it.

Home court was the key. It all went back to February 29 and that regular-season game. Honestly, I don't believe we would have won Game 7 in Portland. It shows you something. People say the regular season doesn't count in the NBA, but there it is. I think that regular season game put more doubt in Portland's minds than they ever realized.

I had a little tear in my eye after we stopped celebrating. But deep down, I also knew the monkey would never be off my back until I won the whole thing. I kept returning to what I'd been saying to all my boys, saying to the organization, what I told Kobe, what I told B. Shaw: "We make it back to the finals, we're gonna go all the way."

That night I rode around L.A. and enjoyed being The Man. They had a party at Good Bar, a club on Sunset Boulevard where a lot of celebrities hang out. Everybody's congratulating me. "Yeah, dog."

I'm in the club, drinking water, I got on my bling-bling jewelry. I'm happy. I'm flexing in my Rolls-Royce, the music is going, the deejay is yelling into the microphone, "There's the man who led us to the finals and threw down that dunk."

I'm playing it off, smiling. I'm not ready to put my killer-instinct face on yet because I know we got four days left before we play Game 1 against Indiana at the Staples Center.

I remember it was warm that night, maybe 75 degrees. I drove home with the breeze hitting me in the face, thinking about how much I loved this town.

When I walked into the Staples Center before Game 1, everything was decorated. They put special logos on the floor. They put them on your jerseys. "NBA Finals 2000." It's a basketball series, but it also feels like this big party that everyone in the world is invited to. Guess who hosted in 2000? Shaq Daddy.

With Reggie Miller saying Indiana was going to "shock the world," a lot of the hype around the finals came down to Hoosiers against Hollywood. NBC was taking that to the bank. I prepared as usual, got and studied my Rik Smits tape. I already knew Rik feared me because I dominated him in the Eastern Conference finals in

1995. (See, before I became the "Great Test of the West," I was the "Beast of the East.") But I don't want to disrespect Rik's game. So I check out what he's doing.

Rik is 7'4" and knows how to score. He takes you outside for that jumper, pulls you away from the basket. Phil was worried about that, so he puts A.C. on him, which was a good move. A.C. sticks him. He fronts Rik because he knows Rik has bad hands.

I'm guarding Dale Davis, and I'm not really worried; I know his game.

The Pacers meanwhile have decided they don't want to double-team me. By now, they should know better. Cats don't double me, I'm pulling out 33 moves on each block. So, usual Game 1. I go to work. I do what I do. They're trying the Hack-a-Shaq at the end, but I shut them up. I have 11 points in the first quarter. Reggie's struggling, can't hit a shot. He ends up making just 1 of 16. In the second half, Indiana's trying to come back. With the Pacers down by 2, Reggie goes baseline for a strong move. I catch his shot and send it back to the floor. We end up blowing them out, 104–87.

I had 43 points and 19 rebounds. I had made 21 of 31 shots.

Here and now, all these months later, I still can't believe the Pacers didn't use more than one player to guard me. After the game, someone asked how would I defend against myself. "I wouldn't," I said. "I would just home. I would fake an injury or something."

My father had flown in from Orlando before the series started. Between Games 1 and 2, we sat and talked, although there wasn't a lot of conversation. Phil's message was simple: "You're here again, dominate. You know what you got to do." He knew I was ready to go. He saw it in my eye.

In Game 2, the Combo was clicking. Kobe and I were playing well together. Then, with less than four minutes remaining in the first quarter, we had some real misfortune. Kobe was on the right wing, going for a jumper. Jalen Rose was guarding him. Kobe came down on Jalen's ankle and had to be helped off. The arena held its breath.

Now, I knew we needed Kobe to win the title, but playing without him was something we were used to. Remember, we started the season without him and went 12–3. And once again, we showed our depth. Glen started dropping in 3-pointers. He made 5 of 6. Everybody was stepping up. In the second half, Larry Bird paid me the ultimate compliment: knowing he couldn't stop me inside, the Hack-a-Shaq was back.

I ended up taking a finals-record 39 free throws. I missed a few. OK, I missed 21. But I made most of the important ones down the stretch, including 9 of 16 in the fourth quarter.

The game turned into a marathon. Reggie started to find his stroke. All of a sudden, it was a close marathon. Lakers 99, Pacers 96, less than a minute left. I got the ball in the middle of the lane. Before Sam Perkins could foul me, I turned and spotted Robert Horry cutting under the basket. I passed the rock to Horry and he made a nice reverse layup, and got fouled to boot. After he made the free throw, it was 102–96, Good Guys, with 58.8 seconds left.

I started motioning for the crowd to stand. We were about to go up 2–0 on our home floor.

I finished with 40 points, 24 rebounds, 4 assists and 3 blocked shots. I could have had 61 if I made my free throws.

Now it's off to boring Indiana for the next three games.

We stayed in a hotel about forty minutes away from downtown. Phil was very clear about what he wanted from us. "We need one or two games there," he said. "After we get one, then we can talk about getting two; but we need to win one game there. I don't care what game it is, you win one game."

The Conseco Fieldhouse, the new home of the Pacers, looks like an overgrown high-school gym. Old red brick. Yellow, faded newspaper clippings hanging on the wall. Trophy cases with jerseys of Oscar Robertson and John Wooden. Actually, that was planned. They built the Conseco like the arena from the last scene of the movie from *Hoosiers,* when that little white dude from the 1950s hit the shot to win the championship. You walk into that place, and it's like going back in time. They start the pregame introductions with all this history about Indiana basketball. Then the screen goes black and all you see is one sentence: "In 49 other states, it's basketball," followed by, "but this is Indiana."

I've been to a lot of arenas with a lot of crazy pregame shows. But that one gave me goose bumps. Their crowd wasn't as loud as Sacramento's, but they made noise. Especially after their team went up 18 points on us in Game 3.

Kobe wanted to play, but he couldn't play because of his sprained ankle. The Lakers medical staff wanted to rest him up, get ready for Game 4. Reggie and Jalen Rose were going off. Hitting jumpers, leading the fast break. We just let down and started forcing the ball inside. I got 33 and 13, but the only numbers that mattered were Indiana 100, Lakers 91. Austin Croshere, some fundamental cat we'd hardly heard of before he started busting our asses, was just killing us with jumpers and strong drives.

We're not panicking though. Phil reminds us, starts stressing, "All right, two games left. We need either one of these games or both of them. But we have to get one."

Leading up to Game 4, there's only one question on everyone's mind: Will Kobe play? He basically answered the question during the morning shoot-around with reporters. "Is there any circumstance under which you might not take the court tonight?" someone asked.

Kobe looked at all the people sitting in front of him real cool. "Any snipers in the room?" he said.

Uh-oh, the Big Little Brother is suiting up.

Now, I'm a big fan of Classic Sports. I'll watch any old game from the past, especially a finals game that goes back and forth between Magic and Bird. When I retire, I expect to see Game 4 of the 2000 finals on Classic Sports. This game was like two kids hitting each other in a pillow fight, until one gets woozy and drops. Except no one dropped. There were ten lead changes in the fourth quarter alone. Reggie was pulling threes out of you-know-where. I was drop-stepping inside, powering my way around Smits and Dale Davis or spinning and hitting my jumper. Kobe started slowly, but he didn't end that way.

We were leading by 3 points with less than a minute left when Sam Perkins hit a bomb on the right baseline to tie the game. We both had chances to win in regulation. I came out on Indiana's tiny point guard, Travis Best, on the Pacers' last possession. He ended up shooting an air ball. Then I missed a sky hook right of the free-throw line at the buzzer. It was tied 104–104. We were going to OT. I had gotten some stupid fouls early in the game and went over Rik's back in the opening minutes of the extra period. As I walked off the court, I could hear the Pacers' radio announcers: "And Shaq is gone!"

Up to that point, I had scored 152 points and grabbed 77 rebounds in the series. I don't think we're going to automatically lose the game, but I am a little worried. Then I felt this little tap on my butt. I turned around. It was Kobe.

"Don't worry about it," he said. "I got you, big dog."

Did he just say what I heard him say? Kobe wants this game. He wasn't a kid anymore. He was the man. And he had an amazing game. He scored 8 of his 28 points in overtime, crossing up Mark Jackson and hitting jumpers. Every time Indiana cut the lead to 1 point, Kobe would keep it at 3 points with some clutch shot. In the final seconds, B. Shaw drove the lane and missed a runner. But there was Kobe, swooping in under the hoop and putting back a reverse layup all in one motion with 5.8 seconds to go.

And after Robert Horry got his hand in Reggie Miller's face on the final shot, a 3-pointer that missed, we had an unreal 120–118 win. Kobe raised his arms up and I came over to hug him and tell him how proud I was of him. We were one game from the championship, all because Kobe Bryant wanted that game more than anyone.

Kobe said afterward that was the game he had always dreamed about as a little kid. That's what having a great one-two punch is about. If Shaq can't do it, then the other guy steps up and does it.

Back in the Laker days, if Magic didn't show up, then Kareem would show up. We were following tradition.

I watched Game 4 again over the summer, and I saw this one jumper Kobe made. He arched his wrist back in a follow-through motion and started back-pedaling, his tongue hanging just a little bit out of his mouth. Now, I've always hated comparisons with other players. But when I saw that, I had only one thought.

This cat looks just like Mike. Just like him.

So we're up three games to one, and we did what Phil wanted: got one game in Indiana. Everybody was talking about the series being over, but they forgot about one thing: Ten days earlier, we were playing Game 7 against Portland. We had them down 3–1, too.

And now the Glen Rice story starts heating up, causing a little distraction.

After his wife came out and killed Phil for not playing him and having a personal vendetta against him, we're taking the bus back from practice and everybody is whispering, "What's wrong with his wife?" It's really trippy because Glen is in a contract year, and now GMs around the league are probably thinking they don't want to deal with Mrs. Rice. I mean, guys are saying, "Yo, he must not want that money. She's costing him every time she opens up her mouth."

Glen was mad at the hotel, so nobody said nothing to him.

Finally, the next day, Phil went in front of the team.

"Enough," he said. "I'm not going back and forth. All we need is one game."

I eventually went up to Glen. "Listen, just play one game, and then after you get that ring, then they'll either have to pay you or you can go somewhere else," I said. "But it won't matter; you'll have the ring. Don't even worry about it, brother."

I'm trying to be sympathetic, telling him, "I know they're not treating you right. I know they don't call your plays. I know they don't think you can play defense. But listen, all we need is one more game. You'll have a ring, you'll be in history, be known as one of the greatest shooters."

Glen shook his head. "All right, all right," he said. "Whatever."

The Glen Rice controversy is not why we lost Game 5.

Larry Bird had only one more loss left and he was stepping down after three seasons as the Pacers' coach. I could tell the Pacers wanted that game for Larry, and knew Indiana was gonna come out strong. Also, Reggie had some good games in the series, but he really hadn't woke up yet.

He did that night.

They made their first six 3-pointers, and we ended up getting drug like a dog, losing 120–87. It was our worst loss of the year. Not that I wanted to lose that game, but when I think back, I'm glad the Pacers didn't go out with losing the championship on their home court. Because I like Larry. It just wouldn't be right if Coach Bird lost his last game in Indiana. I wasn't thinking about that at the time. But when I look back, I'm kind of glad they showed up that strong for Larry in the last home game of the season. Maybe that's corny, but it's how I feel.

And remember, all Phil was saying was we needed one or two. So on the plane, guys were upset that we got beat by 33 points. Their attitude was, "We gonna win it at home."

Game 5 was on a Friday and Game 6 was not scheduled until Monday. We didn't even have a regular practice. We watched tape and, with two chances at home to win a title, talked about the golden opportunity.

Phil ended the last practice by looking each one of us in the eye. "OK, this is the dream we've been waiting for," he said. "Let's go do it."

The Lakers were about to play their 105th game of the season. From October 1, 1999 to June 19, 2000, I had just completed my longest and hardest season of basketball. I tried to block out everything and focus on getting my beat-up body ready for Game 6. Shen fixed me up with some acupuncture. The team masseuse worked my muscles. I did a lot of stretching and drank a lot of water. I also blocked out anybody who called for tickets or favors. I had one thing on my mind.

From the night we beat Portland in February, we were considered the NBA's best team. But it took a lot of work to get there and even more work to stay there. The play-offs told us something about ourselves. Yeah, we showed heart, blowing out Sacramento in Game 5, coming back against Portland in Game 7, and winning Game 4 in Indiana with me on the bench in overtime. But we also didn't have a killer instinct and could go to sleep on teams before a series was over. Going into Game 6, we were 14–8 in the play-offs. In two months, we'd lost more than half as many as we had during the whole, six-month regular season, when we'd gone 67–15.

We might have gone into the play-offs as big-time favorites, but everybody tried to make history against us. People knew we were definitely beatable. It wasn't like that cakewalk San Antonio went through the year before, when they went 15–2 during the lockout play-offs.

By the time everyone arrived to the Staples Center on that Monday night, the chatter had already started in the locker room. "Yo, let's not play with these guys and turn this into another Portland."

My teammates and me came to the arena mad at ourselves. It was time to stop getting cute, thinking we got a cushion and playing around. We couldn't give this team any more life.

Another part of me was nervous and scared. I think I'd only worried about really losing once, when we were about to lose Game 7 to Portland. But this was a different kind of nervousness—being one game away from everything I'd ever wanted as a player.

I wasn't sure things were going to go our way after the first quarter. We weren't playing bad, but Reggie and Jalen were making shots, Croshere and old Sam Perkins were making shots off the bench and it looked like the Pacers were getting bounces.

When Mark Jackson, who's an ordained minister, made a half-court shot to put Indiana up 26–24 after a quarter, I had to scratch my head. We were playing OK, but were down by 3 points at halftime. I thought we might be in trouble. Indiana was making everything. The Lakers had to fight just to stay close in the third quarter, when we went down by 8 points. Going into the fourth we were down 5 points.

But then the game turned.

Like I've always said, what's hot must go cold. Indiana starting missing and we started making. Derrick McKey and Austin Croshere both tried to stop me from getting a layup in the opening minutes of the fourth quarter, grabbing and banging me until I fell to the ground.

But before I went down, I put in a little running floater that gave us our first lead since the last second of the first quarter. Rick Fox stepped up, too. He dropped in a 3-pointer from the left wing with less than nine minutes left, giving us a 4-point lead. Counting that shot, we'd scored the last nine times down the floor.

The Staples Center was starting to get loud, louder than I ever remember. We were up by 7 points midway through the fourth and everyone was starting to feel like we were closing in on a championship. Everyone except Reggie and his boys.

Those cats would not quit. Croshere started knocking down jumpers, hustling. Reggie was all over the place, hitting jumpers and swiping at loose balls. And Jalen Rose gave us something to think about when he knocked down a 3-pointer from the right baseline in front of our bench with 5 minutes left. That shot tied the game and made Phil call a time-out.

I don't remember what was said. I don't even remember if Phil was calm or angry or what. I just remember a feeling. It wasn't like who was going to get the ball, Kobe or Shaq. It wasn't about important strategy. It was about getting the ball in the basket by any means necessary. And it didn't matter how much money a superstar made or how little a role player made; we were going to have to do this together or go down hard.

Of course, I got the ball the next few times down the floor. ☺

Kobe fed me on a fast break and I hit a running layup, got fouled and made the free throw. Uh-oh. Turnaround jumper from the left baseline. Whap! Kobe started heating up, too, making jumpers, pushing his hands to the floor like he was applying pressure.

Rick and Robert Horry were tough, hitting crucial jumpers. The guy I once thought was a sorry-ass role player in Houston (when we met them in 1995 finals) ended up scoring 8 points in the fourth quarter. B. Shaw made some big shots, too.

We're getting close now. About two minutes left and we've got a 3-point lead. On the scoreboard in the arena during a time-out, they showed footage of about a million people outside, waiting to celebrate and go crazy.

We were looking up and getting excited. I called a huddle.

I said, "You see that? Let's go out and win and start playing. Now."

Kobe said, "I got this, I got this. Give me the ball. I got this."

With about 1:20 left, I see David Stern, the NBA commissioner, walking down the stairs toward the floor. I see guys getting the banner. The security guards are holding a rope to keep people from coming onto the floor. They were getting ready for the trophy presentation. For some reason, we start panicking.

"What are they doing?" Robert said.

"Shut up and play," I told him.

I saw Mark Jackson go over to Reggie Miller, trying to get him pumped up.

"You see that? They think they're gonna win. Let's do this."

I don't know if that had anything to do with what happened in the next minute, but it was some coincidence. Down by 3 points and with about 30 seconds left, Reggie is crossing half-court with the ball, and he isn't looking at nothing but the rim. He is cocky.

Of all the players in the league with the game on the line, I think I still fear that dude the most. I can remember being with my cousin Andre one summer, watching a New York-Indiana play-off series. The Knicks were about to win, and we're about to turn the TV off. That dude scored 8 points in the last 19 seconds, pulled out a miracle win at the Garden. He made me choke on a chicken bone that day. I'm serious.

So I always feared him in the clutch. He had just made a big 3-pointer. And now he had that look in his eye, like he wanted to tie the game. He wasn't even close to the 3-point line when he pulled up on the left side. From about 30 feet away, he let go of a bomb.

Too deep. It came out—we got the rebound.

If he would have hit that shot, I think it would have changed the series. I was like, "Phew."

Kobe made four free throws in the final 13 seconds, making the score 116–111. Now we're starting to believe. It's going to happen. I've got little tears in my eyes. I'm trying to hold it in because we're still up only 5 points, but I can feel it. I'm close to winning.

Five . . . four . . . three . . . Reggie takes a shot at the buzzer . . . off the rim. Two . . . one . . .

Purple-and-gold confetti started coming out of the ceiling. Fireworks exploding, people rushing the court like a concert. The next thing I remember was Kobe jumping into my arms and me just holding him up for a few seconds. He then ran over to the press table, jumped up, and started pumping his fists. The whole building is standing and roaring.

My cousin Andre was running onto the court, choking me. The cops were trying to arrest him. I'm trying to tell the cops, "No, he's cool, he's cool."

My boys had told me after I won that they were going to tackle me. Well, they weren't joking. My mother came out to center court. My daughter Taahirah was there. I went over and kissed her and she kissed me back.

By the time I was hugging Glen Rice, tears were just coming down my cheeks. I couldn't keep it in anymore. I was crying in front of the world.

Like I told you already, it wasn't a sad cry or a joyful cry. If I could have found every one of my critics and said, "Now what?" I probably would have. I had that much vindictiveness in me at that moment. "Now what you gonna say?" That was what that was about. Peter Vecsey, Doug Collins, the Hack-a-Shaq inventors, everyone.

I'm not saying I didn't enjoy the moment with my teammates and family and friends, but what I'm saying is, my tears had nothing to do with joy.

I had been in the league eight years. This was the moment I waited for. Growing up, watching Larry and Magic and Michael celebrating, to see Hakeem and Robert Horry celebrating in 1995 when I was with Orlando, I wanted my moment.

I'd held my emotions in for eleven years. Three years in college and eight in the pros. I've always wanted to win. Now it just came out.

I had 41 points and 12 rebounds in that final game, the third time I scored 40 or more points in the finals. My averages of 38 points and 21 rebounds helped me get the MVP award for the series. I didn't think about it until later, but I'd won the triple crown. MVP of the regular season, All-Star Game and the finals.

It was a hard-fought game. Indiana didn't give up. They brought the best out in us. Some people said it was one of the better series they had seen in a while. In his last game, Larry Bird gave me some more props, which in my book, added to his legend. "He was just too much for us," he said about me. "Shaq was awesome the whole series. He's the most dominating player in our league."

Then things settled down on the court, and they brought the little podium out for us to stand on and receive the trophy from Stern. My mom joined me right in the middle of my teammates. We all had our championship T-shirts and hats on.

NBC's Ahmad Rashad gave me the microphone. "I want to thank you all for believing in us," I told the crowd. "We're going to get one next year, too." They roared again.

All this dream-season stuff sank in more after we left the court. I ran into the locker room and dudes were spraying people with champagne. It was burning my pores. We started jumping up and down like little kids, singing that song, "Y'all goin' make me lose my mind, Up in here, Up in there."

This summer, I was watching a video of our season. Rick Fox was interviewed. He said something about all the time we were criticized and maligned for not being mature enough to fight through adversity, using all these big words I never use. He said when you fail as a group, there's no better way to celebrate than with those you fought with, for the same common goal.

The last thing Rick said? "All the pain washes away with a championship."

The whole time he was talking, I was nodding my head.

It was just so crazy in the locker room, everyone spraying champagne and shouting and hugging. I wanted a few minutes to myself so I could cry and think about things. But the NBA wanted to take advantage of marketing opportunities. Andy Bernstein, one of the league photographers who I trust the most, sat me and Kobe down next to the ball and the trophy.

I had two gold balls next to me; the MVP trophy and the championship trophy.

"Congratulations, you deserve it, big guy," Phil Jackson said when he hugged me.

Earlier in the year, I remember him saying, "The reason why I came out of retirement is because I like you guys and I got tired of seeing you guys lose. That's why I took this job." I don't know why, but I remembered him saying that the night we won.

It was the Lakers' seventh championship and the first since the Showtime days of Magic, Kareem and Worthy in 1988. Magic, who's now a part owner of the Lakers, took pictures with me and Kobe. He said, "We did it. We did it. Get a look at the next dynasty."

Then Kobe and I had a few minutes where it was just me and him. Like I said, after the birthday game in March, we became real tight. That was good 'cause Big Brother and Little Brother finally did it.

I'm sure he's been wanting a championship. His father never got one when he played in the league. I'm sure he's been wanting it just as much as I've been wanting it. We were happy.

"Thanks, big dog," he said.

"Thank *you*," I told Kobe.

We were a historical one-two punch now. We're always linked by history and all that on paper, but that doesn't count. With a title, now we know we're historical.

"Finally got one," I said, sitting there with both trophies, completely exhausted. "Finally got one."

Then Dale Brown came out there and gave me a hug. I was pretty excited to see my college coach. After encouraging me to go pro because I kept getting fouled so much, he was one of the few people who understood all the emotions I was feeling.

"Finally, all those guys that criticized you, now they can't say anything," he said. "I know how hard you worked. You used to come to my house at night and get the key to the gym and go work on your game when you couldn't get into the clubs. They never appreciated you enough. Now they finally show you some respect and appreciation."

I turned around to thank him some more, and he was gone. Dale is like that. One minute he's there, the next he's like a ghost.

Will Smith and Jack Nicholson congratulated me. Larry Bird, too. That made the championship even more meaningful.

Snoop Doggy Dog came in the locker room, cursing, probably drunk. "We did it," he said. "We did it."

That's L.A. for you.

By now, the champagne was really burning my pores and the cigar smoke was burning my eyes. Because of all the press conferences and picture taking, it took us two hours to get out of the arena.

I didn't even see the rioting outside that ended up with two LAPD cars burned and turned over.

I walked out of the arena and one of officers says, "All right, we gonna give you an escort to the highway." As I walked out of the Staples Center with my family and friends, I just had one thought:

"Damn, that was fun!"

I got home way past midnight. No one was there. It was just me and Thomas, my chef. I was full of adrenaline, couldn't sleep. I watched TV all night. ESPN. CNN. Nba.com. I probably saw the highlights a hundred different times, over and over. I still couldn't sleep.

Thomas woke up at 4:30, 5:00 in the morning. He looks at me like, "What are you doing?"

"Can't sleep."

"You hungry?"

Got to love having a personal chef who wakes up at 4:30 in the morning.

Thomas made me some prime rib and a Shaq Daddy sandwich. It's like a po' boy sandwich from Louisiana, but with my own little touches. Fried shrimp, mayonnaise, ketchup, and cheese. I'm getting hungry just talking about it. By that time, I had taken all the ginseng I could handle. I wanted real food.

Leonard called me the next day about all the shows and media people who wanted me as a guest.

"OK," I said. "You got ten days, I'll do whatever you want for ten days. I'm tired and beat up as hell. After that, I go on vacation."

I told Leonard, in the immortal words of Tom Cruise in *Mission Impossible 2,* "I'm going on vacation. If I tell you where I'm going, then it won't be a vacation."

After those ten days were over, I took my boys to Las Vegas. That was my present to everyone. I gave them $10,000 each to gamble. Some won; some lost. We partied all night. I'm staying up so late, I'm starting to get headaches.

Enough already. The party is over. I got to go back to Orlando, chill and recharge my batteries. Do some hunting, ride around on my motorcycle and Sea-Doo. Get away for a while.

My last memory before I left L.A. was the day we had the championship parade. Before all the festivities began, I had to pay a little visit to the LAPD.

First, I called up my accountant, Lester.

"Look, Lester, you're probably going to get a little upset, but I just committed $42,000 to buy a new police car, for the two that were damaged in the riot," I said.

Lester said, "Why are you doing that? The police department, the city and the county have a lot of money. You don't need to do that. Why don't the Lakers do that?"

I stopped him. "Lester, trust me. Between the goodwill that's going to come out of it by me doing it, the amount of publicity that I'm going to get that you couldn't pay for, trust me; this is the best $42,000 we'll spend this summer."

The Lakers were embarrassed into picking up the second car. They felt they had to buy it. By the time I made the decision, Lester had been listening to the radio and TV all day, hearing about, "Isn't Shaq a great guy?"

He called me up. "This was an ingenious move," he said.

Thank you.

I could have gone anywhere and asked for help. I could have gone to Pepsi, I could have even gone to Bill Gates and said, "Listen, why don't you throw in one of them new navigational things?"

But it was something that had to be done quickly. I had the money, and I've always had respect for the police. So it made sense.

After I presented the checks, I showed up for the parade. At first, I was a little disappointed. There were only 1,000 people hanging around. But then the guy told me to get on the bus—and everything changed.

I saw at least a million people on our way to the park. When I got up on the podium to speak, I felt like I was in the movie *The Warriors*.

(FYI: *The Warriors* was this great teen gang movie that took place in New York. Cyrus was the leader of this one gang, the Warriors. In one scene where all the gangs meet up in Central Park, he looks out over everyone and says real loud, "Can you dig it? Can-you-dig-it?")

So in a real, loud baritone voice, I yelled to the crowd, "Can you dig it? Can you dig it?"

A lot of cats didn't know what I was talking about, but the homeboys knew, because afterwards I went to a club and some cat came up to me, said, "You crazy, man. You did that stuff from *The Warriors*."

Everything about the parade was beautiful. A beautiful day. Perfect setting.

When I looked out on the crowd, all of a sudden it hit me: We were champions.

Time Out

Shaqfari

Thomas Gosney
Orlando, Florida
August 14, 2000

We got off the helicopter early this morning. It was Shaq, me, Joe Cav-allero, his personal assistant in Florida and his high-school point guard, Charlie Muff, Shaq's friend who works with his T.W.I.S.M. clothing line, and some dude from New York.

The boss, dressed in heavy jeans, a vest and boots, was taking us all hunting for a day on a private game reserve in Frostproof, Florida. We called up some private helicopter company to take us out there. Our pilot was a former tail-gunner in Vietnam. Seeing Shaq fit his body into this little cockpit area was pretty damn funny. When the helicopter took off and we started whizzing along the Florida Everglades, he got on the headset and started humming the theme song from Magnum, P.I.

"This is agent Double-Double 34," Shaq was saying. "We've got a situation here. We're taking off to investigate."

You might say my boss is a big kid. In fact, the nickname his friends gave him is "Big." I never much thought about it, but it kind of fits. Like the movie starring Tom Hanks, he just won't grow up.

After about a forty-minute flight to the hunting lodge in the middle of nowhere, Shaq gets out and meets our hosts. Now, just imagine the scene: a 7'1", 330-pound black man walking out of this teeny helicopter to meet these hunting-lodge guys from Florida's outback—everyone decked out in their camouflage and baseball caps.

"Nice to meet ya, Shaq," one of the guides said. "Damn, son, you are a big un'."

It was like Newark meets Hee-Haw. Funny as hell. Or as Shaq said, "Imagine a guy from the projects ending up down here. Pretty frickin' amazing."

As soon as he got there, he was making jokes. He walked into the lodge and noticed all the photos on the wall were of white people. "I might be the first brother here," Shaq said. "Ever."

After he went and took some target practice, he said, "I can see the headlines tomorrow: Shaq Accidentally Shoots Himself, Forced to Retire. Goes out with a Bang." He called this big jeep we took out into the woods the "Homeboy Hunter's Delight." He wanted to put rims on it and insert a sound system.

A few hours went by before Shaq found a trophy red stag. After going through the brush and the forest, he finally took aim and fired. The deer wasn't dead, and the hunting guide asked if Shaq wanted him to put him out of his misery, to make what hunters call a "clean kill."

Shaq said "No," and said he would do it.

All of a sudden, he takes off his jacket. It was like the scene in The Matrix when the security guards ask Keanu Reeves if he's got any metal on him when the detector goes off. In The Matrix, Keanu opens up his trench coat and has about five guns. Well, Shaq only had one strapped to him, but it was this huge gold-plated handgun called a Desert Eagle. Weighs about 20 pounds. When the guides saw it, their mouths about hit the ground.

"Hell, Shaq, I didn't know you had that there goldfinger," one of the guides said.

Another went, "That must be your homeboy special."

Some people might be disturbed in knowing the best player in the game today hunts animals. But Shaq quickly put the animal out of its misery.

He's the most conscientious hunter I've known. The PETA group, the People for Ethical Treatment of Animals, won't take much stock in that. But it's true.

He's never hunted on a wildlife preserve or ever shot an animal out of season. If he hunts on a private game preserve, he always pays for any animal he has taken. The hunting clubs Shaq goes to are not simple target practice. Sometimes you spend days looking for a buffalo. He'll go through weeds and bushes, whatever he has to do to find the animal. Shaq also won't hunt unless he knows there is an arrangement between the hunting club and a local charity to donate the meat to the charity.

Any real hunter will tell you: You don't go out in the woods to get out your aggressions and empty a round on a helpless animal. It's not the killing aspect as much as being with nature, enjoying beautiful animals and, yes, respecting the animals. We hunt only specific ones at specific times. We don't sit there and hunt deer in the summertime. We hunt them only after they've mated and only if the populations are high in a certain area and hunting is approved. Just like the bears in Yellowstone, Montana, have to be controlled to balance ecology, deer populations have to be also be controlled. The best part for Shaq is that when he gets out in nature, nobody cares about the basketball game, how many points he scores. He's just another person enjoying the outdoors.

Joe and I got him into hunting about two years ago. Karl Malone always used to brag about hunting—Karl has hunted in Alaska—and Shaq finally got curious.

One day he went boar hunting with Joe. He was just sitting by the cornfield, waiting for the wind and all of a sudden he heard this rumbling in the bushes. That's all it took. He was hooked.

As he told me once, "Hunting is not about being aggressive. It's about sitting, relaxing, concentrating, aiming at the thing. I'm not out there trying to shoot up the woods. I'm just out there sitting, chillin', just looking at the nature. I'll be looking at the 'gators, at the birds and then all of a sudden, a buffalo shows up. And I'm like, "Let's get him."

Shaq would never endanger a species.

Shaq is a proud pet owner. He loves dogs and currently has two in Los Angeles, a rottweiler and a pit-bull mutt. A few years ago, in Orlando, he was very attached to a pit bull named Die Hard. One morning he let the dogs out early. When Die Hard didn't come back, he wondered what had happened. Joe found him later, bitten in half by an alligator. Shaq probably could have taken out a few 'gators behind his house, but he thought better of it. He had Die Hard cremated and put into an urn. The dog's ashes rest on a shelf in his Orlando home.

When someone once asked why he likes to hunt, Shaq said, "I'm real. I'm an adult. When my kids get older, if they want to hunt I'll tell them, 'Sure, son, you can hunt. These are the rules. You follow them. Take the gun course. Learn safety. Be respectful of the outdoors.' "

But, again, the animal-interest groups are going to read this and be upset. My boss is who he is. The day he hired me away from the Hyatt hotel chain to be his personal chef was one of the best days of my life.

It's been a great job, cooking for a big kid. Everywhere he goes, he touches people. He smiles and everybody else smiles with him. I could tell you so many stories, but one of my favorites actually involves hunting. Three days after he won the championship, we went hunting sheep on a private ranch outside of Riverside, California. Besides getting a few wild boars, Shaq also got a very rare breed of goat, called a Barbados four-horned goat. Two of the horns actually turned inward toward the goat's cheekbones, so it looks almost frightening.

This goat is a freak of nature. The Latinos are very superstitious about it. It's almost part of their religion. They actually refer to it as "The Goat of the Devil" or "Devil Goat." They won't go near it.

So Shaq goes out, gets a boar, and all of a sudden sees the Barbados four-horned goat. He shoots and kills the thing. On the way back to the lodge, where the Hispanic men are waiting to clean the animals, Shaq jumps in the back of the pickup truck. He stands up and holds up the goat.

Remember when Arnold Schwarzenegger held up James Earl Jones's head in Conan the Barbarian? That's what it looked like. Or maybe Medusa. Anyway, he holds it up in the air like he's performing some ceremony and yells real loud, "Behold, I have killed the Devil Goat. Me, Shaq, I have killed the Devil Goat. You are all free."

Every one of those guys started bowing down, saying, "Viva Shaq! Viva Shaq! Oh, Shaq, he killed the goat of the devil."

That was the best.

Shaq killed the devil goat, so they were all free.

(Note: By the way, no animals were harmed in the writing of this book.)

12

The Future

Two months after we won the championship, some of my friends and family were at my house in Orlando. I popped the tape of Game 6 into the VCR. With everyone watching, I did my own commentary and made fun of certain people. But when the game went into the fourth quarter, I started getting into it again. The feelings I had from that final night were still inside me.

About thirty seconds before the buzzer went off, I just took the tape out and walked out of the living room. Everyone sitting around went, "What are you doing? Here comes the best part."

Maybe I didn't want my friends to see me crying on the screen, not with me watching right there. Maybe I was worried about crying again. All I know is, I've been programmed to deal with a lot of things in life. But my emotions aren't one of them.

I took the tape into my office and hid it under my couch.

No sense in reliving the past, I figured. After all, I had another season to get in shape for, another season of great expectations. I can always look at that tape after I retire.

When people asked me if I have proved something by winning a title, I usually say, "Somewhat."

In this world we live in, in order for me to get my true respect as a great big man, I probably have to outdo all the other big men. Kareem has what, five rings? Magic has five? Jordan has six. In order for me to have my name mentioned in the presence of those guys, they'll probably expect me to win a couple more titles. Which is cool.

Before you can get two, you've got to get one, and at least I've got one. I can tell you this: I'm gonna be trying to get two, three, four and five if I can. I'm not gonna stop now. I'm gonna keep my hunger and desire. I'm not gonna start shooting jumpers. I'm still gonna be the same 'bow-in-the-throat me until I can't do it anymore.

Because if you change what made you successful, everything will go wrong. I can't do that. I've never been about that. For example, Leonard called me last summer and said, "They want you to be on the Sydney Olympic team. You don't even have to practice."

I couldn't go to the Olympics like that. We would lose.

The night I cried, I let go of a lot of the rage inside me. All the bad feelings I had toward the people who told me I couldn't do it sort of melted away.

I'm not about making people eat their words or bow down in front of me because they were wrong about the person and the player they thought I was. But they should know that I'm not a quitter. I never quit. I owe that to my family background. Even though I'm from Newark, at heart I'm a military child.

Losing made me hungry, and I had to persevere. The more I lost in the play-offs, the more I appreciated winning a championship. Everything happens for a reason. Everything just fell in place. We were on a mission. The year 2000. Huh? The millennium. Yeah, it was my turn. It's déjà vu, too, because the Lakers won in 1990, right? Ten years later.

(Oh, wait. The Bulls won in '90? All right, Phil won in '90, and he won in 2000. It's still déjà vu. Just a different vu.)

Everyone remembers Showtime. I knew they had great tradition and great history. And I knew when I came to L.A., I would have big shoes to fill. To have my name mentioned someday in the same breath as a Jerry West, Magic, Chamberlain, Kareem, Worthy, would be an honor. When it's all said and done, I want to have won a couple of rings and I want my jersey hanging up there in the rafters. Getting my jersey retired would be nice.

I'm sure that in 2030, if the NBA is still going on, some kid will be at his first basketball game, and he'll see those jerseys. "Daddy, who was West?"

"A white boy who was cold," his father will say.

"Who was Kareem?"

"Skyhook, Muslim brother."

"Who was Magic?"

"He was the first big guy to bring the ball up the court like that. You see how that guy's 7'2", he's running the point, calling plays, shooting threes? He's nothing. Magic did that."

"Who was Wilt?"

"Wilt was like the first big, mean guy. Real big. Strong. Once scored 100 points in a game."

"Daddy, who was Shaq?"

"Well, son, after Wilt played, you know, there was a lot of . . . Then Shaq. Shaq was sort of like Wilt. He did a lot of things. He scored 70 points in a game twice. One time he did it on his birthday. Then, the next year, he came back and did it again. Great player, him and this young guy named Kobe.

"Oh, there's Kobe, right there. He's kind of old now. He's about fifty-two. But in his day . . ."

The dad will buy the kid a program, and that's how he'll learn about history.

When I first got to L.A., I didn't know who Gail Goodrich was. Never heard of him. Then I started watching his highlights. He was all right. Yeah, Gail had a nice game.

I would give kids advice, but I just turned twenty-nine. A lot of people would say that's too young to be writing about yourself, that you should live a little more. But as you've seen in these pages, I've seen a lot, done a lot, and been through a lot.

I will say this: Nobody wanted a championship more than me.

I've been getting bashed for eight years. I fell down for eight years. One of those years, I fell so bad it was embarrassing, got swept in the finals, four and out.

Sometimes I still think I'm bitter about the people who got on me when I was young and immature and finding my way. Even now, I ask my friends about all the people saying, "Hey, congratulations. Glad you brought it back to L.A., I love you. You're the best."

I wonder if we would have lost what those people would say. I mean, I know what they would say.

"Hit a damn free throw."

Maybe I should put that aside. As I get older, I'm less hung up on it. But I still think about that stuff.

I just never understood why people have to knock young players so much. When you are told how great you're going to be one minute, and then people start to turn on you, it throws a wrench in your world. I've seen a lot of people in my position get stressed out, depressed, start doing drugs, start acting crazy and turning on family members. That wasn't me.

I guess part of the reason I got killed all the time was because my popularity came before I achieved anything in the league. Before I even got to the NBA, I was Reebok's answer to Jordan and Nike. When Mike left the game after my second year, everyone started looking at me to sell the product. The endorsement deals, the movies and the albums, those were supposed to be for someone who won a title. I never looked at it like that. I was just a kid in his early twenties, trying to enjoy life while working and earning a living at the same time. I wanted to try it all. Everything was new. I tried to listen to so many people.

I still don't understand why you have to win it all to be considered doing your job in sports. The guys on the other twenty-eight teams are losers? I'm sorry. That's not right. And until we get more perspective and understand that, you're going to have a lot more young kids wondering why everyone is criticizing and not allowing them time to grow up and learn to be a champion.

Like I said, the first one was to shut people up. The second one's gonna be for me. I do believe I'm gonna start having some real fun now. The year 2001 is gonna be a new beginning for me. In my career, I've started over every four years. So next year I'm gonna try to bring it all out. No, I'm not gonna act crazy, get selfish, or ignore what Phil says. But now that my name is solidified in history, I can play a little.

I don't even think Phil knows all the tricks I have in my game. I will be the greatest big man Phil has ever coached. But I have a little Magic in me, too. Remember what Magic used to do when he had a little feisty guard playing him tight? He turned sideways. And then he just stayed basic. He used to dribble sideways, use his height to look over his man, and when his man went one way, he would spin and go the other.

That could be me. A guy my size, I'm pulling out all the tricks. All of them. It's a shame people don't know I have that in my game. It will be a shame if I never really get to show that.

Now that I've got a ring, I might have to show what I can do. I might have to bring out a little somethin'-somethin'.

It's a thin line, I know. Especially as a big man. If I put the ball between my legs, I'd better do something good with it. If I put it between my legs and dribble off my foot, I'm done. Phil yanks me.

"What the hell are you doing?! What the hell are you doing?!"

You're probably thinking, "Why doesn't Shaq keep working on his free throws and break out the tricks later?"

Hey, if I made them all, it wouldn't be fair. ☺

What am I going to do after I give up the game? Hopefully, I'll have a couple of businesses. I would still love to be a restaurant owner. I've already got my little Internet businesses going on. I don't know what I would do, but I don't think I would be in basketball.

Marriage? I have a lot of friends who are married. I've seen a lot of marriages in the NBA. Marriage is a job. That life might have to come after my career.

My idea of a marriage is to live king-and-queen style. I'm working hard now, setting myself up for the future so I don't have to do anything the day I get married. It will be a dream for me. Wake up, talk to the boys, "All right sons, don't be acting stupid in school today. Teacher told me you . . ."

I'll pick the kids up from school. My wife will be working. She'll come home; we'll play with the kids.

"All right, get in the gym. I don't want to hear you guys talking. Battle right now. One-on-one."

Just be a normal dad.

I live the kind of lifestyle where my wife wouldn't have to cook. You don't have to clean, you don't have to do the stuff that your mom did, that my mom did. You don't have to do none of that. Just stay fine. If you want to work, it's optional, up to you.

I would like to retire at age thirty-five, meaning this will be my last contract. The only thing that would make me retire sooner is if the game isn't fun anymore. I'm not worried about the Hack-a-Shaq. If I have to take the law into my own hands every now and then and pay the consequences, then that's what I have to do.

When I first came into the league, I used to jump at every pump fake. Now my knee bothers me sometimes. I don't have the same lift as I once had. I know that when I'm thirty-two and thirty-three, there will probably be a youngster coming in, twenty-four or twenty-five. He will have much more energy. Might even be a little bit bigger, a little better. Once it's time, it's not fun and I can't dominate anymore, then I'll be ready to give it to the next dominant big man.

Hey, eventually everything in life goes cold. It has to. Hopefully, I can go out with a bang. Jerry West went out with a bang, winning a championship his last season. I hope to win a couple more and just say, "You know what? That's it. I quit. I don't want to play no more." They'll have nothing to say.

I don't want to win one now and then have seven more disappointing seasons, because then they're gonna say, "Shaq's a great player, got one championship. But then, after that, never again."

For all the young players trying to find their way in the NBA, my only advice is: Experience is the best teacher. I just pray they have a good head on their shoulders and hope that they don't get caught up in the life—'cause this life doesn't last forever. It really is a fairy tale. So take care of yourself. Take care of your money. Someday the luxuries will be gone. But your family and true friends never leave.

You know what would be great? I'd like a kid to ask about me one day and have his father take him aside.

"Come watch this tape," he'll say.

I just want my name to be solidified in the history books. So when a youngster sees my name, he's trying to move my name out the way. That would be nice.

They raised the championship banner last November and presented us with our rings. I didn't keep mine. I gave it to my pops. In a way, I'm not only living my dreams; I'm living his dreams.

I said it before, and I'll say it again. My father could play. Not many people know that. He was always on the army team, shooting jumpers, banging guys in the paint, always fundamental. My father was cold. Butchy was his nickname.

He never took his game to the next level because life got in the way. He was from the 'hood. He had two kids from another relationship, me, my mama. At some point, he just said, "Enough already, I'm gonna join the army and earn a living for my family."

He worked. He sacrificed. He raised me.

The day after we won the championship, I called him.

"You made it, you listened," he said. "Now you're a part of history, just like I knew you would be."

He kept going on. "You take care of business. You're a family man. You have beautiful kids. You're a positive person. You don't get into trouble. Congratulations, you deserve it. Now enjoy it. Take a vacation, don't do anything."

There was a pause on the phone. And then the Sarge broke down and cried.

He said, "Thank you for listening. I love you."

I might make myself a copy of my championship ring, but I will not keep the original. It belongs to Philip. The next one I'll probably keep. But the first one is for him.

Thank you, Daddy.

I love you, too.